ADVANCE

"Up to now, most atheists have simply criticized religion in various ways, but the point is to dispel it. In *A Manual For Creating Atheists*, Peter Boghossian fills that gap, telling the reader how to become a 'street epistemologist' with the skills to attack religion at its weakest point: its reliance on faith rather than evidence. This book is essential for nonbelievers who want to do more than just carp about religion, but want to weaken its odious grasp on the world."

—**Jerry Coyne**, Ph.D., author of *Why Evolution Is True*

"There is nothing else on the market like this book that helps atheists talk believers out of their faith. Every atheist interested in doing so, or who talks to believers about faith at all, should read it. It's both needed and brilliant!"

—**John W. Loftus**, author of *Why I Became an Atheist* and *The Outsider Test for Faith*

"Boghossian has provided an indispensible chart book for all of us who must navigate the rising sea of magical thinking that is inundating America today."

—**Victor Stenger**, Ph.D., author of *God: The Failed Hypothesis* and *God and the Atom*

"Excellent application of science, philosophy, and strategy for breaking through ideological and psychological barriers to freethought, all in terms anyone can understand and apply. Delightfully novel and controversial, this is the kind of thing I've long wanted and we need more of: bringing practical philosophy to the common man and woman."

—**Richard Carrier**, Ph.D., author of *Sense and Goodness Without God*

"This book is a feisty, tough-minded attempt to undo what the author sees as the profound damage done to society by faith. There is something here that lots of people are likely to get angry about: liberals, academics, feminists, psychologists, politicians, progressives, and libertarians—and everybody in between. The book is a Molotov cocktail of ideas, arguments, policy proposals, thought experiments, encouragements, and denunciations."

—**Steven Brutus**, Ph.D., author of *Religion, Culture, History*

"A brave, clear book, crammed with useful insights. Boghossian's call for honest, evidence-based thinking has implications far beyond its focus on debates about God and religious faith. *A Manual for Creating Atheists* is a strong challenge to ideology and propaganda, wherever we find them."

—**Russell Blackford**, author of *Freedom of Religion and the Secular State and* co-author of *50 Great Myths About Atheism*

"A 'how-to' book for the ages. Boghossian manages to take a library's worth of information and mold it into a concise and practical tome to guide through the murky waters of magical thinking, docking the reader safely on the shores of reason, logic, and understanding. I thoroughly enjoyed reading this, and highly recommend it."

—**Al Stefanelli**, author of *A Voice of Reason in an Unreasonable World*

"This is a manual that we can use in our everyday interaction with those infected by the faith virus. The skills and concepts are both practical and learnable. As the founder and Chairman of the Board of RecoveringfromReligion.org, I recommend that all of our facilitators and leaders not only read and share this book, but actually learn how to use the questioning and dialogue techniques Dr. Boghossian illustrates. It will help you avoid common mistakes and give greater value to the conversations you have with the religious."

—**Darrel Ray, Ed.D.**, author of *The God Virus* and *Sex and God*

"The fact is, this book is perfect. It's simple, and (most importantly) accessible. The same techniques it outlines can be used in all walks of life—from social justice issues to boardroom negotiations. It does what no other atheist/skeptic book has done in the past: it gives you somewhere to go to after you've read everything and said, 'well, that was fascinating, where the hell do I go to now?' It works. It really does."

—**Jake Farr-Wharton,** author of *Letters to Christian Leaders*

"Since atheism is truly Good News, it should not be hidden under a bushel. Peter Boghossian shows us how to take it to the highways and the byways. I love it!"

—**Dan Barker**, co-president of the Freedom From Religion Foundation

A MANUAL FOR CREATING ATHEISTS

Peter Boghossian

Foreword by Michael Shermer

PITCHSTONE PUBLISHING
DURHAM, NORTH CAROLINA

Pitchstone Publishing
Durham, NC 27705
www.pitchstonepublishing.com

To contact the publisher, please e-mail info@pitchstonepublishing.com

Front cover design by Corey Van Hoosen, coreyvanhoosen.com
Author photo courtesy of Steve Eltinge

Printed in the United States of America

Library of Congress Cataloging-in-Publication Data

Boghossian, Peter G. (Peter Gregory)
A manual for creating atheists / Peter Boghossian ; foreword by Michael Shermer.
    pages cm
Includes bibliographical references and index.
ISBN 978-1-939578-09-9 (pbk. : alk. paper)
1. Atheism. 2. Rationalism. 3. Faith and reason. 4. Religion—Controversial
literature. I. Title.
 BL2747.3.B587 2013
 211'.8—dc23
                            2013019026

To Michael Shermer and Sam Harris

"Never be a spectator of unfairness or stupidity . . . the grave will supply plenty of time for silence."

—Christopher Hitchens, *Letters to a Young Contrarian*

"The idea, therefore, that religious faith is somehow a sacred human convention—distinguished, as it is, both by the extravagance of its claims and by the paucity of its evidence—is really too great a monstrosity to be appreciated in all its glory."

—Sam Harris, *The End of Faith*

CONTENTS

BORN-AGAIN ATHEIST

In 1971, my senior year at Crescenta Valley High School in Southern California, I accepted Jesus into my heart and became a born-again Christian, repeating aloud the gospel passage from John 3:16 (emblazoned on countless sporting event banners by faithful fans): "For God so loved the world, that he gave his only begotten Son, that whosoever believeth in him should not perish, but have everlasting life."

Everlasting life. Wow. That's quite a claim, and as we skeptics like to say, "extraordinary claims require extraordinary evidence." Is there extraordinary evidence for the claim that accepting Jesus of Nazareth bestows upon the believer eternity? No. Is there even any ordinary evidence for this extraordinary claim? No. There is no evidence whatsoever, as to date not one person who has died has returned to report a celestial realm where a first-century carpenter resides with his father—God. Let's think this claim through as a person of reason and science might:

1. Christians claim that God is omniscient, omnipotent, omnipresent, and omnibenevolent—all knowing, all powerful, all present, and all good, creator of the universe and everything in it including us.

2. Christians believe that we were originally created sinless, but because God gave us free will and Adam and Eve chose to eat the forbidden fruit of the knowledge of good and evil, we are all born with original

sin as part of our nature, even though we did not commit the original sinful act ourselves.

3. God could just forgive the sin we never committed, but instead he sacrificed his son Jesus, who is actually just himself in the flesh because Christians believe in only one god—that's what monotheism means—of which Jesus and the Holy Spirit are just different manifestations. Three in One and One in Three.

4. The only way to avoid eternal punishment for sins we never committed from this all-loving God is to accept his son—who is actually himself—as our savior. So . . .

God sacrificed himself to himself to save us from himself. Barking mad!

And why do we need to be saved? Because of that original sin thing, which stems from commandment number 3 of the decalogue: "Thou shalt not bow down thyself to them, nor serve them: for I the LORD thy God am a jealous God, visiting the iniquity of the fathers upon the children unto the third and fourth generation of them that hate me." Yikes! The sins of the fathers are to be born by their children's children's children? What sort of justice is that? This goes against half a millennium's worth of Western jurisprudence.

This all sounds positively daft, but when you are in the religious bubble everything makes sense and there is no such thing as chance, randomness, and contingencies. Things happen for a reason and God has a plan for each and every one of us. When something good happens, God is rewarding us for our faith, our good works, or our love of Christ. When something bad happens, well, God does work in mysterious ways you know. As Brian Dalton said through his character "Mr. Deity" in explaining to "the boy" Jesse/Jesus who upbraided Mr. Deity for erasing most of the prayers left on his voice mail:

> Look, if somebody prays to me and things go well, who gets the credit? Me! Right? But if they pray to me and things don't go well, who gets

the blame? Not me! So . . . it's all good. I'm gonna mess with that by steppin' in and putting my nose where it doesn't belong?

Inside the bubble the explanatory filter works at every level, from the sublime to the ridiculous, from career opportunities to parking spots. I thanked God for everything, from getting me into the Christian-based Pepperdine University (my grades and SAT scores were unspectacular) to finding a parking place at theaters and restaurants. In the Christian worldview there is a place for everything and everything is in its place, and believe it or not when you are committed to that belief system it is internally consistent and logically coherent . . . as long as you don't look too closely and you are surrounded by others who are also in the bubble.

When you step outside of the bubble, however, and encounter people who employ reason and science in their lives, the internal logic unravels. I'm talking about the kind of reason and logic called "Street Epistemology" by the philosopher Peter Boghossian in his brilliant treatise on creating atheists. Peter Boghossian's book is precisely what I—and millions of other people who were born again during this period of American history that saw the rise of the Religious Right and the evangelical movement— needed to cut through the obfuscating jargon of what is called Christian apologetics, which I swallowed hook, line, and poisonous lead sinker.

Sure there were academic treatises and philosophical tomes on the arguments for and against God's existence and the central tenets of the Christian religion, but there was nothing like the book you hold in your hands, aptly titled *A Manual for Creating Atheists*. Had I read this book when I was a neophyte Bible-thumper I would have saved scores of people from my incessant door-to-door evangelizing, and spared my patient and loving family members (who were surely at their wits' end with me) endless mini-sermons about Jesus and the Good Book that carried his gospel. If I started reading *A Manual for Creating Atheists* as a Christian I would have been an atheist by the time I finished it.

Peter Boghossian's *A Manual for Creating Atheists* is the perfect companion to Richard Dawkins' *The God Delusion*. They should be bundled like an atheist software package to reprogram minds into employing reason instead of faith, science instead of superstition. Religion is still a powerful force in the world and the majority of humans still adhere to one faith or another (but which is the right one?). But this is changing thanks to rational thinkers and brave activists such as Peter Boghossian, who has helped lead the fastest growing religious movement in America called the "nones"—those who check the box for "none" when asked about their religious faith. We are the nones, and we are growing, and in the long run we will triumph because we have on our side reason and science, the best tools ever devised for understanding the world.

—**Michael Shermer**
Altadena, California

CHAPTER 1

STREET EPISTEMOLOGY

---

street /strēt/
Noun: A public thoroughfare.

e·pis·te·mol·o·gy /i-ˌpis-tə-ˈmä-lə-jē/
Noun: The study of knowledge.

This book will teach you how to talk people out of their faith. You'll learn how to engage the faithful in conversations that help them value reason and rationality, cast doubt on their beliefs, and mistrust their faith. I call this activist approach to helping people overcome their faith, "Street Epistemology." The goal of this book is to create a generation of Street Epistemologists: people equipped with an array of dialectical and clinical tools who actively go into the streets, the prisons, the bars, the churches, the schools, and the community—into any and every place the faithful reside—and help them abandon their faith and embrace reason.

A Manual for Creating Atheists details, explains, and teaches you how to be a street clinician and how to apply the tools I've developed and used as an educator and philosopher. The lessons, strategies, and techniques I share come from my experience teaching prisoners, from educating tens of thousands of students in overcrowded public universities, from engaging the faithful every day for more than a quarter century, from over two decades of rigorous scholarship, and from the streets.

Street Epistemology harkens back to the values of the ancient philosophers—individuals who were tough-minded, plain-speaking, known for self-defense, committed to truth, unyielding in the face of danger, and fearless in calling out falsehoods, contradictions, inconsistencies, and nonsense. Plato was a wrestler and a soldier with broad shoulders. He was decorated for bravery in battle (Christian, 2011, p. 51). Socrates was a seasoned soldier. At his trial, when facing the death penalty, he was unapologetic. When asked to suggest a punishment for his "crimes," he instead proposed to be rewarded (Plato, *Apology*).

Hellenistic philosophers fought against the superstitions of their time. Lucretius, Sextus Empiricus, Epictetus, Marcus Aurelius, and others combated the religious authorities of their period, including early versions of Christianity (Clarke, 1968; Nussbaum, 1994). They thought the most important step was to liberate people from fear of tortures of the damned and from fear that preachers of their epoch were spouting. Hellenistic philosophers were trying to encourage stoic self-sufficiency, a sense of self-responsibility, and a tough-minded humanism.

Street Epistemology is a vision and a strategy for the next generation of atheists, skeptics, humanists, philosophers, and activists. Left behind is the idealized vision of wimpy, effete philosophers: older men in jackets with elbow patches, smoking pipes, stroking their white, unkempt beards. Gone is cowering to ideology, orthodoxy, and the modern threat of political correctness.

Enter the Street Epistemologist: an articulate, clear, helpful voice with an unremitting desire to help people overcome their faith and to create a better world—a world that uses intelligence, reason, rationality, thoughtfulness, ingenuity, sincerity, science, and kindness to build the future; not a world built on faith, delusion, pretending, religion, fear, pseudoscience, superstition, or a certainty achieved by keeping people in a stupor that makes them pawns of unseen forces because they're terrified.

The Street Epistemologist is a philosopher and a fighter. She has savvy and street smarts that come from the school of hard knocks. She relentlessly helps others by tearing down falsehoods about whatever enshrined "truths" enslave us.[1]

But the Street Epistemologist doesn't just tear down fairytales, comforting delusions, and imagined entities. She offers a humanistic vision. Let's be blunt, direct, and honest with ourselves and with others. Let's help people develop a trustfulness of reason and a willingness to reconsider, and let's place rationality in the service of humanity. Street Epistemology offers a humanism that's taken some hits and gained from experience. This isn't Pollyanna humanism, but a humanism that's been slapped around and won't fall apart. Reason and rationality have endurance. They don't evaporate the moment you get slugged. And you will get slugged.[2]

The immediate forerunners to Street Epistemologists were "the Four Horsemen," each of whom contributed to identifying a part of the problem with faith and religion. American neuroscientist Sam Harris articulated the problems and consequences of faith. British evolutionary biologist Richard Dawkins explained the God delusion and taught us how ideas spread from person to person within a culture. American philosopher Daniel Dennett analyzed religion and its effects as natural phenomena. British-American author Christopher Hitchens divorced religion from morality and addressed the historical role of religion. The Four Horsemen called out the problem of faith and religion and started a turn in our thinking and in our culture—they demeaned society's view of religion, faith, and superstition, while elevating attitudes about reason, rationality, Enlightenment, and humanistic values.

The Four Horsemen identified the problems and raised our awareness, but they offered few solutions. No roadmap. Not even guideposts. Now the onus is upon the next generation of thinkers and activists to take direct and immediate action to fix the problems Harris, Dawkins, Dennett, and Hitchens identified.

A Manual for Creating Atheists is a step beyond Harris, Dawkins, Hitchens, and Dennett. *A Manual for Creating Atheists* offers practical solutions to the problems of faith and religion through the creation of

Street Epistemologists—legions of people who view interactions with the faithful as clinical interventions designed to disabuse them of their faith.

Hitchens may be gone, but no single individual will take his place. Instead of a replacement Horseman, there are millions of Horsemen ushering in a new Enlightenment and an Age of Reason. You, the reader, will be one of these Horsemen. You will become a Street Epistemologist. You will transform a broken world long ruled by unquestioned faith into a society built on reason, evidence, and thought-out positions. This is work that needs to be done and work that will pay off by potentially helping millions—even billions—of people to live in a better world.

For the reader eager to get started talking others out of their faith, the tendency will be to skip to chapter 4. This is a mistake. The early chapters are designed to give you an understanding of the mechanism of belief. Effective interventions depend upon understanding core ideas and definitions covered in chapters 2 and 3.

NOTES

1. Other falsehoods include faith as a virtue; the importance of passionate belief; radical subjectivity; cognitive, cultural, and epistemological relativism; metaphysical entities that scrutinize and then ultimately punish or reward us; men who allegedly received revelations in the desert, or through golden plates; not blaspheming and being sensitive and respectful to the faith-based delusions of others; feeling shame in not knowing; unreflective injecting of pervasive egalitarianism into our judgments; unsupported beliefs about what happens to us after we die, etc.

2. On September 10, 2010, my friend, Steven Brutus, gave the graduation speech for The Art Institute of Portland at the Gerding Theater in Portland, Oregon. I've included portions of it here because it perfectly sums up the vision of Street Epistemology:

    Hard-boiled means that you look at things straight on. You play it straight. You don't sugarcoat it, you don't play it cute, you don't pull your punches. You look at the cold, hard truth. You lay things out truthfully. That's your healthy skepticism. You become the investigator—you have to be your *own* private investigator—you're the detective—so you better learn how to handle yourself. You're going to go to some tough places, the other side of the tracks, and there's going to be some bad guys around—some tough cookies, some palookas and gorillas and femme fatales and some snakes. . . .

The tough guy adheres to a moral code in a world that has no moral code. It has no moral values—basically no values at all. The tough son-of-a-bitch stands for something, unlike pretty much everything around him. He's a stand-up guy in a sit-down, shut-up world. Philip Marlowe in particular is all about hanging on to his decency and humanity in a world that's chipping away at his soul, at his spirit and honor. The tough-guy hero is always an exception, a lone wolf—she's independent, strong, brave, self-reliant—they're a little bit on the outside, they're isolated, estranged, they're out there on the margins—pretty close to *amoral* territory. But he's always got a stance, a code, a worldview. They've seen it all—not much shocks them—they've been around the block—these are principled people. . . .

What makes them the exception is that they're tough, they hang in there, they won't go down for the count. But not *just* that—it's also that they're fighting for something—*fighting the good fight*—they're not in it for themselves—they're principled, they've got their pride, their honor, their dignity. But they never talk about it. They don't tell you how great they are, they don't tell you what great stuff they're doing for you—they just do it. They don't preach. They act.

[T]he tough guy hero is "inner directed"—he has what psychologists call an "inner locus of control"—the opposite of an "external locus of control"—he's not going to worry too much about what the next guy thinks of him. He knows that he's got to get his game face on, tough things out on his own, stand on his own two feet, put his pants on one leg at a time.

I am . . . talk[ing] about toughening up and finding some strength in yourself to be self-confident and able to take some hits and to stay in the game—to come back from setbacks—to be resilient.

Socrates . . . said that wisdom is the key to happiness. Socrates was a skeptic about happiness, because we do not possess wisdom—no one he knows has wisdom. I guess I should say that whatever it is that you have learned from teachers—including me—and I hope it is a great deal—it is not *wisdom*. That you will have to search for in the school of hard knocks and—if you find it—it's going to be something you earn on your own—you'll have to learn it on your own—it will also be on your own terms. But tell the rest of us about it, if you find it—tell everyone—help as many people as you can.

CHAPTER 2

FAITH

This chapter has two parts. The first part clears up the terms "faith," "atheist," and "agnostic." It does so by offering two definitions of faith: "belief without evidence" and "pretending to know things you don't know." It then disambiguates "faith" from "hope." Once the meanings of these terms have been clarified, the second part of the chapter articulates faith as an epistemology, underscores the fact that faith claims are knowledge claims, and then briefly articulates the problems and dangers of faith.

THE MEANING OF WORDS: FAITH, ATHEIST, AND AGNOSTIC

As a Street Epistemologist, you'll find subjects will attempt to evade your help by asserting that *every* definition of faith offered is incorrect and that you "just don't understand" what faith really is.

When pressed, the faithful will offer vague definitions that are merely transparent attempts to evade criticism, or simplistic definitions that intentionally muddy the meaning of "faith." More common still are what Horseman Daniel Dennett terms "deepities."

A deepity is a statement that looks profound but is not. Deepities appear true at one level, but on all other levels are meaningless. Here are some examples of deepities:

"Now faith is the substance of things hoped for, the evidence of things not seen." (Hebrews 11:1)

"Faith is not to have a perfect knowledge of things; therefore if ye have faith ye hope for things which are not seen, which are true." (Alma 32:21)[1]

"Faith is the act in which reason reaches ecstatically beyond itself." (Tillich, 1957, p. 87)

"Faith is faith in the living God, and God is and remains a mystery beyond human comprehension. Although the 'object' of our faith, God never ceases to be 'subject.'" (Migliore, 1991, p. 3)

"Making faith-sense tries to wed meaning and facts. You can start with either one, but it is important to include the claims of both." (Kinast, 1999, p. 7)

"Having faith is really about seeking something beyond faith itself." (McLaren, 1999, p. 3)

. . . and additionally, virtually every statement made by Indian-American physician Deepak Chopra. For example, Chopra's tweets on February 7, 2013, read:

"The universe exists in awareness alone."

"God is the ground of awareness in which the universe arises & subsides"

"All material objects are forms of awareness within awareness, sensations, images, feelings, thoughts"

One could easily fill an entire book with faith deepities—many, many authors have. Christians in particular have created a tradition to employ deepities, used slippery definitions of faith, and hidden behind unclear language since at least the time of Augustine (354–430).

The word "faith" is a very slippery pig. We need to get our hands on it, pin it to the ground, and wrap a blanket around it so we can have something to latch onto before we finally and permanently subdue it. Malleable definitions allow faith to slip away from critique.[2]

Two Definitions of Faith

The words we use are important. They can help us see clearly, or they can confuse, cloud, or obscure issues. I'll now offer my two preferred definitions of faith, and then disambiguate faith from hope.[3]

faith /fāTH/

1. *Belief without evidence.*

> "My definition of faith is that it's a leap over the probabilities. It fills in the gap between what is improbable to make something more probable than not without faith. As such, faith is an *irrational* leap over the probabilities."
>
> —John W. Loftus, "Victor Reppert Now Says He Doesn't Have Faith!" (Loftus, 2012)

If one had sufficient evidence to warrant belief in a particular claim, then one wouldn't believe the claim on the basis of faith. "Faith" is the word one uses when one does not have enough evidence to justify holding a belief, but when one just goes ahead and believes anyway.

Another way to think about "belief without evidence" is to think of an irrational leap over probabilities.[4] For example, assume that an historical Jesus existed and was crucified, and that his corpse was placed in a tomb. Assume also that eyewitness accounts were accurate, and days later the tomb was empty.

One can believe the corpse was missing for any number of reasons. For example, one can believe the body arose from the dead and ascended to heaven, one can believe aliens brought the body back to life, or one can believe an ancient spirit trapped in the tomb merged with the corpse and animated it. Belief in any of these claims would require faith because there's insufficient evidence to justify any *one* of these particular options.

Belief in any of these claims would also disregard other, far more likely possibilities—for example, that the corpse was stolen, hidden, or moved.

If one claims knowledge either in the absence of evidence, or when a claim is contradicted by evidence, then this is when the word "faith" is used. "Believing something anyway" is an accurate definition of the term "faith."

faith /fāTH/

2. *Pretending to know things you don't know.*

Not everything that's a case of pretending to know things you don't know is a case of faith, but cases of faith are instances of pretending to know something you don't know.[5] For example, someone who knows nothing about baking a cake can pretend to know how to bake a cake, and this is not an instance of faith. But if someone claims to know something on the basis of faith, they are pretending to know something they don't know. For example, using faith would be like someone giving advice about baking cookies who has never been in a kitchen.

As a Street Epistemologist, whenever you hear the word "faith," just translate this in your head as, "pretending to know things you don't know." While swapping these words may make the sentence clunky, "pretending to know things you don't know" will make the meaning of the sentence clearer.

To start thinking in these terms, the following table contains commonly heard expressions using the word "faith" in column one, and the same expressions substituted with the words "pretending to know things you don't know" in column two.

"FAITH"	"PRETENDING TO KNOW THINGS YOU DON'T KNOW"
"My faith is beneficial for me."	"Pretending to know things I don't know is beneficial for me."

"I have faith in God."	"I pretend to know things I don't know about God."
"Life has no meaning without faith."	"Life has no meaning if I stop pretending to know things I don't know."
"I don't have enough faith to be an atheist."	"I don't pretend to know things I don't know enough to be an atheist." Alternatively, if atheist is defined as "a person who doesn't pretend to know things he doesn't know about the creation of the universe," the sentence then becomes, "I don't pretend to know things I don't know enough to be a person who doesn't pretend to know things he doesn't know about the creation of the universe."
"You have faith in science."	"You pretend to know things you don't know about science."
"You have faith your spouse loves you."	"You pretend to know things you don't know about your spouse's love."
"If everyone abandoned their faith, society would devolve morally."	"If everyone stopped pretending to know things they don't know, society would devolve morally."
"My faith is true for me."	"Pretending to know things I don't know is true for me."
"Why should people stop having faith if it helps them get through the day?"	"Why should people stop pretending to know things they don't know if it helps them get through the day?"
"Teach your children to have faith."	"Teach your children to pretend to know things they don't know."

"Freedom of faith."	"Freedom of pretending to know things you don't know."
"International Faith Convention"	"International Pretending to Know Things You Don't Know Convention"
"She's having a crisis of faith."	"She's having a crisis of pretending to know things she doesn't know." Alternatively, "She is struck by the fact that she's been pretending to know things she doesn't know."

Disambiguation: Faith Is Not Hope

Faith and hope are not synonyms. Sentences with these words also do not share the same linguistic structure and are semantically different—for example, one can say, "I hope it's so," and not, "I faith it's so."

Thought Challenge!

In my May 6, 2012, public lecture for the Humanists of Greater Portland, I further underscored the difference between faith and hope by issuing the following thought challenge:

Give me a sentence where one must use the word "faith," and cannot replace that with "hope," yet at the same time isn't an example of pretending to know something one doesn't know.

To date, nobody has answered the thought challenge. I don't think it can be answered because faith and hope are not synonyms.

The term "faith," as the faithful use it in religious contexts, needs to be disambiguated from words such as "promise," "confidence," "trust," and, especially, "hope."[6][7] "Promise," "confidence," "trust," and "hope" are not knowledge claims. One can hope for anything or place one's trust in anyone or anything. This is not the same as claiming to know something. To hope for something admits there's a possibility that what you want may not be realized. For example, if you hope your stock will rise tomorrow, you are not claiming to know your stock will rise; you want your stock to rise, but you recognize there's a possibility it may not. Desire is not certainty but the wish for an outcome.

Hope is not the same as faith. Hoping is not the same as knowing. If you hope something happened you're not claiming it did happen. When the faithful say, "Jesus walked on water," they are not saying they *hope* Jesus walked on water, but rather are claiming Jesus actually did walk on water.

Atheist

"I contend we are both atheists, I just believe in one fewer God than you do."

—Stephen F. Roberts

Of all the terms used in this book, none is more problematic, more contentious, more divisive, or more confusing than the term "atheist."

This confusion is understandable given that the word "theist" is contained in the word "atheist." It is thus natural to assume a type of parallelism between the two words. Many of the faithful imagine that just as a theist firmly believes in God, an a-theist firmly disbelieves in God. This definitional and conceptual confusion needs to be clarified.

"Atheist," *as I use the term*, means, "There's insufficient evidence to warrant belief in a divine, supernatural creator of the universe. However, if I were shown sufficient evidence to warrant belief in such an entity, then I would believe."[8][9] I recommend we start to conceptualize "atheist" in this way so we can move the conversation forward.

The atheist does *not* claim, "No matter how solid the evidence for a supernatural creator, I refuse to believe."[10] In *The God Delusion*, for example, Horseman Dawkins provides a 1–7 scale, with 1 being absolute belief and 7 being absolute disbelief in a divine entity (Dawkins, 2006a, pp. 50–51). Dawkins, whom many consider to be among the most hawkish of atheists, only places himself at a 6. In other words, even Dawkins does not definitively claim there is no God. He simply thinks the existence of God is highly unlikely. A difference between an atheist and a person of faith is that an atheist is willing to revise their belief (if provided sufficient evidence); the faithful permit no such revision.

Agnostic

Agnostics profess to not know whether or not there's an undetectable, metaphysical entity that created the universe. Agnostics think there's not enough evidence to warrant belief in God, but because it's logically possible they remain unsure of God's existence. Again, an agnostic is willing to revise her belief if provided sufficient evidence.

The problem with agnosticism is that in the last 2,400 years of intellectual history, *not a single argument* for the existence of God has withstood scrutiny. Not one. Aquinas's five proofs, fail. Pascal's Wager, fail. Anselm's ontological argument, fail. The fine-tuning argument, fail. The Kalām cosmological argument, fail. All refuted. All failures.[11]

I dislike the terms "agnostic" and "agnosticism." I advise Street Epistemologists to not use these terms. This is why: I don't believe Santa Claus is a real person who flies around in a sleigh led by reindeer delivering presents. I am a Santa Claus atheist. Even though there's nothing logically impossible about this phenomenon, I'm not a Santa Claus agnostic. (That is, a large man in a red suit delivering presents at the speed of light is not a logical contradiction.) "Agnostic" and "agnosticism" are unnecessary terms. Street Epistemologists should avoid them.

EPISTEMOLOGY AND KNOWLEDGE CLAIMS

Now that the terms "faith," "atheist," and "agnostic" have been clarified, we can have a meaningful discussion about "belief without evidence" being an unreliable way to navigate reality. We can also examine the dangers of formulating beliefs and social policies on the basis of insufficient evidence.

Faith Claims Are Knowledge Claims

The term "epistemology" comes from the Greek "episteme," which means "knowledge," and "logos," which means "reason and logic" and "argument and inquiry" and therefore, by extension, "the study of." Epistemology is a branch of philosophy that focuses on how we come to knowledge, what knowledge is, and what processes of knowing the world are reliable.

Conclusions one comes to as the result of an epistemological process are knowledge claims. A knowledge claim is an assertion of truth. Examples of knowledge claims include: "The moon is 52,401 miles from the Earth," "My fist has a greater diameter than a soda can," and "The Azande supreme God, Onyame, created the world and all lesser gods."

Faith is an epistemology.[12] It's a method and a process people use to understand reality. Faith-based conclusions are knowledge claims. For example, "I have faith Jesus Christ will heal my sickness because it says so in Luke" is a knowledge claim. The utterer of this statement is asserting Jesus will heal her.

Those who make faith claims are professing to know something about the external world. For example, when someone says, "Jesus walked on water" (Matthew 14:22–33), that person is claiming *to know* there was an historical figure named Jesus and that he, unaided by technology, literally walked across the surface of the water. "Jesus walked on water" is a knowledge claim—an objective statement of fact.

Much of the confusion about faith-based claims comes from mistaking objective claims with subjective claims. Knowledge claims purport to be objective because they assert a truth about the world. Subjective claims are not knowledge claims and do not assert a truth about the world; rather, they are statements about one's own unique, situated, subjective, personal experiences or preferences.

Think of subjective claims as matters of taste or opinion. For example, "Mustard on my hot dog tastes good," "John Travolta is the greatest actor who's ever lived," and "The final season of *Battlestar Galactica* wasn't as good as the first two seasons." These are subjective statements because they relate to matters of taste. They are not statements of fact about the world. They do not apply to everyone. Contrast these statements with, "The Dalai Lama reincarnates." This statement is a knowledge claim. It's an assertion of truth about the world that is independent of one's taste or liking; it's a faith claim masquerading as a knowledge claim, a statement of fact.

Faith claims are knowledge claims. Faith claims are statements of fact about the world.

Faith Is an Unreliable Epistemology

"Your religious beliefs typically depend on the community in which you were raised or live. The spiritual experiences of people in ancient Greece, medieval Japan or 21st-century Saudi Arabia do not lead to belief in Christianity. It seems, therefore, that religious belief very likely tracks not truth but social conditioning."

—Gary Gutting, "The Stone," *New York Times*, September 14, 2011

Faith is a failed epistemology. Showing why faith fails has been done before. And it's been done well (Bering, 2011; Harris, 2004; Loftus, 2010; Loftus, 2013; McCormick, 2012; Schick & Vaughn, 2008; Shermer, 1997; Shermer, 2011; Smith, 1979; Stenger & Barker, 2012; Torres, 2012; Wade, 2009). There's no need to recapitulate this vast body of scholarship. Instead, I'll briefly explain what I find to be one of the principal arguments against faith.

If a belief is based on insufficient evidence, then any further conclusions drawn from the belief will at best be of questionable value. Believing on the basis of insufficient evidence cannot point one toward the truth. For example, the following are unassailable facts everyone, faithful or not, would agree upon:

1. There are different faith traditions.

2. Different faith traditions make different truth claims.

3. The truth claims of some faith traditions contradict the truth claims of other faith traditions. For example, Muslims believe Muhammad (570–632) was the last prophet (Sura 33:40). Mormons believe Joseph Smith (1805–1844), who lived after Muhammad, was a prophet.

4. It cannot both be the case that Muhammad was the last prophet and someone who lived after Muhammad was also a prophet.

5. Therefore: *At least* one of these claims *must* be false (perhaps both).

It is impossible to figure out which of these claims is incorrect if the tool one uses to do so is faith. As a tool, as an epistemology, as a method of reasoning, as a process for knowing the world, faith cannot adjudicate between competing claims ("Muhammad was the last prophet" versus "Joseph Smith was a prophet"). Faith cannot steer one away from falsehood and toward truth.

This is because faith does not have a built-in corrective mechanism. That is, faith claims have no way to be corrected, altered, revised, or modified. For example, if one has faith in the claim, "The Earth is 4,000 years old," how could this belief be revised? If one believes that the Earth is 4,000 years old on the basis of faith, then there's no evidence, reason, or body of facts one could present to dissuade one from belief in this claim.[13]

The *only* way to figure out which claims about the world are likely true, and which are likely false, is through reason and evidence. *There is no other way.*

THE DANGER OF FAITH

"No amount of belief makes something a fact."

—James Randi

The pretending-to-know-things-you-don't-know pandemic hurts us all. Believing things on the basis of something other than evidence and reason causes people to misconstrue what's good for them and what's good for their communities. Those who believe on the basis of insufficient evidence create external conditions based upon what they think is in their best interest, but this is actually counterproductive. In the United States, for example, public policies driven by people who pretend to know things they don't know continue to hurt people: abstinence-only sex education, prohibitions against gay marriage, bans on death with dignity, corporal punishment in schools, failure to fund international family planning organizations, and promoting the teaching of Creationism and other pseudosciences are but a few of the many misguided conclusions wrought by irrationality.

The less one relies on reason and evidence to form conclusions, the more arbitrary the conclusion. In aggregate, conclusions that result from a lack of evidence can have incredibly dangerous consequences. The Taliban, for example, have rooted their vision of a good life on the Koran. By acting on what they perceive to be divine injunctions revealed to God's Prophet, they think they're creating a good life and a good society. They are not.[14] [15] Consequently, the conclusions they act upon— covering women and beating them, beheading people who have rival interpretations of the Koran or who act in ways they deem un-Islamic, perpetrating violence against females who seek an education, denying citizens basic freedoms, executing people for blasphemy—take them away from a good life. They've misidentified *the process* that will allow their community to flourish because they've identified and used faith, not evidence and reason, as a guide.

How do we know the society the Taliban created has not led to human flourishing? By virtually every modern metric: exports versus imports, literacy, economic aid, public health, life expectancy, infant mortality, household income, GDP, Happy Planet Index, etc. Afghanistan under the Taliban was an unmitigated catastrophe. It is not in anyone's interest, particularly the people who live under their tyranny, to have created a dystopian, premodern, misogynistic theocracy.[16] (If you don't think they created a dystopia, or if you're a relativist and think they created a society that's merely different, not better or worse, from Denmark, for example, then there's nothing I can say to you. Nothing I write in this book will persuade you.)

The vast majority of people use faith to understand the world, to guide their actions, and to ground their institutions. Countries like Saudi Arabia, Yemen, Mauritania, Somalia, Sudan, and Iran adhere to Islamic law (sharia) as the basis for state law. This is a problem that would be unimaginable in its scope and severity were it not for the fact that we're currently witnesses to this epistemic horror show, such as the beheading of homosexuals, blasphemers, adulterers, and apostates and radically disproportionate treatment of individuals based upon their gender.

Yet there is hope. Faith is slowly falling into disrepute. The forces of unreason are diminishing in number. Thousands of new Horsemen, Street Epistemologists, are emerging.

DIG DEEPER

Books

Sam Harris, *The End of Faith* (Harris, 2004)

Stephen Law, *Believing Bullshit* (Law, 2011)

John W. Loftus, *The Outsider Test for Faith* (Loftus, 2013)

Michael Shermer, *The Believing Brain* (Shermer, 2011)

Al Stefanelli, *A Voice Of Reason in an Unreasonable World: The Rise of Atheism On Planet Earth* (Stefanelli, 2011)

Victor Stenger, *God and the Folly of Faith: The Incompatibility of Science and Religion* (Stenger, 2012)

Lawrence Wright, *Going Clear: Scientology, Hollywood, and the Prison of Belief* (Wright, 2013)

Videos

Peter Boghossian, "Jesus, the Easter Bunny, and Other Delusions: Just Say No!" http://www.philosophynews.com/post/2012/02/14/Jesus-the-Easter-Bunny-and-Other-Delusions-Just-Say-No.aspx

Peter Boghossian, "Faith: Pretending to Know Things You Don't Know," http://www.youtube.com/watch?v=qp4WUFXvCFQ

Jerry Coyne, "Why Science and Faith Are Incompatible: My Talk in Edinburgh," http://whyevolutionistrue.wordpress.com/2012/12/26/why-science-and-faith-are-incompatible-my-talk-in-edinburgh/

QualiaSoup's YouTube channel, "UK Secular Humanist Discussing: Science & the Natural World, Critical Thinking, Atheism, Philosophy, Religion," http://www.youtube.com/user/QualiaSoup

The Atheist Experience, "The Atheist Experience is a weekly cable access television show in Austin, Texas geared at a non-atheist audience. Every week we field live calls from atheists and believers alike, and you never know what you're going to get!" http://www.atheist-experience.com

Thunderf00t's YouTube channel, "The true beauty of a self-inquiring sentient universe is lost on those who elect to walk the intellectually vacuous path of comfortable paranoid fantasies," http://www.youtube.com/user/Thunderf00t

NOTES

1. The Book of Alma is one of the books in the Book of Mormon. The complete title is "The Book of Alma: The Son of Alma."

2. Religious belief is very often defended through the use of clever semantics. There are some important things to note about these dodges. When a person of faith is questioned over one or more specific, illogical tenets of their belief, they often respond with, "Well, of course I don't believe that," leaving the Street Epistemologist at a disadvantage since the believer continues to profess their unaltered faith-based belief regardless. If pressed further, the believer will either respond with deepities or with a somewhat different version of "why" they continue to believe despite a lack of evidence. This entrenched position results in a cycle of indefinite repetition. My sense is that those who use meaningless words to protect their emotional ties to faith are engaging in self-deception. (This type of "conversation" is not two-sided; it is a monologue masquerading as a dialogue.)

    The emotional satisfaction of religious belief vitally depends upon the beliefs being taken literally; the epistemic defense of such beliefs crucially depends on taking them nonliterally. This type of cognitive disruption does not bode well in the search for truth.

What nearly all *sophisticated* believers do is simultaneously deceive themselves while alternating between two stances: they absolutely don't believe in *that*—of course he didn't walk on water—while voicing unflappable conviction about *this*—the world was created by a higher power. When defending epistemically, they characterize the belief as not literally requiring the existence of a Special Person ("God loves us" means "Love is important," "Love prevails in the end," etc.), but then as soon as they have satisfied the epistemic challenge, they reframe the belief more literally ("God loves us" means "There is a Special Person who loves us").

I think this latter issue is far more important to address than critics of faith realize, and it is probably a more common phenomenon (not limited to intellectuals) than one might think. It is at least a part of what the believer is doing when replying to criticism by simply and mysteriously saying, "You just don't understand." The other part is, "You lack detailed familiarity with the culture, history, and theology of my religion."

This is a separate issue, and is often enough true, though the response to that is like replying to someone who points out *Star Trek* is fiction by saying, "You wouldn't say that if you had the detailed and rich experience of being a Trekkie that I have," which is, of course, absurd.

3. Hebrews 11 defines faith, "Now faith is the substance of things hoped for, the evidence [elenchus] of things not seen." What is interesting is the use of the term "elenchus" in this passage.

"Elenchus" in Homer (8th century) is variously: to put to shame, to treat with contempt, to question with the aim of disproving, with the aim of censure, accusation, to accuse someone and perhaps to convict him—oftentimes in uses where superior officers dress down rank-and-file soldiers. In courts of law the term is also used: to bring charges, to bring accusations, but also to bring proofs, evidence, to offer convincing proofs. Pre-Socratics like Parmenides (early 5th century) use it as Socrates does: as argument, scrutiny, cross-examination for the purpose of refutation or disproof.

In Koine, the verb *elencho* is "I accuse, rebuke, reprove," and also "I expose, I show to be guilty, I prove" (in the sense of putting the lie to a public statement). It's in John 3:20; 1 Cor 14:24; Eph. 5:11, 13; James 2: 9. Souter's Lexicon of the New Testament lists elenchus as "proof, possibly a persuasion" (Souter, 1917). This evidence points to a straightforward fact: in the Apostolic Age, the word elenchus expands in an important new context to take on the sense that is on stage in Hebrews 11, that is, people began using the word in a new way. They advocated, practiced, and helped make a success of using the word "elenchus." Socrates used this term to indicate a rigorous process of argumentation by strict application of logic. In the new sense elenchus is used as conviction or persuasion or some other species of willing and satisfied affirmation—without argument—without going through the Socratic process of rigorous argumentation.

Socrates earned the right to claim a conclusion from philosophical examination. The anonymous author of Hebrews writes instead that faith is the assurance of things hoped for, and the conviction or persuasion (elenchus) of things not seen. If Socrates were to hear this phrase, I imagine he'd say, "This may be conviction, but it is not an argument, not a cross-examination and test by scrutiny, but is a jump without any justification—without proof, and without earning it. Where is the virtue in this?"

4.   For more, see American mathematician James A. Lindsay's, "Defining Faith via Bayesian Reasoning" (Lindsay, 2012). Lindsay provides a cogent analysis of faith using Bayes' theorem.

5.   The exceptions to this are those people who are not pretending. These individuals are either delusional, or they're victims of a wholesale lack of exposure to alternative ideas and different epistemologies. In the latter case, many people in the Islamic world fall into this category. For example, most of the people in Saudi Arabia are not pretending to know something they don't know about the Koran. They've never encountered nor been given an opportunity to genuinely engage in competing ways of understanding reality. In a very real sense, they're epistemological victims. Additionally, anyone reared by fundamentalist parents deserves credit for the exceptional struggle from indoctrination to enlightenment.

6.   A recent move by apologists is to avoid the use of the word "faith" entirely, and instead to use the word "trust." Given that the word "faith" is inherently problematic, I think this is an excellent strategy. The counter to this, however, is identical: "Without sufficient evidence how do you know what to trust?" If the response is, "There's sufficient evidence," then your reply should be, "Then you don't need faith."

7.   In this vein, I've also heard faith defined as, "An attitude about things we don't know." When asked to spell out the nature of this attitude, it seems to be a kind of confidence or assurance or untroubled conviction, which in normal parlance is what we associate with the attitude of a person who has

adequate justification for saying, "I know."

The problem with defining faith as "an attitude about things we don't know" is that it functions in exactly the same way as an attitude about things we do know. From a critical perspective the question is, "How can an attitude that does not have sufficient justification to warrant belief work in the same way as an attitude that flows from actually having sufficient justification to warrant belief?" And the straightforward answer is: it cannot.

Because people adopt this kind of attitude it's therefore fair game to call them on this and say, "You are not justified in this assurance or conviction that you have. And the fact that you are not worried about it shows that you have not aimed your intellectual honesty at this attitude—in fact, you seem to be afraid or unwilling to do this—when the honest thing would be to say, 'My faith is not like knowledge, it is not justified, but is something else . . . maybe (charitably) a choice.'"

8. An alternative definition of "atheist" is: a person who doesn't pretend to know things he doesn't know with regard to the creation of the universe.

9. Some noted atheists, like American historian Richard Carrier, view atheism as an identity (Carrier, 2012). Others, like Horseman Sam Harris, do not. My opinion is that self-identification as an atheist is a personal choice. (Personally, I'm more interested in balancing my home and work lives, or in getting a full night of sleep.)

I am frequently asked if atheism is part of my identity. My answer is always, "No." As odd as it may seem, given this book, my career, and my speaking engagements, atheism is not a part of my identity. My lack of belief in leprechauns is also not part of my identity. I don't define myself by what I don't believe or what I don't do. I don't do a lot of things. I don't practice tai chi. The lack of tai chi in my life is also not part of my identity.

I do not define myself in terms of opposition to other people: I don't refer to myself as an atheist even though the vast majority of people do not consider themselves atheists.

When friends who are atheists come to our home, we don't sit around talking about the fact that there's insufficient evidence to warrant belief in God. We also don't talk about the fact that we don't do tai chi.

I don't identify as an atheist because nothing extra-epistemological is entailed by the fact that I do my best to believe on the basis of evidence. Neither my reasoning nor my conclusion about the probability of a divine creator means I'm a good guy, or I'm kind to my dog, or I'm a patient father, or I have an encyclopedic knowledge of science fiction, or I'm fun to have at a party, or I am good at jiu jitsu. If "good critical thinker" were to be substituted with "atheist," then perhaps it would be clear that atheism entails nothing beyond the fact that one doesn't believe there's sufficient evidence to warrant belief in God.

Whether a person is an atheist or a believer is immaterial with respect to morality, and yet, moral ascriptions are frequently made to atheists and to the faithful. For example, currently there's a (hopefully) short-lived movement called Atheism+. Among Atheism+'s tenets are social justice, support for women's rights, protesting against racism, fighting homophobia and transphobia, critical thinking, and skepticism (McCreight, 2012). The problem with this is, as Massimo Pigliucci writes, "a-theism simply means that one lacks a belief in God(s). . . . That lack of belief doesn't come with any positive position because none is logically connected to it" (Pigliucci, 2012). Many people try to make atheism into something it's not. Atheism is not about racism, homophobia, or not practicing tai chi; it's simply about not having enough evidence to warrant a belief in God. Atheism is about epistemology, evidence, honesty, sincerity, reason, and inquiry.

Finally, perhaps because I don't view atheism as an immutable characteristic, like eye color, I don't consider it an identity. I'm willing to change my mind if I'm presented with compelling evidence for the existence of a God or gods. I can understand why many theists consider belief a part of their identity, as they often claim that they're unwilling to change their minds. One may be more likely to consider something a part of one's identity if it's not subject to change.

10. In an e-mail I asked American physicist and best-selling author Dr. Victor Stenger where he places himself on the Dawkins' God Scale. Vic replied, "8. It's not a matter of belief. It's a matter of knowledge. I have knowledge beyond a reasonable doubt that there is no God" (personal correspondence, August 15, 2012). For more on why he thinks this, see *God: The Failed Hypothesis* (Stenger, 2007).

11. Aquinas' five proofs: (1) motion (as nothing moves itself there must be a first, unmoved mover), (2) efficient causes (something must exist that is not caused), (3) possibility and necessity (because everything that's possible to exist must not have existed at some point, then there must be something that necessarily exists), (4) gradation of being (because gradation exists there must be something that occupies the highest rung, perfection) (5) design (because natural bodies work toward some end, an intelligent being exists to which natural things are directed).

For more on Pascal's Wager, see footnote 11 in chapter 4.

Anselm's ontological argument, from *Proslogion II*: "Thus even the fool is convinced that something than which nothing greater can be conceived is in the understanding, since when he hears this, he understands it; and whatever is understood is in the understanding. And certainly that than which a greater cannot be conceived cannot be in the understanding alone. For if it is even in the understanding alone, it can be conceived to exist in reality also, which is greater. Thus if that than which a greater cannot be conceived is in the understanding alone, then that than which a greater cannot be conceived is itself that than which a greater can be conceived. But surely this cannot be. Thus without doubt something than which a greater cannot be conceived exists, both in the understanding and in reality."

For more on the fine-tuning argument, see footnote 5 in chapter 7.

For more on the Kalām cosmological argument, see footnote 3 in chapter 7.

12. One of my Arts and Sciences colleagues asked me, "If faith doesn't have the earmarks of an epistemology, why call it an epistemology? For an epistemology to be an epistemology, must empirical evidence play a significant role?" What he was getting at was that with faith, because empirical evidence does not play a role (or as philosophers say, faith "fails to satisfy the conditions" of an epistemology), why call it an epistemology?

There are many epistemologies, like rationalism and pragmatism, which do not rely upon empirical evidence. Descartes, for example, has a rationalist epistemology. For Descartes, reason by itself without any experience of the world is a source of knowledge. I don't have to go out in the world—I can be a brain in a vat attached by electrodes to a computer, and just from the process of thought alone I can come to knowledge about the world. That's basically a rationalist position. Hume, Locke, and Berkeley would deny that position and respond, "No, by itself reason can organize experience but it's not a source of knowledge about experience. There's only one source of knowledge about experience and that is empirical content, an encounter via the senses with the physical empirical universe."

Historically, Kantians are yet another school. Their position is that both rationalism and empiricism are correct in different ways. For Kant, concepts without experience are empty but experience without concepts is blind; knowledge is a combination of the organizing function of the mind and sensory input.

Then there's the pragmatist school, fallibilism, and also intuitionist positions that allow for different kinds of knowledge. All of these schools define knowledge slightly differently.

Faith is an epistemology because it is used as an epistemology. It is epistemology as use; people use faith as a way to know and interpret the world. For example, approximately a third of North Americans think the Bible is divinely inspired, and more than half think it's the actual word of God (Jones, 2011). It's a common belief among Americans that angels or spirits guided the hands (depicted by Caravaggio's 1602 "Saint Matthew and the Angel"), or whispered in the ear (seen in Rembrandt's 1661 "The Evangelist Matthew Inspired by an Angel," Giovanni Girolamo Savoldo's 1534 "Saint Matthew and the Angel," and Guido Reni's 1640 "St Matthew and the Angel"), of the Gospel writers. Consequently, the faithful root many of their beliefs in the authenticity of the Bible. That faith is unreliable, or discredited, only makes faith unreliable or discredited; it does not entail that faith is not an epistemology.

Part of the confusion on the part of those who don't use faith to navigate reality is that they understand that faith is an obviously unreliable process of reasoning. Consequently, they either don't view faith as an epistemology, or they don't think others *really* use it as an epistemology. They view it as something else, something weird, something other, something personal, something malicious, perhaps even something redemptive.

But at its root, faith remains an epistemology. It is a process people use to understand, interpret, and know the world.

Faith produces knowledge claims. Claims that arise out of epistemologies unmoored to reason are exactly like other claims that arise out of other epistemologies—they are assertions of truth about the world. Faith claims may be endemically flawed, bizarre, or highly implausible, but they are still knowledge claims.

13. An exception is the so-called Satanic verses from the Koran. In his early suras, Muhammad made compromises with popular, preexisting goddess worship; later he revoked these verses—calling them Satanic verses—and created a new principle permitting newer revelations to supersede earlier revelations. Thus there is another way to figure out which claims about the world we should accept and which are likely false, though not through reason or evidence. The new principle is based upon the latest revelation. Later suras in the Koran supersede earlier suras. Unfortunately, many of the more militant suras are found later in the Koran.

14. I've never understood such claims of the faithful—in this example, Muslims

who state that other Muslims do not have the correct interpretation of the Koran. Once one buys into a system of belief without evidence, it's unclear on what basis one could make the claim that there's a correct or incorrect interpretation of the Koran.

15. There are many ways we can rationally determine what's in our own interest and what sort of communities we should construct. For example, in *The Theory of Justice*, American philosopher John Rawls offers us thought experiments to reason our way to an ideal political and economic system (Rawls, 2005). He details ways to create mutually agreed upon principles of justice.

16. One doesn't have to look to the most extreme examples to find other instances of people misconstruing what's good for them. Fad diets are a more pedestrian and close-to-home example. A few years ago I met someone at a local gym who ate pounds of watermelon everyday in the hope that this would help him lose weight and regain his health. He didn't lose weight and he didn't regain his health. He didn't manage to do either because eating pounds of watermelon every day is almost certainly not an activity that will lead one to health or to sensible weight loss.

CHAPTER 3

DOXASTIC CLOSURE, BELIEF, AND EPISTEMOLOGY

"The call to an examined life is about changing the way people think."

—Steven Brutus, *Religion, Culture, History* (2012)

"Change minds and hearts will follow."

—Peter Boghossian

You're almost ready to begin your work as a Street Epistemologist. However, before you start talking people out of their faith, you'll need a primer on the following: (1) the reasoning away of unreasonable beliefs; (2) the forces that contribute to closed belief systems; (3) the factors that cause people to lend their beliefs to the preposterous; and (4) the likely reaction to treatment by individuals (they'll be upset!). You'll also need a crash course in epistemology.

"ALL MEN BY NATURE DESIRE TO KNOW"

In Book 1 of *Metaphysics*, Aristotle writes, "All men by nature desire to know." Aristotle, while reflecting on the thoughts of Plato and Socrates, argues that for an examined life to emerge we need questions *and* a hunger to pursue those questions. Absent any desire to know one is either certain or indifferent.

Socrates said that a man doesn't want what he doesn't think he lacks. That is, if you believe you have the truth then why would you seek another truth? For example, if your unshakable starting condition is that the Ten Commandments are the final word on morality, or that the Koran is the perfect book that contains all the answers you'll ever need, or that all human beings descended from Manu, you stop looking. Certainty is an enemy of truth: examination and reexamination are allies of truth.

In ancient Greece, Chaerephon went to the Oracle at Delphi and asked who was the wisest man in Greece. The Oracle said that no one is wiser than Socrates. Socrates thought perhaps the Oracle—The Pythia—was saying that all men are ignorant. On the surface this was what she was saying, but she was also saying that understanding that we're ignorant, and having a desire to know, are virtues.

Aristotle is correct: all people by nature are driven to know. Humans have an inborn thirst for knowledge. When we speak to others we're interested to know what they think and why they think the way they do. When we see a physical process at work in the world we're curious about it—we want to know why the cream makes the design in the coffee it does, and why the leaf falls in the wind in a particular way. We have an inborn curiosity about people, natural phenomena, and our lives. Children in particular desire to know.

Faith taints or at worst removes our curiosity about the world, what we should value, and what type of life we should lead. Faith replaces wonder with epistemological arrogance disguised as false humility. Faith immutably alters the starting conditions for inquiry by uprooting a hunger to know and sowing a warrantless confidence.

If it's true that the unexamined life is not worth living, then the realization of our own ignorance begins our intellectual and emotional work. Once we understand that we don't possess knowledge, we have a basis to go forward in a life of examination, wonder, and critical reflection.

Among the goals of the Street Epistemologist are to instill a self-consciousness of ignorance, a determination to challenge foundational beliefs, a relentless hunger for truth, and a desire to know. Wonder, curiosity, honest self-reflection, sincerity, and the desire to know are a solid basis for a life worth living.

The Street Epistemologist seeks to help others reclaim their curiosity and their sense of wonder—both of which were robbed by faith. A human being can live a life without questioning, but as British philosopher John Stuart Mill (1806–1873) wrote, "It is better to be a human being dissatisfied than a pig satisfied; better to be Socrates dissatisfied than a fool satisfied." The sense of moving your intellectual life forward and feeding the hunger to know are a vital part of the human experience.[1]

Academicians frequently talk about confirmation bias and a hermeneutic circle—when interpreting something, our assumptions dictate what we feel, hear, see, and experience. For example, many years ago when I lived in New Mexico, I was in a doctor's waiting room with three strangers and an oddly oversized painting on the wall. The painting depicted a scene in which settlers, who had just disembarked from a large ship on the coastline, were peacefully greeted by Native Americans. The young woman to my left started a discussion about what a wonderful painting it was, mentioning that she was studying art in school. An older man to her left said that he found it to be offensive, and talked about his Native American heritage. The other man talked about how the ship in the painting was not historically accurate, and went on to speak about what the ships actually looked like. Each person brought her or his life experience to the interpretation of the painting.

Socrates and Nietzsche prescribed a different kind of interpretative experience, one in which we're not just finding and confirming our existing biases, but also attacking them. Whenever we have a chance to peek at our prejudices and see our own biases and underexamined assumptions, we have an opportunity to attack those assumptions and to rid ourselves from the presumption of knowledge. Examining and thoughtfully criticizing our biases, our interpretations, and what we think we know, is an opportunity for wonder to reemerge.

As a Street Epistemologist, one of your primary goals is to help people reclaim the desire to know—a sense of wonder. You'll help people destroy foundational beliefs, flimsy assumptions, faulty epistemologies, and ultimately faith. As Austrian philosopher Ludwig Wittgenstein says in *Philosophical Investigations* (§118): "What we are destroying is nothing but houses of cards and we are clearing up the ground of language on which they stand." When you destroy a house of cards you have a view of reality that's no longer obstructed by illusions.

Helping rid people of illusion is a core part of the Street Epistemologist's project and an ancient and honorable goal. Disabusing others of warrantless certainty, and reinstilling their sense of wonder and their desire to know, is a profound contribution to a life worth living.

REASONING AWAY THE UNREASONABLE

"Faith and reason are often—and justly—treated as irreconcilable opposites, despite Pope John Paul II's famous argument (in the aptly entitled *Fides et Ratio*) that the two are alternative ways of arriving at the same truths. After all, faith is by definition the belief in something regardless or even in spite of evidence, while as David Hume famously put it: 'A wise man proportions his belief to the evidence.'

It would seem to follow that someone's faith couldn't possibly be moved by reason. Thankfully, it turns out that this is empirically not the case. There is both ample anecdotal and occasional systematic evidence of people shedding their faith through—in part—a process of reasoning. For instance, in their book, *Amazing Conversions: Why Some Turn to Faith & Others Abandon Religion*, Bob Altemeyer and Bruce Hunsberger examine how the typical time course unfolds in both directions (i.e., acquiring or losing one's faith) and find striking asymmetries. Non religious people who convert often do so as a result of a sudden, highly emotional event, either a personal one (e.g., the death of a loved person) or a societal one (e.g., the 9/11 attacks). However, the most likely path to un-faith is slower, taking years to unfold, and going through a lot of readings, conversations, and reflection.

When I was living in the Bible Belt I knew several people who illustrated this latter path. Often the initial spark was provided by reading a secular author who wrote in a non-threatening manner (the typical example was Carl Sagan), or by being exposed to small but nonetheless disconcerting cracks in one's own religious teachings (e.g., being told by your preacher that your friends will go to hell because of such a trivial thing as singing in church).

There is clearly a need for more systematic psychological and sociological studies of the relation between faith and reason, but the evidence so far is clear: people can and do change their mind in response to reasonable argument. The problem is, it takes a long time, repeated exposure to similar ideas by different sources, and possibly also a particular personality that includes a propensity to reflect on things."

—Italian-American biologist and philosopher Massimo Pigliucci

One of the premises of this book is that people can be reasoned out of unreasonable beliefs. Not all scholars agree. In "Why Is Religion Natural?" French anthropologist Pascal Boyer argues against the idea that people have religious beliefs because they fail to reason properly (Boyer, 2004).[2] Ending his article with the famous quotation from Irish writer Jonathan Swift, "You do not reason a man out of something he was not reasoned into," Boyer argues that it is unlikely that religious beliefs can be argued away.

I disagree. Here's the evidence and several counterarguments:

1. Individuals *have* been argued away from religion. Many people who have recovered from religion have self-reported that they've been reasoned out of their religious belief. Former preachers have even gone on to become evangelical atheists: Hector Avalos, Dan Barker, Kenneth W. Daniels, Jerry DeWitt, Joe Holman, John W. Loftus, Teresa MacBain, Nate Phelps, Robert Price, Sam Singleton, etc. These individuals now successfully use lessons from their past, alongside reason and argument, to help others leave religion.

2. If the focus is on religion, as opposed to faith, Boyer may be partially correct in stating that *religion* can't be "reasoned away." Trying to

reason away religion would be like trying to reason away one's social support, friends, hobbies, comforting songs, rituals, etc. This is why Street Epistemologists shouldn't attempt to separate people from their religion, but instead focus on separating them from their faith. Reasoning away faith means helping people to abandon a faulty epistemology, but reasoning away religion means that people abandon their social support network.

3. Subsequent to much of Boyer's work, an interesting 2012 study, *Analytic Thinking Promotes Religious Disbelief*, showed, as the title states, that analytic thinking does in fact lead to religious disbelief (Gervais & Norenzyan, 2012). While mechanisms of religious disbelief and various factors that contribute to disbelief are not entirely understood at this time, the authors demonstrated that improvements in analytic processing translate into an increased likelihood of religious *dis*belief. In other words, if one gains a proficiency in certain methods of critical reasoning there is an increased likelihood that one will not hold religious beliefs.

4. Finally, many apologists (especially American theologian William Lane Craig) have had considerable success reasoning people into holding unreasonable beliefs (Craig, n.d.). This is a despairing statement about the effectiveness of the faithful's tactics. There are entire bodies of apologist literature detailing how to reason and persuade unbelievers into faith.

Boyer's criticisms notwithstanding, the problem of faith is *at least* partially a problem of reasoning. People can be reasoned out of unreasonable beliefs.[3] In fact, people frequently change their religious beliefs independent of reason, moving with abandon from one faith tradition to another.

BELIEVING THE PREPOSTEROUS

"I believe because it is absurd."

—Tertullian (197–220)

"I mean that we do not infer that our faith is true based on any sort of evidence or proof, but that in the context of the Spirit of God's speaking to our hearts, we see immediately and unmistakably that our faith is true. God's spirit makes it evident to us that our faith is true."

—William Lane Craig, *Hard Questions, Real Answers* (2003, p. 35)

There are five reasons why otherwise reasonable people embrace absurd propositions: (1) they have a history of not formulating their beliefs on the basis of evidence; (2) they formulate their beliefs on what they thought was reliable evidence but wasn't (e.g., the perception of the testament of the Holy Spirit); (3) they have never been exposed to competing epistemologies and beliefs; (4) they yield to social pressures; and (5) they devalue truth or are relativists.

Most people like to think that in their epistemic lives they accord beliefs to reason and evidence. That is, the less reason and evidence they have, the less confident they are about their conclusions and what they believe. But sometimes reason and evidence are not closely connected to belief. That is, individuals formulate their beliefs on the basis of other influences like parochial education, peer pressure, or community expectations—all potent forces not subjective to the pressure of evidence.

In some cases, individuals have damaged their thinking not only because they've habituated themselves to not proportioning their beliefs to the evidence, but also because they actually celebrate the fact that they don't do so. For example, in matters relating to religion, God, and faith, believers are often told ignorance is a mark of closeness to God, spiritual enlightenment, and true faith. (The Street Epistemologist should spend considerable time working within these contexts. This is where you're needed most. These interventions will be challenging but can be profoundly rewarding.)

Over time, you'll develop diagnostic tools that will enable you to quickly place someone in one of the above five categories. You'll then be able to tailor the intervention accordingly.

DOXASTIC CLOSURE

The word "doxastic" derives from the Greek *doxa*, which means "belief." I use the phrase "doxastic closure," which is esoteric even among seasoned epistemologists and logicians, in a different and less technical way than it's used in philosophical literature. I use the term to mean that either a specific belief one holds, or that one's entire belief system, is resistant to revision.[4] Belief revision means changing one's mind about whether a belief is true or false.

There are degrees of doxastic closure. At the most extreme degree of closure, one has a belief and/or a belief system that is fixed, frozen, and immutable, and therefore is less open to revision. The less one is doxastically closed, the more one is willing and capable of changing one's belief.

One can become doxastically closed with regard to any belief, regardless of the content of the belief. One can be closed about a moral belief ("We shouldn't torture small children for fun"), an economic belief ("Markets don't need regulation"), a metaphysical belief ("I am not a brain in a vat"), a relational belief ("My boyfriend loves me"), a scientific belief ("Global climate change is anthropogenic"), a faith-based belief ("A woman without a husband is like a dead body," Śrīmad Bhāgavatam 9.9.32), etc.

A Recipe for Closure

In *The Big Sort*, American sociologist Bill Bishop argues that we cluster in politically like-minded communities (Bishop, 2008). That is, we seek out people and groups with ideologies similar to own—we like to be around people who value what we value. One consequence of clustering is to further cement the process of doxastic closure; when surrounded by "ideological likes," even far-fetched beliefs become normalized. It is assumed, for example, "It's normal to believe what I believe about polygamy. Everyone believes this about polygamy, and those who don't are just wackos." Clustering thus increases the confidence value that we implicitly assign to a belief—we become more certain our beliefs are true.

Further complicating this clustering phenomenon is what American online organizer Eli Pariser terms "filter bubbles" (Pariser, 2012). A "filter bubble" describes the phenomena of online portals—like Google and Facebook—predicting and delivering customized information users want based upon algorithms that take preexisting data into account (e.g., previous searches, type of computer one owns, and geographical location).

Consequently, and unbeknownst to the user, the information users see is in ideological conformity with their beliefs. For example, if you've been researching new atheism by reading or watching Horsemen Hitchens and Dawkins, and you Google "Creationism," the search algorithm takes into account your previous searches, then gives you very different search results from someone who's previously visited Creationist Web pages, researched Christian apologist videos, or lives in an area of the country with high rates of church attendance (e.g., Mississippi).

This puts users in a type of bubble that filters out ideologically disagreeable data and opinions. The result is exclusive exposure to skewed information that reinforces preexisting beliefs. This is doxastic entrenchment. "It's all over the Internet," or "I'm sure it's true, I just Googled it this morning and saw for myself," gains new meaning as one is unwittingly subject to selective information that lends credence to one's beliefs as confirming "evidence" appears at the top of one's Google search.

Combine clustering in like-minded communities with filter bubbles, *then* put that on top of a cognitive architecture that predisposes one to belief (Shermer, 2012) and favors confirmation bias, *then* throw in the fact that critical thinking and reasoning require far more intellectual labor than acceptance of simple solutions and platitudes, *then* liberally sprinkle the virulence of certain belief systems, *then* infuse with the idea that holding certain beliefs and using certain processes of reasoning are moral acts, and *then* lay this entire mixture upon the difficulty of just trying to make a living and get through the day with any time for reflection, and voilà: Doxastic closure![5]

DOXASTIC OPENNESS AND THE SELF-CONSCIOUSNESS OF IGNORANCE

Doxastic openness, as I use the term, is a willingness and ability to revise beliefs.[6] Doxastic openness occurs the moment one becomes aware of one's ignorance; it is the instant one realizes one's beliefs may not be true. Doxastic openness is the beginning of genuine humility (Boghossian, under review).

Awareness of ignorance is by definition doxastic openness. Awareness of ignorance makes it possible to look at different alternatives, arguments, ways of viewing the world, and ideas, precisely because one understands that one does not know what one thought one previously knew. The tools and allies of faith—certainty, prejudice, pretending, confirmation bias, irrationality, and superstition—all come into question through the self-awareness of ignorance.[7]

In your work as a Street Epistemologist you'll literally talk people out of their faith. Your goal is to help them by engendering doxastic openness. Only very rarely will you help someone abandon their faith instantly. More commonly, by helping someone realize their own ignorance, you'll sow seeds of doubt that will blossom into ever-expanding moments of doxastic openness.

IMMUNE TO STREET EPISTEMOLOGY?

As a Street Epistemologist, you will encounter individuals whose beliefs seem immune to reason. No matter what you say, it will appear as if you're not breaking through—never creating moments of doxastic openness.

This section will unpack the two primary reasons for this appearance of failure: either (1) an interlocutor's brain is neurologically damaged, or (2) you're actually succeeding. In the latter case, an interlocutor's verbal behavior indicates that your intervention is failing—for example, they're getting angry or raising their voice, or they seem to become even more entrenched in their belief. Such protests may actually indicate a successful treatment. (Of course, it's possible that the believer has an argument that she has not yet raised in the conversation, but there's no way to address an unvoiced argument.)

1. Delusion and Doxastic Closure

Some delusions are not beliefs (Bortolotti, 2010). For example, some people who have experienced a traumatic head injury suffer from Capgras delusion—they believe that familiar people, like their husband, and sisters and brothers, are really imposters. Other individuals are afflicted by Cotard delusion—they believe they are dead (literally). It is not possible to talk people out of these delusions.

> Street Epistemologists should set the realistic goal of helping the faithful become more doxastically open. Sow the seeds of doubt. Help people to become less confident in what they claim to know, and help them to stop pretending to know things they don't know. In time, with more interventions behind you, you'll hone your skills and increase your ambitions. Ultimately, in your wake you'll have created not only people freed from the prison of faith, but also more Street Epistemologists.

In instances of damage to the brain, no dialectical intervention will be effective in eliciting cognitive and attitudinal change. These and other conditions like some strokes, intracranial tumors, or Alzheimer's disease affect the brain and are beyond the reach of nonmedical interventions. In short, if someone is suffering from a brain-based faith delusion your work will be futile.

2. Primum non nocere ("First, do no harm")

> "[Faith] causes us to distort or even ignore objective data [as such] we often ignore all evidence that contradicts what we want to believe."
>
> —John W. Loftus, *The Outsider Test for Faith* (2013)

When people are presented with evidence that contradicts their beliefs, or are shown that they don't have sufficient evidence to warrant beliefs, or learn that there's a contradiction in their beliefs (the trees could not both come before Adam, Genesis 1:11–12 and 1:26–27, and after Adam, Genesis 2:4–9), or come to understand that their reasoning is in error, they seem to cling to their beliefs more tenaciously.

Does this mean your intervention has backfired? Have you unintentionally made their epistemic situation worse? Have you cemented doxastic closure? No.

Interesting lines of research by Sampson, Weiss, and colleagues illustrate this phenomenon in the context of psychotherapy (Curtis, Silberschatz, Sampson, Weiss, & Rosenberg, 1988; Gassner, Sampson, Weiss, & Brumer, 1982; Horowitz, Sampson, Siegelman, Weiss, & Goodfriend, 1978; Norville, Sampson, & Weiss, 1996; Sampson, 1994; Silberschatz, Curtis, Sampson, & Weiss, 1991;

Doxastic pathology is especially evident in faith-based beliefs. That is, faith-based beliefs occupy a special category of beliefs that are particularly difficult to revise. Helping people revise a faith-based belief, or to abandon faith entirely, presents a host of challenges not usually encountered in other belief domains; even with politics, which trades in competing ideologies, a belief change can be facilitated more readily. This is because many factors are working to cement doxastic closure with regard to faith-based belief systems: society treats faith as a virtue, religious organizations actively spread faith, faith has evolved mechanisms to shield it from analysis, there are cultural taboos with regard to challenging people's faith, and faith communities actively support members' beliefs. (Tax-exempt status has allowed faith to become big business, but unlike faith, big business is always in the spotlight and under constant criticism.)

Weiss & Sampson, 1986.) Researchers posited that short-term psychotherapy helps individuals escape from pathogenic beliefs. A pathogenic belief is a belief that directly or indirectly leads to emotional, psychological, or physical pathology; in other words, holding a pathogenic belief is self-sabotaging and leads one away from human well-being. Examples of such beliefs are, "I'm unlovable, I'll always fail in romance," "I'm pathetic, weak, and worthless, and without Christ's love I couldn't quit drinking on my own," and "Without Scientology and auditing, I'll never be able to limit the effects of the trauma ruining my life."

Based upon data with human subjects, psychiatrists have posited that therapeutic interventions work by creating an environment where the therapist continually frustrates a pathogenic belief; this causes the patient to redouble their efforts to prove the pathogenic hypothesis. For example, a patient's pathogenic hypothesis is that people don't like her. She goes to her therapist, sits down in her office and says, "It's such a cold room in here. You never have flowers. My other therapist had cut flowers." She expects or even wants the therapist to confirm her pathogenic hypothesis and respond, "Well, I don't like you either," but instead the therapist says, in proper psychoanalytic technique, "Tell me more about your feelings of coldness here." This response causes the patient to further redouble her efforts to seek a rejection, and she becomes even more wedded to her pathogenic hypothesis. Consequently, the patient might say, "I'm really disturbed by the fact that you don't have flowers. That's incredibly thoughtless of you."

The patient's verbal behavior makes it appear that she's getting worse, but actually she's getting better. While she appears to double down and become more strident, she's actually becoming more self-aware. (We see this in Book I of *The Republic* with Thrasymachus, toward the end of the *Meno* with Anytus, in the *Hippias Major* with Hippias, in the *Gorgias* with Polus and Callicles, and in the *Euthyphro* with Euthyphro. In the *Clitophon*, often rejected as non-Platonic because it's so uncharacteristic, Clitophon denounces Socrates for not really making people virtuous. In the cave allegory at the beginning of Book VII of *The Republic*, Socrates says that those in the cave will become angry at the one who tells them that all they see are shadows—and will try to kill him if they can lay their hands on him. Through Socrates's questions people become more assertive the more they doubt, or rather the more assertive they become the more reason one has to suppose they are unsure.)

For the Street Epistemologist, the conclusion to draw from increasingly resolute verbal behavior is that if you make headway into someone's epistemic life—in helping them to question their beliefs, and the way they come to acquire knowledge—you may observe the opposite in their utterances and behavior. Once you expose a belief or an epistemology as fraudulent, you're likely to hear statements of greater confidence. It seems that Street Epistemology has made your client more doxastically closed, when in fact this strident verbal behavior indicates a glimmer of doxastic openness.

If you're worried that your intervention has made someone's epistemic life more disconnected from reality because they seem more resolute after treatment—don't be. Their verbal behavior is a natural and expected consequence of Street Epistemology. What appears to be doxastic closure is really doxastic openness.

BELIEF, EPISTEMOLOGY, AND "ACTING ACCORDINGLY"

"No one goes willingly toward the bad."

—Socrates in *Protagoras*

Helping someone value and use an epistemology that brings their beliefs into alignment with reality is no guarantee that their behavior will follow suit; this failure to see behavioral change can dishearten nascent Street Epistemologists. You've invested time and energy helping someone abandon their faith, and then to your surprise they mention they were just at temple last week. How is it someone can recognize they have a flawed epistemology but fail to act by not changing their behavior? (An answer perhaps is the supportive community surrounding the faithful.)

Having a reliable epistemology doesn't guarantee that one will act accordingly. There are many reasons people might not act upon their conclusions. Chief among these are:

1. *Moral disengagement.* Canadian-American psychologist Albert Bandura developed interesting research around what he termed moral disengagement (Bandura, 1990, 1999, 2002). For Bandura, one could know what to do, but then not do it because one morally cut oneself off—disengaged—from the action. For example, I'd really like new headphones. While in the changing room at the gym, I see a new pair of unguarded headphones. I'd feel bad about taking them, but I shut down and divorce myself from what I know I should do

and take them anyway. This is an example of moral disengagement because I knew what the right course of action was, but morally I cut myself off from doing what was right to instantly get what I wanted.

2. *Akrasia.* The ancient Greeks used the word *akrasia*, which means "lack of command over oneself" or, in common parlance, "weakness of will." One could know what one should do—not cheat on one's spouse, for example—but one may not be able to muster the will to do so.

3. *Social benefits and pressures.* People adhere to certain behaviors so that they can receive benefits like respect, recognition, friendship, and solidarity from their community. For example, a person in a public restroom plans to immediately leave after urinating, but when someone comes out of a stall they feel compelled to wash their hands. In this instance a person may also exhibit a behavior in order to avoid shame.

In many cases, individuals may also be pressured into participating in faith rituals. Failure to acquiesce may mean being stigmatized (Jehovah's Witnesses call this "disfellowshipping" and "shunning") or worse (Scientologists denigrate apostates by calling them "squirrels," and countless fallen members have reported instances of relentless harassment, including aggressive legal action).

Sooner or later in your practice as a Street Epistemologist, you'll disabuse someone of their faith and they'll behave as if nothing happened. Do not let this deter you. There are many factors that prevent one from leaving a faith tradition, pull one back into a faith tradition, or, even after one has abandoned faith, push one to stay connected with a religious community. These factors are largely outside of your control.

What is not beyond your control are the number of people you engage and your desire to constantly improve your interventions. By making Street Epistemology your default communicative interaction, you'll reach more people and improve the effectiveness of your interventions. Over time, failure to engender doxastic openness will become increasingly rare.

Intervention 1

I was at a natural food store waiting in line when the woman ahead of me struck up a conversation. She was in her late 30s, had wavy hair, and wore relaxed clothing (RC). The conversation started when she asked me something, twice, but I didn't hear her.

PB: I'm sorry. I didn't hear you. I'm deaf in one ear.

(We briefly discussed her initial question regarding moving the item divider.)

RC: May I ask, were you born deaf or did something happen?

PB: Sure. Funny you should ask. A few years ago I woke up and couldn't hear out of my left ear. I just assumed it was wax. I asked my wife to check it out—she's a medical doctor—and she told me to see a specialist right away. I was diagnosed with sudden, unilateral, idiopathic hearing loss.

RC: I'm really sorry to hear that.

(We briefly talked about living with hearing loss and treatment.)

RC: Have you tried acupuncture? I ask because I'm an acupuncturist.

(She handed me her card. I took it and read it. She was a Doctor of Naturopathic Medicine.)

PB: No. I haven't tried it because it doesn't work.

(I held the card.)

RC: Oh, it works all right. I know it works.

PB: Really? How do you know it works?

RC: Because I've cured people of illnesses. I've seen it work.

PB: Do you think selection bias has anything to do with that?

RC: No.

PB: What illnesses have you cured?

RC: Everything. You name it, I've cured it.

PB: Parkinson's, Ebola, autism?

RC: I've never treated anyone with those.

PB: But if someone came in with one of those illnesses, could you cure them?

RC: I don't know. I could try.

PB: Let's take something more pedestrian, like my hearing loss. Could you cure it?

RC: If I did, would you believe me?

(I was at the cashier and RC stood off to the side.)

PB: Yes. And once you did, I'd personally fly you out to every children's hospital in the world. Frankly, if you could cure these illnesses it's monstrously immoral not to and should be a criminal offense. My feeling is that you're a decent and kind person. I don't think you'd withhold inexpensive treatment from people who needed it. If you really believe acupuncture works, why don't you volunteer your services?

RC: There are acupuncturists at hospitals all over Portland—

PB: You're right, there are. And acupuncture still doesn't work.

RC: I don't understand why you're so confident it doesn't work.

PB: Because there's no evidence for it. In fact, there's actually evidence *against* it. You should read Bausell's *Snake Oil Science* (Bausell, 2007).

RC: There are *a lot* of studies that support acupuncture. I've seen them and I know from my experience it works.

PB: Name one.

(Pause)

RC: I can't think of one right now.

PB: But yet you're confident that there's literature out there that supports the efficacy of acupuncture.

RC: Absolutely.

(End of the conversation)

Intervention 2

I had the following discussion with a professor (OM) who teaches at an evangelical university. He's smart and Christian, and surprisingly he claims to base his religious beliefs on evidence. The conversation begins in medias res.

PB: So I just want to be clear. You're 100 percent sure that Jesus Christ is the Son of God—

OM: Yes.

PB: You're also certain that the claims in the Bible constitute sufficient evidence to warrant belief. I don't want to mischaracterize your position. This is correct, yeah?

OM: Yes, that's correct.

PB: Okay. Just so that I can understand this, and I'm sorry if I'm not getting it—

OM: You're fine.

PB: Okay, thanks. So, you think that there was an actual man named Jesus—

OM: Definitely.

PB: Okay, and he more or less behaved as it's written in the Bible. Is that correct?

OM: He did what the Bible said that he did. Yes.

(We discussed some of the alleged miracles Jesus performed and whether what's written in the Bible constitutes reliable evidence.)

PB: Okay, and this is the part I have a hard time understanding. You believe that there's sufficient evidence to warrant belief in these things, right?

OM: Yes, as I've said.

PB: Okay, so for all evidence-based beliefs, it's possible that there could be additional evidence that comes along that could make one change one's beliefs. What evidence would you need to make you change your mind?

(Responding instantly)

OM: The bones of Christ.

(Which would mean Jesus didn't ascend to heaven and the myth would be exposed as such.)

PB: The bones of Christ would make you doubt?

OM: Absolutely.

PB: But how would you know they were the bones of Christ?

(Long pause)

PB: I mean let's say a famous archeologist said, "We've found Christ's bones in this ancient tomb in Israel." Wouldn't you ask how he'd know they were the bones of Christ?

OM: I certainly would.

PB: And what answer would satisfy you?

(Looking at me as if he didn't understand)

PB: I mean, what would he have to say to you to convince you that they were indeed the bones of Christ?

OM: Well, I don't really know. I'd have to see why he said that.

PB: I don't understand how you could not have a response to something so central to your life. So you're not sure what would make your belief falsifiable?

OM: I am sure. As I told you, the bones of Christ.

PB: But what evidence would it take to satisfy you that they were actually the bones of Christ? If you could never know—or if there would be no way for you to know—that they were the bones of Christ, then your belief isn't falsifiable. If your belief isn't falsifiable then do you really believe on the basis of evidence?

(Brief pause)

PB: I don't say this lightly, but I don't think you're being sincere. You know that there's absolutely no evidence one could present that would make you change your mind.

OM: There is. I already told you.

PB: But you don't believe that. That's verbal behavior. You've created impossible conditions and you're okay with that? That's not the intellectual attitude one has when forming one's beliefs on the basis of reason and evidence.

(Silence)

PB: Here's what I don't get. Why don't you just say that you're not open to evidence and that you're going to believe anyway? Isn't that a more honest and sincere way to live your life?

OM: I told you. I am open to evidence. I'm willing to hear what someone would say.

PB: I don't believe you. You're pretending that you're open to evidence but you're not really open to evidence.

OM: I am open to evidence, but you're not open to faith.

PB: This isn't about me being open to faith; this is about you being open to evidence. You've just told me you're open to evidence, but when pressed you can't provide details of that evidence. Specifically, what would that evidence look like?

OM: Faith is belief in things hoped for that reason points toward.

PB: That's a deepity. Let's get back to the question at hand. If a famous archeologist announced that he'd discovered the bones of Christ, what evidence would you need to believe that he was telling the truth?

(End of the conversation)

DIG DEEPER

Articles

Brock and Balloun, "Behavioral Receptivity to Dissonant Information" (Brock & Balloun, 1967)

David Gal and Derek Rucker, "When in Doubt, Shout! Paradoxical Influences of Doubt on Proselytizing" (Gal & Rucker, 2010)

Book

Cass Sunstein, *Going to Extremes: How Like Minds Unite and Divide* (Sunstein, 2009)

Videos

Peter Boghossian, "Walking the Talk," https://www.youtube.com/watch?v=9ARwO9jNyjA

Peter Boghossian, "Critical Thinking Crash Course," http://www.youtube.com/watch?v=A7zbEiNnY5M

NOTES

1. The Danish philosopher Kierkegaard writes that anxiety is a key human experience. Most people are afraid of feeling anxiety, and they'll do anything they can to distract themselves from it. What Kierkegaard means is that if you want to live a full, meaningful human life—catch hold of anxiety and don't let it go. Use anxiety to follow your thoughts as a guide to see where it leads you. Don't try to escape. Let it energize your life; let it bring you awareness not only of your ignorance but also of your desire to understand moments in every experience. At least for Kierkegaard, holding onto anxiety is a key to a fulfilled life.

2. When people aren't reasoned into their faith, it is difficult to reason them out of their faith.

Many people of faith come to their beliefs independent of reason. In order to reason them out of their faith they'll have to be taught how to reason first, and then instructed in the application of this new tool to their epistemic condition. The totality of this endeavor is indeed challenging, but a goal of the Street Epistemologist is to provide people with hope. Reason has emancipatory potential.

There's something to be said for Pascal Boyer's account in *Religion Explained* that can help to understand this strategy (Boyer, 2001). Boyer is one of the leading figures in what can generally be referred to as neurotheology. Thinkers like Jonathan Haidt, Michael Gazzaniga, and Boyer, research in the areas of anthropology, linguistics, cognitive science, neurology, experimental psychology, etc. They're all moving in similar directions, which is to seek reductive explanations for the appearance of religion in human affairs. They provide interesting albeit speculative answers to a range of related questions: Where did religion come from? What purpose does it serve? How can these issues be viewed from the standpoint of evolutionary biology? In what way does religion help the survival of the fittest? What is religion's survival value from a cultural standpoint? Why do human cultures invariably develop religious superstitions and ideologies?

3. There's a vast body of literature in sales, marketing, and advertising about persuasion and convincing people to buy products they don't need. Entire industries revolve around figuring out how to influence consumers' purchasing behavior. For more on these industries and the techniques they use, I recommend two PBS Frontline documentaries: *The Persuaders* and *The Merchants of Cool*.

4. An interesting but highly technical paper that relates attitudes about information sources to doxastic attitudes is Baltag, Rodenhäuser, and Smets's "Doxastic Attitudes as Belief-Revision Policies" (Baltag, Rodenhäuser, & Smets, 2011). They write, "This paper explores the idea that an agent's 'information uptake' (i.e., what she does with some new informational input) depends substantially on her *attitude* towards the source of information: her assessment of the reliability of the source" (p. 1). Their research is applicable to faith-based beliefs formed on the perception of the evidential accuracy of ancient texts. This article also opens up potential new interventions that target attitudes toward sources of information.

Additionally, I'd recommend social psychologist Arie Kruglanski's body of work on what he terms "the need for closure." Kruglanski has published interesting, though not entirely accessible for a lay audience, articles about the importance of being closed-minded.

5. Another type of doxastic closure involves ego and narcissism. For example, there are times when we're too narcissistically involved in our conclusions, when our egos have been involved in a judgment, when we've spat out an opinion we've held for a long time, or when we don't want to consider objections because we like to win arguments. It's important not just to be aware, but also to be sincere when asking ourselves why we hold the beliefs we do. Sincerity is indispensible not just in leading an examined life, but also in having meaningful relationships.

6. The less pedantic sounding terms "snapping" (Dubrow-Eichel, 1989, p. 195) and "unfreezing" (Kim, 1979, p. 210) have been used to describe the moment of successful deprogramming when subjects cognitively leave religious cults.

7. In an interesting study, Orenstein relates religious belief and church attendance to belief in the paranormal (Orenstein, 2002). Orenstein makes this interesting and overlooked observation: "A particularly intriguing comparison in these data is between religious variables and educational attainment. There have been numerous calls for upgrading science education in order to combat paranormal beliefs. . . . However, the effects of education are so small that it appears that values and faith rather than rationality are the driving factors in paranormal belief. Moreover, if paranormal beliefs are as closely attached to religious beliefs as these data indicate, were the schools to present a skeptical position regarding the paranormal, they would run the risk of arousing a religiously-based opposition. Some observers suggest that the legitimacy of science itself is under attack by supporters of the paranormal" (Orenstein, 2002, p. 309).

In *The Believing Brain*, American author Michael Shermer discusses how science education does next to nothing to undermine belief in the paranormal (Shermer, 2011). Shermer demonstrates that this effect is related to science content, not process. This is why, Shermer argues and I agree, that we need to teach people how to think like scientists (see Shermer's Skepticism 101 program: http://www.skepticblog.org/2011/08/30/skepticism101/) and not just have them memorize science facts (Shermer, personal correspondence, August 16, 2012).

CHAPTER 4

INTERVENTIONS AND STRATEGIES

"There's evidence that religious belief is something that people go into quite quickly, but come out of rather more slowly. True, almost no one is instantly reasoned out of belief. But that's not to say people cannot be reasoned, or cannot reason themselves, out of a particular religious belief. I have talked to many who have left religious belief behind, and it turns out that a willingness to think critically and independently has almost always played a pivotal role."

—Stephen Law

"As Christian teachers, students, and laymen, we must never lose sight of the wider spiritual battle in which we are all involved and so must be extremely wary of what we say or write, lest we become the instruments of Satan in destroying someone else's faith."

—William Lane Craig, *Hard Questions, Real Answers* (2003, p. 34)

This chapter will provide you with tools and intervention strategies to begin your work as a Street Epistemologist. It covers basic principles of effective dialectical interventions designed to help people abandon their faith. These tools and strategies are pulled from diverse bodies of peer-reviewed literature, including those dealing with exiting cults, effective treatments for alcoholics and drug addicts, and even salient pedagogical interventions. In my work as a Street Epistemologist, I deploy the general strategies described in this chapter in conjunction with my principal treatment modality, the Socratic method, discussed in the following chapter. Ultimately, you'll need to personalize and tailor these techniques and strategies to account for the person with whom you're speaking, the context, and your own personality and style.

In the United States alone, we have a standing "army" of more than half a million potential Street Epistemologists ready to be empowered, given the tools, and let loose to separate people from their faith. Approximately 312 million people live in the United States. Five percent of the U.S. population does not believe in God (CBS News, 2012). If only five percent of these 15.6 million nonbelievers become Street Epistemologists and actively try to rid the faithful of their faith affliction, then 780,000 Street Epistemologists can be informally deployed to deliver millions of micro-inoculations (of reason) to the populace on a daily basis.

PART I: INTERVENTIONS

Your New Role: Interventionist

"The deprogrammer is like a coach, or a 'horse whisperer' who convinces the wary animal that crossing a creek to leave an enclosed area is not so dangerous."

—Joseph Szimhart, "Razor's Edge Indeed" (2009)

"Deprogramming, a methodology of inducing apostasy, relies heavily on this need for alternatives to the cultic interpretation of reality. After dissonance has been induced, or even as a method for inducing it, deprogrammers typically present a brainwashing model of conversion and membership in religious cults. This is a type of medical model which essentially absolves individuals of responsibility for making their original commitment, for staying with the movement. . . . It also holds out . . . the promise of a viable existence apart from the movement in which the individual will come to again experience independence and intellectual freedom. This facilitates apostasy similar to the way the adoption of a competing religious world view does. Such a model or paradigm provides a cognitive structure with which individuals can reinterpret the cultic world view and their respective experiences in it as well as anticipate a life outside it."

—L. Norman Skonovd, *Apostasy* (1981, p. 121)

Your new role is that of interventionist. Liberator. Your target is faith. Your pro bono clients are individuals who've been infected by faith.

Street Epistemologists view every conversation with the faithful as an intervention. An intervention is an attempt to help people, or "subjects" as they're referred to in a clinical context, change their beliefs and/ or behavior. Subjects start with a faith-based belief or a faith-based epistemology. You administer a dialectical treatment with the goal of helping them become less certain and less confident in their faith commitment (or perhaps even cured of faith entirely).

You will, in a very real sense, be administering a dialectical treatment to your conversational partners in a similar way that drug addicts receive treatment for drug abuse. Drug addicts come into the detox center in state X, undergo treatment, and then leave the facility in state Y, hopefully improved. You will not be treating drug addicts—you will be treating people who have been infected with the faith virus.

I view nearly every interaction as an intervention.[1] I am intervening in my interlocutor's thought process to help him think more clearly and reason more effectively. Socrates says thought is a silent conversation of the soul with itself. This means that when I'm intervening in someone else's thinking, it's not that different from thinking things out in my own head.

Talking to myself and talking to other people are alike—they are both interventions and opportunities. Even if my interactions are only three or four minutes, they still present an opportunity to help someone jettison faith and live a life free of delusion.

When you view your interactions as interventions, as opposed to confrontations or debates, you gain the following:

- It will help you to step back and exhibit more objectivity in your interventions. This will be useful because your passions won't drive the treatment and you'll be more likely to model behaviors you want others to emulate, such as being trustful of reason and willing to reconsider a belief.

- It's more likely you'll earn success if you view what you're doing as an intervention and consider a person of faith as someone who needs your help—as opposed to passing judgment. A positive, accepting attitude will translate into an increased likelihood of treatment effectiveness.

- You're less likely to be perceived as an "angry atheist," upset with the believer because you—and by extension all atheists—are "angry without God(s)." Apologists have gone to great length to advance this narrative, and if your subject even senses a hint of anger it could complicate their treatment, significantly slow their progress, and even calcify or feed the faith virus. American author Greta Christina writes about atheism and anger in her book, *Why Are You Atheists So Angry? 99 Things That Piss Off the Godless* (Christina, 2012).

- Viewing conversations as interventions will also help you listen closely and learn from each intervention. In turn, this increases the likelihood that the subject will change her behavior. It can also make you a better Street Epistemologist because you'll be able to improve future interventions.

- Anyone witness to the intervention sees the proper treatment modality in action, and may go on to help others. Everyone is a potential Street Epistemologist.

- Interventions are not about winning or losing; they're about helping people see through a delusion and reclaim a sense of wonder. On a personal level, you'll likely find deeper satisfaction in helping people than in winning a debate.

Model Behavior

"If we could change ourselves, the tendencies in the world would also change."

—Mahatma Gandhi

"Don't just tell me what you want to do, show me."

—Matt Thornton, community activist

If you are reading this book you probably already possess attitudes that predispose you to rationality, like a trustfulness of reason (American Philosophical Association, 1990, p. 2) and a willingness to reconsider (American Philosophical Association, 1990, p. 2). (For a list of the attitudinal dispositions and a definition of the ideal critical thinker, please see appendix A.) These are the core attitudinal dispositions, along with the creation of nonadversarial relationships (Muran & Barber, 2010, p. 9), which Street Epistemologists should model for the faithful.[2]

Don't portray the universe as a binary value—you're either with us or against us. Helping people to think clearly and to reject unreliable epistemologies is not another shot across the bow in the culture wars. Your discussions with the faithful are a genuine opportunity for you to help people reason more reliably and feel less comfortable pretending to know things they don't know. They also present an opportunity for *you* to further develop a disposition conducive to anchoring beliefs in reality.

Keep in mind the possibility the faithful know something you don't, that they may have a reliable method of reasoning that you've overlooked, that there's a miscommunication, or that they can somehow help *you* to think more clearly. As long as you keep in mind the possibility someone may know something you don't, and as long as you're open to changing your mind based upon evidence and reason, you'll eliminate much of the potential for creating adversarial relationships, and avoid becoming that against which you struggle.

In the middle to latter stages of one's journey to reason, many people often ask themselves, "What now? What do I do now that my faith has been shown to be false?" The Street Epistemologist's attitude, language, and behavior model what former believers can do: trust reason, stop pretending to know things they don't know, be open to saying, "I don't know," be comfortable with not knowing, and allow for the possibility of belief revision.

DOXASTIC OPENNESS

"If you are a person of the same sort as myself, I should be glad to continue questioning you: If not, I can let it drop. Of what sort am I? One of those who would be glad to be refuted if I say anything untrue, and glad to refute anyone else who might speak untruly; but just as glad, mind you, to be refuted as to refute, since I regard the former as the greater benefit."

—Socrates in *Gorgias*

Whenever one is arguing against X, the danger is that one becomes unreflectively counter-X. One of the most insufferable things in discussions with the faithful is the experience of speaking to someone who's doxastically closed. When someone suffers from a doxastic pathology, they tend to not really listen to an argument, to not carefully think through alternatives, and to lead with their conclusion and work backward (this is called "confirmation bias").

The moment we're unshakably convinced we possess immutable truth, we become our own doxastic enemy. Our epistemic problems have begun the moment we're convinced we've latched on to an eternal, timeless truth. (And yes, even the last two sentences should be held as tentatively true.) Few things are more dangerous than people who think they're in possession of absolute truth. Honest inquirers with sincere questions and an open mind rarely contribute to the misery of the world. Passionate, doxastically closed believers contribute to human suffering and inhibit human well-being.

Street Epistemologists enter into discussions with an open and genuine attitude from the start—even if there's no reciprocity.[3] If someone knows something you don't know, acknowledge that you don't know. The Street Epistemologist never pretends to know something she doesn't know. Often the faithful will attempt—intentionally or otherwise—to make you feel "less" because you don't know what they're pretending to know.

There is one piece of advice I can provide to help you overcome this social or personal feeling of inadequacy—the kind of feelings some beginning Street Epistemologists may feel in their initial interventions with the faithful. You need to become comfortable with not knowing and not pretending to know, even though others may ridicule you or attempt to make you feel inadequate for not pretending to know something they themselves are only pretending to know.

PART II: STRATEGIES

Avoid Facts

"Facts don't necessarily have the power to change our minds. In fact, quite the opposite . . . when misinformed people, particularly political partisans, were exposed to corrected facts in news stories, they rarely changed their minds. In fact, they often became even more strongly set in their beliefs. Facts . . . were not curing misinformation. Like an underpowered antibiotic, facts could actually make misinformation even stronger."

—Joe Keohane, "How Facts Backfire" (2010)

People dig themselves into cognitive sinkholes by habituating themselves to not formulate beliefs on the basis of evidence. Hence the beliefs most people hold are not tethered to reality.[4] For an individual with a personal history of not placing a high value on the role of evidence in belief formation, or not scrutinizing evidence, it is extremely difficult to subsequently engender a disposition to believe on the basis of evidence. Thus, it is of little use to bring in facts when attempting to disabuse those in the precontemplative stage of their faith-based beliefs. If people believed on the basis of evidence then they wouldn't find themselves in their current cognitive quagmire.

When I teach beginning Street Epistemologists how to help rid the faithful of their affliction and anchor their beliefs in reality, one of the most difficult strategies to get across is: do not bring particular pieces of evidence (facts, data points) into the discussion when attempting to disabuse people of specific faith propositions. Many rational, thoughtful people think that somehow, magically, the faithful don't realize they are not basing their beliefs on reliable evidence—that if they were only shown solid evidence then voilà, they'd be cured! This is false. Remember: *the core of the intervention is not changing beliefs, but changing the way people form beliefs*—hence the term "epistemologist." Bringing facts into the discussion is the wrong way to conceptualize the problem: the problem is with epistemologies people use, not with conclusions people hold.[5]

The futility of trying to persuade the faithful by way of evidence is particularly conspicuous in fundamentalists and in people who experience severe doxastic pathologies. For example, if a fundamentalist believes the planet is 4,000 years old, there's absolutely no evidence, no set of facts, no data, one can show her to disabuse her of this belief.[6] The belief the planet is 4,000 years old is based on another belief. That is, one doesn't believe the Earth is 4,000 years old without a supporting belief structure, for example, the Bible. The supporting belief structure acts as the soil in which individual beliefs are germinated and eventually grow roots.

The introduction of facts may also prove unproductive because this usually leads to a discussion about what constitutes reliable evidence.[7] This is a reasonable and important issue, but one not often encountered in the context of a Street Epistemologist's intervention.

Nearly all of the faithful suffer from an acute form of confirmation bias: they start with a core belief first and work their way backward to specific beliefs. For example, if one starts with a belief in Christ as divine, any discussion of evidence—tombs, witnesses, etc.—will almost always be futile. Any piece of contradictory evidence one brings into the discussion will never be sufficient to warrant a change in belief.

Contradictory evidence will be discarded as anomalous, offensive, irrelevant, preposterous, or highly unlikely.

Every religious apologist is epistemically debilitated by an extreme form of confirmation bias.[89] Gary Habermas, for example, exemplifies this cognitive malady. Habermas (Habermas, 1996, 2004) alleges to believe—and I think he actually does believe—that there's sufficient evidence to warrant belief in an historical Jesus, and the miracles attributed to him (Habermas, 1997), and that Jesus rose from the dead. Yet when confronted by basic, rudimentary objections (people lied, someone ransacked the tomb, the witnesses were unreliable), he takes the most remote logical possibility and turns that into not just a probability but an actuality. He does this because he starts with a foundational belief first—Christ's divinity and the truth of scripture—then conveniently sidesteps logic and reasons backward from his belief. By starting with a belief first and working backward, his beliefs make perfect sense to him as well as those who begin with the same belief.

Another example of confirmation bias occurs when someone tells their pastor, for example, that they're having doubts about their faith. Their pastor in turn tells them to read the Bible and pray about it. This is asking someone to start with their belief first and see what happens—what will happen is that their belief will strengthen. Similar advice is given to Muslims, called *dhikr* or *zikr*, which translates to remembering Allah in one's heart. Muslims "achieve" this by continuously repeating a phrase, like "Allah Akbar" (God is Great), "Subhan' Allah" (Glory be to Allah), or other such phrases, to strengthen their devotion.

Doxastic closure almost always results from pressures independent of evidence. Therefore you should avoid facts, evidence, metaphysics, and data points in discussions with those suffering from faith-based forms of doxastic closure. It won't advance their treatment. It won't help subjects to abandon their faith. What will help is maintaining your focus on epistemology and using the techniques discussed here and in the next chapter on Socratic questioning.

THE STRUCTURE OF BELIEFS: TARGET THE FOUNDATION

The overrated French philosopher Jacques Derrida has a famous line that before one can deconstruct a tradition, one must really understand that tradition. Similarly, before one can help others to overcome false beliefs, it's important to understand the structure of belief within the context of an epistemological intervention.

In philosophy, the two primary schools regarding belief (epistemic) justification are coherentism and foundationalism. Coherentists think belief statements are justified if they cohere or comport with other statements within the belief system. For example, think of the movie *The Matrix*. According to the coherentist view, if you're in the matrix you're justified in believing what appears to be a table is actually a table because other points of reference indicate that the table is in fact a table.

Foundationalists argue that specific beliefs are justified if they're inferred from other beliefs. Descartes is a good example of a foundationalist. He starts with the fact that he exists as the foundation for his beliefs: "I think therefore I am." Descartes constructs additional propositions based upon this proposition. For example, once he establishes the reliability of his senses, he then constructs propositions about the accuracy of his perceptions of the world—when he perceives something clearly and distinctly he's not deceived. Descartes and other foundationalists come to know the world by basing their beliefs on fundamental and often irreducible propositions.

Coherentism doesn't work in the context of a belief intervention because artifacts in one's epistemic landscape (an ancient text, one's feelings, one's experiences) are used to refer to each other. For example, subjects will emphatically state that their personal experiences confirm The Urantia Book is true, and that their feelings are also confirmatory evidence. Using a coherentist model, it's impossible to break through and meaningfully engage The Urantia Book, or one's feelings, etc., because of the circular nature of justification. That is, each artifact is justified by other artifacts, yet does not receive justification from any outside source. Thus, from inside a coherentist system everything makes sense—exactly as if one were in the matrix.

Street Epistemologists should use a foundationalist paradigm when deconstructing a subject's faith.

Foundationalism and Houses

It's helpful to conceptualize the structure of belief architectonically—a belief system is like a large house. There are foundational beliefs at the base of the house that hold up the entire edifice. There are also secondary and tertiary beliefs that act as scaffolding for the structure—these beliefs are important to give coherence and solidity to the structure but they are dispensable to the structure's support.

To demolish a building, start with the base. Take out the support beam and the entire structure will fall. Faith is the base. Faith holds up the entire structure of belief. Collapse faith and the entire edifice falls.

TARGET FAITH, NOT RELIGION: FAITH IS THE FOUNDATION

Here's where I part ways with the Four Horsemen—who have relentlessly attacked and undermined religion. And by all accounts they've been tremendously successful at exposing the fraudulent nature and dangers of religion. I'm advocating that we move the conversation forward by refocusing our attacks primarily on faith. By undermining faith one is able to undermine almost all religions simultaneously, and it may be easier to help someone to abandon their faith than it is to separate them from their religion. Your interventions should target faith, not religion.

One of my personal and professional goals, and a goal of this book, is to create Street Epistemologists. To do this, I'm providing easy to use tools that help move people away from faith and toward reason, rationality, and the key dispositions that accompany an examined life. The greatest obstacle to engendering reason and rationality is faith. When faith falls, edifices built upon and around faith will also collapse.

Religion is a social experience (Höfele & Laqué, 2011, p. 75; Moberg,

1962). Religious structures (churches, mosques, synagogues, temples) are places where people come together in friendship, love, trust, and community to do things that are fun, meaningful, and satisfying, that are perceived to be productive, or that grant solace. Communal celebrations of life milestones—birth, adulthood, marriage, death—are also significant social experiences. In church, for example, many people make new friends, play bingo in community halls, engage in casual sports with a team, sing songs with their friends and with strangers, date, etc. This is how the vast majority of believers experience their religious life—as a communal and social event that adds meaning, purpose, and joy to their lives (Argyle, 2000, p. 111).

Attacks on religion are often perceived as attacks on friends, families, communities, and relationships. As such, attacking religion may alienate people, making it even more difficult to separate them from their faith.

One of my students asked me if a person could be rational and go to church. I responded, "Can one be rational and sing songs? And read poetry? And play games? And read ancient texts? Of course. One can do all of these things and be rational." Religion is not necessarily an insurmountable barrier to reason and rationality. The problem is not that people are reading ancient texts. I read Shakespeare with my son. I don't, however, think that Iago, Hamlet, and Lear were historical figures. I also don't derive my ultimate moral authority from Shakespeare's works. I don't want to kill people who have rival interpretations of Shakespeare's plays. Nor do I attempt to bring Othello into decisions at the ballot box.

TARGET FAITH, NOT GOD: FAITH IS THE FOUNDATION

Trying to disabuse people of a belief in God (a metaphysical conclusion that comes about as a result of a faulty epistemology) may be an interesting, fun, feel-good pastime, but ultimately it's unlikely to be as productive as disabusing people of their faith. Attempting to disabuse people of a belief in their God(s) is the wrong way to conceptualize the problem. God is the conclusion that one arrives at as a result of a faulty reasoning process (and also social and cultural pressures). The faulty reasoning process—the problem—is faith.

Positing make-believe metaphysical entities is a consequence of a deeper epistemological problem. Belief in God(s) is not the problem. Belief without evidence is the problem. Warrantless, dogged confidence is the problem. Epistemological arrogance masquerading as humility is the problem. Faith is the problem. Belief in an imagined metaphysical entity—God—is a symptom of these larger attitudinal and critical thinking skill-based deficiencies, one that is supported and made possible primarily by faith, and also by social and cultural elements and institutions that are covariant with, and supportive of, faith. Belief in God is one consequence of a failed epistemology, with social and cultural mechanisms that both prop up this metaphysical belief and stifle epistemological challenges.

Faulty epistemologies are at least part of the reason people believe in God. Faulty epistemologies also contribute to constructing religious institutions that in turn perpetuate, nourish, and sustain one of the principal reasons for their existence in the first place—faith. Theism and atheism are both late developments that occur when the world of prehistoric rites is toppled by the discovery of writing and the beginning of intellectual traditions—including faith traditions and skeptical traditions. Faith is not a cause of religion (Brutus, 2012). Faith is an idea that appears in many religious traditions. Skepticism is an idea that appears in countertraditions. Faith and skepticism emerge together.

Attempting to disabuse people of a belief in God usually takes the counterproductive model of a debate. This is the wrong strategy and is highly unlikely to help people overcome their delusions (it may even force them into deeper doxastic closure and make them better debaters and thus more able to rationalize bad ideas). By targeting belief in God, you also run the risk of modeling the wrong behavior—the behavior of being doxastically closed—of having a closed belief system and an inability to revise *your* beliefs. This is not the behavior a Street Epistemologist should model in order to elicit behavioral change. You should be modeling doxastic openness—a willingness to revise your beliefs.

Targeting belief in God may be perceived as a type of militancy, particularly about things that cannot be known, and may push people even further into their faith-based delusions as a consequence of your perceived metaphysical extremism. In your interventions you can avoid this trap by targeting faith, not God.

If You Must *Disabuse People of Belief in God* . . .

Many readers won't heed my suggestion to target faith (epistemology) instead of God. People like to debate the existence of a God, and that's understandable as it's a clear, easy to hit, oversized bull's-eye. The Street Epistemologist doesn't just aim to hit the bull's-eye, but instead aims to raze the target and the entire field upon which the target rests. Wannabe Street Epistemologists don't have the patience or just want to enjoy the "sport" of debate.

But if you must disabuse people of a belief in God, then it's important to consider your objectives because there will be no win, no victory. About the best that can be expected is that your subject will experience a shift in confidence over God's existence. Thus, knowing that my advice will not be heeded, I'll briefly lay out one broad strategy for undermining someone's confidence in God.

In arguments about the existence of God, consider victory conditions. A victory is lowering the probability your subject assigns to the existence of God on the Dawkins' Scale, with 1.0 representing an absolute belief in God and 7.0 representing an absolute belief that there is no God. For example, if someone starts out at a 1.0, you can attempt to help them arrive at a 1.1, or even a 2.0. (While it is possible to help subjects achieve a 6.0, a belief that God's existence is highly improbable, this is overly ambitious.)

Early in the intervention, explicitly ask subjects to assign themselves a number on the Dawkins' Scale. At the end of the intervention ask them to again assign themselves a number. By doing so you can test the effectiveness of your intervention. It may be possible for you to figure out what works and what doesn't, and then adjust your approach accordingly.

Planting seeds of doubt and even moving someone 0.1 on the Dawkins' Scale should be considered a meaningful contribution to their cognitive life. (One consequence of thinking more clearly and learning how to reason is that one will place less confidence in one's conclusions. That is, one will assign one's beliefs lower confidence values.)

A solid strategy for lowering your conversational partner's self-placement on the Dawkins' Scale, and one that I repeatedly advocate throughout this book, is to focus on epistemology and rarely, if ever, allow metaphysics into the discussion. This is even more important in discussions about God—a metaphysical entity.

In other words, focus on undermining one's confidence in *how* one claims to know what one knows (epistemology) as opposed to what one believes exists (metaphysics/God).[10] Instead of having a discussion about the actual existence of metaphysical entities that can neither be proven nor disproven, direct the discussion to how one knows that these alleged entities exist. (This may also avoid one of the most common retorts among uneducated, unsophisticated believers, "You can't prove it not to be true.")

Target each epistemological claim separately. For example, "I feel God in my heart," or "Literally billions of people believe in God." Do not move on to another claim until the subject concedes that the particular claim in question is not sufficient to warrant belief in God.

Again, it's always advisable to target faith and avoid targeting God.

DIVORCE BELIEF FROM MORALITY

It's crucial to undermine the value that one should lend one's belief to a proposition because of something allegedly noble in the act of believing, or in the act of professing to believe. There's nothing virtuous about pretending to know things you don't know or in lending one's belief to a particular proposition. Having certain convictions—even the belief that one should form one's beliefs on the basis of evidence—is not noble. Formulating beliefs on the basis of evidence and acting accordingly does not make one a better person. It just makes it more likely that one's beliefs will be true and far less likely that one's beliefs will be false.[11] Similarly, not formulating beliefs on the basis of evidence (faith) does not make one a bad person. Aristotle made the distinction between a moral virtue and an intellectual virtue, and working toward developing a reliable epistemology is a step toward developing intellectual virtue.

Street Epistemologists should diligently try to uncouple the idea that the act of belief, the tenacity with which one holds a belief, and the epistemological system to which one subscribes, are moral virtues. Dennett terms this "belief in belief"—the idea that people believe that they should have certain beliefs—and he writes about this extensively in "Preachers Who Are Not Believers" and *Breaking the Spell* (Dennett & LaScola, 2010; Dennett, 2007). The belief that faith is a virtue and that one should have faith are primary impediments to disabusing people of their faith.

Faith is bundled with a moral foundation. Many people, even those who do not have faith, buy into the mistaken notion that faith is a virtue. The perceived association between faith and morality must be terminated. Faith-based interventions need to target and decouple the linkage between faith and morality.

As a Street Epistemologist, one of your treatment goals is to change the perception from faith being a moral virtue (similarly, the idea that belief in a proposition makes one a good person) to faith being an unreliable process of reasoning—that is, from faith being something to which one should morally aspire, to faith being a failed epistemology.

There's not just one correct way to conceptually divorce faith from morality in the minds of the faithful. Contextualizing and understanding the reasons why subjects believe faith claims is important. I've tried many strategies, to various effect. My current preferred ways to begin the disassociation between faith and virtue are:

- By redefining faith as "pretending to know things you don't know." Even though much of the discussion tends to revolve around the meaning of the word "faith," I've found interventions using this strategy to be surprisingly productive. This strategy also provides an opportunity to further disambiguate faith from hope.

- By explicitly stating that having faith doesn't make one moral, and lacking faith doesn't make one immoral. I usually provide examples of well-known atheists most people would consider moral: Bill Gates (for donating his vast fortune to charity) and Specialist Pat Tillman (for abandoning an incredibly promising football career to give his life for his country). I then ask subjects if they can think of any examples of the faithful who are immoral.[12][13]

Many people haven't considered the fact that having faith is unconnected to morality, and so stating it bluntly may achieve a certain "shock and awe" among a particular segment of the faithful. When I treat someone who understands that faith may not be a virtue, but has trouble disassociating the two, I usually steer the conversation back to the definition of "faith" and to faith as an epistemology.

SHORTCUTS

Occasionally, when I'm pressed for time and can't give my interlocutor a comprehensive Socratic treatment (for example, in line at the grocery store), I use two powerful dialectical shortcuts.

First, I'll ask, "How could your belief [in X] be wrong?"[14] I don't make a statement about a subject's beliefs being incorrect; instead, I ask the subject what conditions would have to be in place for her belief to be false.

When the subject is thinking about an answer it's important to listen attentively. On occasion, simply asking this question can cause a moment of doxastic openness, particularly in people who've not reflected extensively on their faith. If the subject asks me to tell them what it would take for me to believe, I respond, "That's a great question. I'd like to hear what you think first, before I tell you what conditions would have to be in place for me to believe." This is also a reinforcing statement in which I reiterate the question. It also invites a response.

Once they've given their response, I thank them. If they've asked me what it would take for me to believe, I'll use a variation of American physicist Lawrence Krauss's example in his debate with William Lane Craig: if I walked outside at night and all of the stars were organized to read, "I am God communicating with you, believe in Me!" and every human being worldwide witnessed this in their native language, this would be suggestive (but far from conclusive as it's a perception and could be a delusion).[15]

Second, I'll ask, "How would you differentiate your belief from a delusion? We have unshakable testimony of countless people who feel in their heart that the Emperor of Japan is divine, or that Muhammad's revelations in the Koran are true. How do you know you're not delusional?"

I've found this quick question to be more effective with specific religious claims, and in particular if people tell me that they feel something in their hearts. Simply causing one to consider that their core beliefs could be delusions may help them recognize the delusions.

In my experience, few people directly answer the question about how they know they're not delusional. (In the case of faith-based beliefs, I'm not sure there is an answer because they're actually suffering from a delusion.) Instead they'll reply, rarely with anger, more often with sincerity, "Well how do you know that your beliefs aren't delusions? How do you know you're not wrong?" To which I respond, "I could very well be wrong about any of my beliefs. I could also misconstrue reality. The difference between misconstruing reality and being delusional is the willingness to revise a belief. If I'm genuinely willing to revise my belief I'm much less likely to think it's a delusion. Are you willing to revise your belief that [insert belief here]"?[16] Posing this as a question is helpful because it gently reinforces the idea that they're harboring a delusion without telling them they're delusional.

MOTIVATIONAL INTERVIEWING

There's an extensive corpus of literature documenting effective treatment modalities across a wide spectrum of psychological and health-related issues—diabetes, alcohol and drug addiction, gambling, etc. The purpose of these approaches is to help counselors to elicit change behavior in their clients.

One of the most effective approaches is Motivational Interviewing (MI) (Miller & Rollnick, 2002). It's beyond the scope of this book to detail the nuances of MI, but there are some core lessons that can help the Street Epistemologist in dialectical interventions:

- Develop nonadversarial relationships

- Help clients think differently and understand what could be gained through change

- "Meet clients where they are"[17] and don't force a change

- Express empathy

- Go with resistance

- Tap into internal change behavior

MI is designed to get around a social problem involved in treating alcoholics and other substance abusers. A problem may occur, for example, when a counselor or physician adopts a moralistic, judgmental attitude toward an individual who is in a state of despair and needs help. This kind of unhelpful posturing is almost always counterproductive and very often results in a complete lack of collaboration between counselor and patient.

The bullet points above help people to avoid this interactive problem. They also hint at much larger and more thematic treatment principles. I strongly encourage Street Epistemologists to read Motivational Interviewing and the surrounding literature with an eye toward faith interventions.

AVOID SHOWING FRUSTRATION

For the unseasoned Street Epistemologist, there's often a tendency toward impatience resulting in frustration, "Why can't he just see his beliefs are ridiculous?" (Szimhart, 2009). Understand from the outset that it's unrealistic to expect a subject will stop pretending to know things she doesn't know on, during, or immediately after her first treatment. Have patience. The fruits of the intervention may come weeks, months, or even years later.

Countless people have either not responded—or responded negatively to—my initial intervention, only to e-mail me, or bump into me on the streets years later and thank me. During some interventions I've been called "Satan" or "The Mouth of the Devil," or told, "You're an evil, sick fuck and I hate you." These same people have later thanked me and even sent me gifts. Their strong reactions weren't really directed at me personally; rather, they came about as a *consequence* of the treatment. When people begin to genuinely question their faith, or when their pathogenic hypothesis is frustrated, they may be unhappy with their

> There is a certain degree of cognitive blamelessness and legitimate epistemic victimization in falling prey to an unreliable epistemology. Like children born into an epistemological community, adults in isolated communities are often not presented with options.

interlocutor. Street Epistemologists should prepare for anger, tears, and hostility. You should also strive to deal with struggling and frustrated individuals with composure, compassion, grace, and dignity.

Model the behavior you want to emulate. Don't become frustrated. Helping people to stop pretending to know things they don't know takes time, usually occurs over multiple treatments, and involves months and months of practice before you become a full-fledged Street Epistemologist.

NOT DENIAL, PRECONTEMPLATION

The Transtheoretical Model of Change is a theoretical model of behavioral change that's been used to inform and to guide interventions (DiClemente & Prochaska, 1998; Grimley, Prochaska, Velicer, Blais, &

DiClemente, 1994). For the Street Epistemologist, the stages of change and some basic terminology may be helpful.

The Transtheoretical Model of change states that behavioral change occurs in a series of stages.

- Precontemplation (not ready to change)

- Contemplation (getting ready to change)

- Preparation (ready to change)

- Action (changing)

- Maintenance (sustaining change)

- Termination (change completed)

The first stage, prechange, is called "precontemplation." Precontemplation is somewhat similar to a state of doxastic closure—the faithful don't even imagine that they need to change because they don't understand that they have a problem.[18] Precontemplative means that one is at the stage before contemplation even begins and thus does not mean denial.

In my experience, many people who consider themselves to be "moderate" in their faith are in the precontemplation stage. I've found that fundamentalists, on the other hand, have given considerable thought to their faith and to their beliefs, and this change model sometimes does not directly apply to them; rather, they're often suffering from an as yet unclassified cognitive disorder.

Contemplative means that people see a need to change their behavior but don't think it can be done, or they're wondering if they should change but they're not really sure. The other stages are less important for the Street Epistemologist, as work will often focus on helping subjects transition from precontemplation to contemplation, or from contemplation to preparation.

In your interventions, one of the first things you should do is make a diagnosis by ascertaining the change stage of your subject. There's no formula for how to do this, but you'll likely have an idea within the first minutes of conversation. You can then, to borrow from the literature on addiction and health, "meet the patient where they are" (Blume, Schmaling, & Marlatt, 2000, pp. 379–384). Are they precontemplative or are they contemplative, or are they determined to do something? With experience, you'll be able to make more accurate diagnoses and consequently tailor your treatments to the subject's stage of change.

Finally, I find the terms "precontemplative" and "contemplative" politically correct but helpful ways of avoiding the negative term "denial," which sounds more permanent and unhelpable. Street Epistemologists are agents of hope. Those who pretend to know things they don't know are not hopeless cases—they are prehope cases.[19]

AVOID POLITICS

It's all too easy to let political issues creep into interventions. At this particular point in U.S. history, many people who self-identify as atheists tend to be Democrats, while the faithful tend to be Republicans (Coffey, 2009; CNN, 2008; Miller, 2006). Don't let this fact impinge upon your interventions. Avoid politics whenever possible.

Street Epistemology is best left uncorrupted by baggage that tends to accompany political issues. Bringing up politics when conducting interventions sidetracks the discussion—which should be about faith.

I've also found that many subjects think attacks on faith are politically motivated. For example, attacks on abortion are attacks on faith by proxy, and subjects adopt a defensive posture that undermines the effectiveness of the treatment. Don't engage topics like abortion, gay marriage, school prayer, stem cell research, pornography, contraception, etc. Often, conclusions one comes to on these issues are consequences of a failed epistemology: faith. Undermine faith and all faith-based conclusions are simultaneously undermined.

MISCELLANEOUS

The following are some miscellaneous tips and suggestions beginning Street Epistemologists may be able to use:

- Just as evangelizing is relationship based (called "Relationship Evangelism"), so too is Street Epistemology (Anderson, 2010; Chambers, 2009). Always be mindful that your relationship with the subject will make or break the treatment.

- When appropriate, relate to your subject by bringing in shared personal experiences. For example, if you were the same religion as your subject, tell them that you too used to hold those beliefs.

- Be mindful of your goals throughout the intervention. Don't get sidetracked by politics or metaphysics; keep the treatment focused on epistemology.

FINALLY

You'll need to tailor these strategies to your personality and to your subject's unique circumstances. Learning to effectively weave these skills into your interventions will take time. Relax. Street Epistemology isn't a race. Over time you'll learn what works for you and what doesn't.

Finally, never forget that subjects don't owe you anything for helping to liberate them of their faith. The Street Epistemologist seeks no gratitude for her efforts.

INTERVENTIONS

Intervention 1: Belief in Belief

I had the following conversation with prison inmates in 2004. This intervention demonstrates Dennett's idea of "belief in belief" (Boghossian, 2004). I like this dialogue because it's brief and because it causes people to adopt the idea that they should "believe in the right stuff."

Researcher [Peter Boghossian]: What is justice?

Inmate 6: Standing up for what you believe in.

Researcher: What if you believe weird stuff? Like one of those lunatics who wants to kill Americans? Or what if you're a pedophile?

(A twenty-second silence)

Inmate 6: I think if you can stand on your own two feet and not care what anyone else thinks about you, and you're willing to fight for it and die for it or whatever, that makes you a man. Whether it's right or not.

Researcher: So being a man would mean to be resolute in your beliefs no matter what? What if you're in the military, like in Rwanda, and you're told to butcher all these people, and you have this skewed idea of loyalty. And you stand up for what you believe, for your country or tribe or whatever, and you just start butchering civilians? Hutus or Tutsis or whoever. Is that just? Does that make you a man?

Inmate 5: Yeah, good point. It happened in Nam [Vietnam].

Inmate 4: What are you saying? That justice isn't standing up for what you believe in?

Researcher: I'm not saying; I'm asking. What is justice? [Inmate 6] said it's standing up for what you believe in. But is it really standing up for what you believe in? Don't you have to believe the right stuff, then stand up for that? No?

Inmate 6: Yeah, maybe. Maybe.

Intervention 2: Kill All Left-handed People

I had to pick up my friend's daughter from choir practice. While I almost never frequent places of worship, I arrived early to use this as an opportunity to deliver interventions to the faithful on their home turf. After a few failed attempts to engage people, I finally found the perfect subject: a well-groomed (WG) young man in his early twenties. He'd been attending this church for the past decade. The conversation begins in medias res.

PB: So just to help me understand, you believe in the Christian God, and the Resurrection, and Redemption, and Original Sin, but you don't believe that there was a physical Adam and Eve or that the Earth is 4,000 years old. And you also don't exactly believe in predestination, but you do believe that your actions here [on Earth] are a good indicator of whether you'll go to heaven or hell, which you believe are real, physical places. You also believe that God answers prayers and that God can communicate with people. And you know this because of a deep, heartfelt "feeling," for lack of a better word. Yeah? Is that about right?

(Chuckling)

WG: Yup, pegged it.

(A brief clarification about what it means that heaven and hell are "physical places.")

PB: So, may I ask you what kind or good things have you done?

WG: Of course.

(He relates a story of an elderly neighbor. He mows his lawn and frequently checks in on him, occasionally picking up needed items.)

PB: And so you do that why? You do that because . . . ?

WG: I do that because Christ died for my sins. Think about what that means. He gave his life so that we could have the possibility of redemption.

PB: So you do that because you're a Christian?

WG: Absolutely.

PB: Okay, great. Thanks. Now I'm curious, you said before that you think God speaks to people. Not just way back when, but even today. Still. Yeah?

WG: There's no question about it—

PB: Okay, cool, sorry to interrupt, but I'm really curious about something. Let's say that God told you to kill all left-handed people and—

WG: God would never ask me to do that.

PB: Okay, but this is just a thought experiment. Just run with me here for a sec. Just to help me understand. I really am trying to figure out where you're coming from. Would you please just run with this just for a minute or two?

WG: Alright, sure. Why not.

PB: Okay, so God tells you to kill all left-handed people. And you're sure, I mean you're *absolutely* freakin' positive it's God. You just feel it in your heart. Would you do so? Would you kill all left-handed people?

WG: Again, God would never tell anyone to do that. Now you—

PB: Okay, but you did tell me you'd just run with this. Just what would you do? I mean I'm not a biblical scholar, but I think in Genesis God told Abraham to sacrifice his son, right?

WG: Yeah, that's right he did. But God stopped him. So I'm sure that it's God? Absolutely sure, as you say? Positive?

PB: Yup, no doubt about it. You feel it in your heart. You know it in your mind. It infuses every fiber of your being. Just like your belief in Christ. God tells you to kill all left-handed people. What do you do? Do you carry out the will of God?

WG: Well, if I'm sure, I mean if I'm absolutely positive, then yes. I would.

PB: Interesting. Thanks for running with me on that. Okay, does it bother you that you'd do that? I mean does it disturb you that you'd be the kind of person that would do something you know is wrong just because God told you to do so?

WG: No. You said I *knew* it was God. If I knew it was God it wouldn't bother me.

PB: Okay, let's run through this so I get it. Let's say that kid over there [gesturing to a late-teen who walked by] is left-handed. Let's say we both saw him sign his name with his left hand. So we follow him into the restroom. And let's say I go along with you because you seem sincere and I too want to carry out God's will. So we follow him into the bathroom. I smash him over the head with that thing [gesturing to a music stand]. He falls down. I give you a knife and tell you to slit his throat while he's down and I run to the door to be a lookout. You cut him open because you're following God's will. Now you really mean to tell me while he bleeds out you wouldn't even feel a little bit bothered by that?

(Pause)

WG: Well if you phrase it like that then sure. But you were talking on a theoretical level. I mean I've obviously never killed anyone before. I don't know what I'd feel. And this is a different circumstance.

PB: I think you do. I think you'd feel like shit. I think you'd regret it. I think you'd feel terrible. But neither here nor there. What if God then said, "Good job, WG. Well done. Now don't stop there, keep it up. You need to kill two more lefties before the sun rises."

WG: What's your point?

PB: I don't really have a point. I'm just trying to figure out the limits of your faith. It seems to me that your faith is limitless. You'd do anything you think that God wanted you to do, including murder innocents. Right? Or am I mischaracterizing your faith commitment?

(Pause)

PB: You're a Christian. You want to go to heaven. To do so it seems that an absolutely *minimum* requirement is to discharge the will of God. So, would you then kill another left-handed person?

WG: Yes, I would. Again, if I'm sure it's God.

PB: Okay, so if there's a conflict between your conscience and what you believe is God's will, your belief that you're doing God's will trumps your conscience?

(Pause)

WG: Yeah. That's right. Yeah. Yeah. That's right.

PB: Okay. And at any point would you ever question your certainty? Would you ever wonder if you're delusional? Maybe mistaken, or drugged?

WG: No, no. Now you just went back on me. You said I *knew* it was God. Now you're changing your story. That's not what you said.

PB: But don't delusional people think they're not delusional? Isn't that the definition of a delusion? You don't know it's a delusion.

WG: Your point being?

PB: Again, I'm not sure I have a point. I'm really just thinking through your beliefs. An admittedly odd question, but what do you think my point is?

WG: I dunno. I'm not sure. Maybe it's that conscience is the most important thing? Or maybe it's some point about God. You know, about God.

PB: Yeah. I'm not sure how you or anyone else could ever be certain that God is talking to you. Just because someone is positive that God speaks to them doesn't mean that God actually spoke to them. They could be mistaken. And just because you feel that Jesus is the Son of God, I'm not sure that you could ever be certain about that either. You could always be mistaken, maybe even delusional. Maybe it's an idea that's germinated and developed in you because of our culture and the way our brains work. I mean lots of people have had feelings that their holy books were true and they can't all be correct. Right?

(Silence)

Intervention 3: Two Churches

The following conversation took place at a fast-food restaurant in Portland, Oregon. An older man had just spoken to two younger women (around eighteen years of age) in what appeared as an intense conversation. I couldn't hear what was said, but being curious, I asked the women what they talked about:

PB: I'm curious, if you don't mind me asking, what did that guy say to you? The conversation looked really heated.

W1: He wanted us to come to his church.

PB: Now? At 8:00 p.m.?

W1: No, no.

PB: What did you say?

W1: We said we already have a church.

PB: Oh. So why didn't you want to go his church? Then you'd have two churches.

(Perplexed)

W2: What?

PB: I mean if having one church is good, maybe having two churches is better. I mean, that way you'd cover some of your bases. What if in your church they're missing something key, but if in this other church they have what your church is missing?

W1: Our church isn't missing anything.

PB: Oh. How do you know that?

W2: Know what? What do you mean?

PB: I mean how do you know that your church has everything you need, or that they've gotten all of the rules right and such, and that his church might have picked up on something that your church overlooked?

W1: What are you talking about?

PB: I'm talking about one reason I think you're going to church. You want to be saved, right? Am I right?

W1: Of course. We are saved.

PB: That's really great. Did they tell you that in your church?

W2: Yeah, kind of.

W1: Yes.

PB: So then if you're already saved, why did that man want you to go to his church?

W1: What?

PB: When you told that man that you went to your own church and that you're already saved, which I assume you told him, why did he then want you to go to his church? Why would he want that? What would be the point of going to his church if you're already saved?

(Long pause)

PB: Why didn't you tell him that he's the one who should be going to your church because you're already saved?

W1: We don't care where he goes to church.

PB: But he obviously cares where *you* go to church. He must think you're not saved or he wouldn't want you to go to his church. So if he thinks you're not saved because you don't go to his church, and you think you are saved because you do go to your church, how do you know you're actually saved? Someone has to be wrong. How do you know it's not you?

W2: Because we know we're saved. We know it.

PB: But he *knows* you're not saved. In fact, I think he's more certain that you're not saved than you are that you are saved.

W2: We're saved. We're saved.

PB: Don't you think it's strange that a fellow Christian would want you to leave your church?

W1: What do you mean?

PB: If you're already saved why would it make any difference which church you go to?

(Pause)

PB: If you're already saved then why would it make any difference which church you go to?

W1: I guess it wouldn't matter.

PB: So if you're already saved, why go to church at all?

(Pause)

W1: I don't really know.

(End of conversation)

DIG DEEPER

Article

Daniel Dennett and Linda LaScola, "Preachers Who Are Not Believers" (Dennett & LaScola, 2010)

Blog

Matt McCormick, "The Defeasibility Test" (McCormick, 2011)

Books

Christopher Muran and Jacques Barber, *The Therapeutic Alliance: An Evidence-Based Guide to Practice* (Muran & Barber, 2010) (Focus on pp. 7–29, 97–210, and 285–320)

Daniel Dennett, *Breaking the Spell* (Dennett, 2007)

William Miller and Stephan Rollnick, *Motivational Interviewing* (Miller & Rollnick, 2002) (Focus on pp. 3–179)

Dan Barker, *Godless: How an Evangelical Preacher Became One of America's Leading Atheists* (Barker, 2008)

For a frightening glimpse into the Christian world of "Relationship Evangelism," see:

Shawn Anderson, *Living Dangerously: Seven Keys to Intentional Discipleship* (Anderson, 2010)

Arron Chambers, *Eats with Sinners: Reaching Hungry People Like Jesus Did* (Chambers, 2009)

Dave Earley and David Wheeler, *Evangelism Is . . .: How to Share Jesus with Passion and Confidence* (Earley & Wheeler, 2010)

NOTES

1. Airplanes offer a fantastic opportunity to practice Street Epistemology—particularly if you fly Southwest Airlines, or any other airline that doesn't have assigned seats. I usually get on the plane a little later and try to sit next to someone reading a religious text. Middle seats are good, as they increase your chance of sitting next to someone of faith.

2. The creation of nonadversarial relationships is a necessary condition for a successful treatment. Trustfulness of reason and willingness to reconsider are two crucial posttreatment attitudes the faithful need in order to make a full recovery.

3. I find this easy to do with rank-and-file believers, but difficult with faith leaders. I'm often left with the suspicion many reflective and published apologists don't genuinely and sincerely believe what they claim to believe. I've always found Dinesh D'Souza to be an example of someone who's insincere; Ravi Zacharias, who appears to me as someone who suffers from pathognomonic delusions, strikes me as someone who's sincere.

    Toward the end of many of my conversations with apologists, I'm left with the feeling that they've often said things or taken positions to justify their beliefs *to themselves*. I find it bizarre during the pauses in our conversation when they wait for my approbation, and seem disappointed when it's not forthcoming.

    Shermer has noted that the smarter someone is the better they are at rationalizing. I think he's correct. Smart apologists are good at generating reasons for why they believe their irrational beliefs are true—and they spend a good deal of their time doing just that.

Rank-and-file believers do not fill their days with thinking about how to defend their faith. The combination of insincerity, intelligence, and intentionally leading or coaxing others into an unreliable epistemology makes it difficult to be open in these communicative engagements.

4. Often, the same people have a lower threshold for what constitutes reliable evidence. For more, see Mele's, *Have I Unmasked Self-deception or Am I Self-deceived?* (Mele, 2009, especially p. 264). The original citation can be found here: Trope, Y., & Liberman, A. (1996). Social hypothesis-testing: Cognitive and motivational mechanisms, in E. T. Higgins & A. W. Kruglanski (Eds.), *Social psychology: Handbook of basic principles* (pp. 237–270). New York: Guilford Press.

5. One way to conceptualize the relationship between belief and evidence is through Israeli-American psychologist and economist Daniel Kahneman's System 1 and System 2 thinking (Kahneman, 2011). System 1 thinking (intuition) is instantaneous, automatic, subconscious, and often has some degree of emotional valence; System 1 thinking is the result of habits and resistance to change. System 2 thinking (reasoning) is much slower, more subject to change, more conscious, and requires more effort.

   Many beliefs are formed on the basis of the System 1 fast-thinking phenomenon. Doxastic closure can come about when people lack the system capacity to reinsert evidence into their System 1 thinking—that is, their System 1 thinking is invulnerable to System 2 thinking. They haven't developed the ability to allow System 2 thinking to penetrate System 1 beliefs.

6. Dawkins explicitly stated that he will not debate creationists (Dawkins, 2006b). Noting Stephen Gould's advice, he writes, "'Don't do it.' The point is not, he said, whether or not you would 'win' the debate. Winning is not what the creationists realistically aspire to. For them, it is sufficient that the debate happens at all. They need the publicity. We don't. To the gullible public which is their natural constituency, it is enough that their man is seen sharing a platform with a real scientist. 'There must be something in creationism, or Dr. So-and-So would not have agreed to debate it on equal terms.'"

I'd go beyond this and state that for a reputable scientist to publicly debate a creationist borders on being unethical. Providing a platform for someone who suffers from a pathogenic belief may push the creationist even further into delusion.

7. For more here, I highly recommend Schick and Vaughn's, "How to Think about Weird Things" (Schick & Vaughn, 2008). Specifically, pp. 179–189 cover the following criteria of adequacy: testability (180), fruitfulness (182), scope (185), simplicity (186), and conservatism (189).

Arguing about what constitutes evidence and what are the criteria for evidence usually results in shifting the discussion into ever-receding tangents. Such shifts are common rhetorical tactics of apologists. If you choose to enter into a discussion about what constitutes reliable evidence, I suggest you carefully read the Schick and Vaughn text.

8. This is particularly true among intelligent, articulate apologists. The more intelligent and articulate the apologist, the more conspicuous and epistemologically enfeebling the confirmation bias.

9. It's very difficult to start from a position of belief neutrality because everyone suffers from some form of confirmation bias—myself included. When I read the work of religious apologists, for example, I find myself incredulous and in a state of perpetual marvel that intelligent, thoughtful people could seriously entertain such hokum. I have to force myself to step back, to intellectually open myself up to looking at their evidence and, more importantly, the process of reasoning that they use to come to their conclusions.

The process of genuinely opening oneself up to competing ideas is vital for one's intellectual life, because it prevents doxastic closure. How one engenders this attitude in the first place, however, is complicated and subject to many personal, psychological, social, and emotional variables.

10. Metaphysical discussions center on the furniture of the universe—what exists or does not exist. Bringing metaphysics into a discussion is usually fruitless and may even be counterproductive, in some cases pushing people further into their faith and metaphysical delusions. Conversations about what

there is, as opposed to how one knows what there is, cannot gain cognitive traction because the entities in question (Gods, angels, demons) have no attributes that leave a footprint in the natural realm. Given this starting condition, there's nowhere for the conversation to move. Consequently, these discussions almost invariably devolve into he said, she said.

One reason many people assign belief in God a high number on the Dawkins' Scale is because they started with metaphysics and worked their way back to epistemology. That is, people started with the belief God exists and then asked themselves how they know this. This is confirmation bias. No discussion of alternative formulations of what there is (maybe there's a God but it's somehow limited, maybe there was a God but in creating the universe it extinguished itself) will divorce this self-interested bond with metaphysics.

11. An interesting question is whether it's even possible to knowingly use an epistemology that will not guide one to the truth. For example, if one knows goat sacrifice will not lead one to the truth about how to build a better car battery, is it possible one can use the process of goat sacrifice and make oneself believe that it is a reliable way to build a better car battery? The opposing views of Clifford and James are helpful here.

Clifford (Clifford, 2007) basically shares the conception of knowledge put forth by Plato in the *Theaetetus*: Knowledge = Justified True Belief. Knowledge is not a fuzzy thing that we can decide to have or not. For Clifford, one can't decide to believe something. You lend your belief to a proposition because you're forced to believe it by, among other things, the thoughtfulness that you have given to the problem. From Clifford's perspective it's not possible to force yourself to believe anything. And if somehow you do manage to force yourself to believe something, then you have a kind of epistemological sickness.

William James takes a very different position (James, 1897). For James, we don't always know things or believe things or regard the world in terms of the appreciation of evidence. Our attitude about how we go about our lives is everything. James went up to his room at his parent's house and pretty much stayed there for years, thinking through questions of belief. James comes to the opposite conclusion from Clifford: one can decide to believe certain things; one can make a decision to believe something; it's healthy for one to do so in certain cases and it would be unhealthy for one to do so in other cases. As a pragmatist, James is saying that his concern isn't whether a belief is true according to some abstract standard of truth; rather, his concern is whether it is going to serve one's purposes in living a fulfilling human life. Thus, James's answer and Clifford's answer are in direct opposition. The issue at stake in this debate is the idea of whether the human part of ourselves can supersede our scientific reasoning or whether some sort of appreciation of scientific evidence should supersede our human feelings.

Choosing to believe a particular proposition is referred to in the philosophical literature as "doxastic volunteerism." While James predates this literature, one of the examples James uses to demonstrate belief choice is in the health arena. One cannot, James argues, "by any effort of our will, or by any strength of wish that it were true, believe ourselves well and about when we are roaring with rheumatism in bed" (James, 1897, p. 5). However, evidence suggests that often people do in fact believe that they are well when they are quite ill (Livneh, 2009; Vos & de Haes, 2007). Whether this is a conscious choice remains unclear. Conversely, often people believe they are sick when they are well.

Among the interesting manifestations of this phenomena are what medical anthropologists term "culture-bound syndromes," which have recently been included in the DSM-IV (Bernstein & Gaw, 1990). Culture-bound syndromes are recognizable diseases only within a specific culture or society. Koro, for example, is the unsubstantiated belief that one's penis is retracting into one's body, and that it will ultimately disappear (Edwards, 1984). Koro is primarily found in China and Southeast Asia, though recently it has appeared in parts of the developing world, and even among the intellectually disabled (Faccini, 2009).

Overlapping and particularly interesting arguments about belief choice, specifically in regard to God, can be found in the literature on Pascal's Wager. Pascal's Wager states that one should bet as if God exists, and consequently believe and live as if God exists, because if one does so then one has everything to gain and nothing to lose. One line of criticism is that one cannot force oneself to believe in God. Harris articulates this in a piece for the *Washington Post* titled, "The Empty Wager" (Harris, 2007). Harris writes, "But the greatest problem with the wager . . . is its suggestion that a rational person can knowingly will himself to believe a proposition for which he has no evidence. A person can profess any creed he likes, of course, but to really believe something, he must also believe that the belief under consideration is true" (Harris, 2007). Many Christian apologists, and even some secular writers (Braithwaite, 1998, pp. 37–44), would disagree.

A common thread among these "God exists" discussions is that one is attempting to force oneself to believe. To my knowledge there have been no empirical studies demonstrating whether it's possible to force oneself to believe in God, or perhaps more effortlessly, to believe trivial propositions (like whether or not a McDonald's hamburger bun has more sesame seeds than a Burger King bun). Furthermore, it is unclear how to test whether it is possible to force oneself to believe in various propositions.

12. Here are a few of the more well-known examples: Ted Haggard (had sex with a male prostitute and used crystal meth), Peter Popoff (exposed by James Randi for using a concealed radio receiver to deceive his flock), Jimmy Swaggart (had sex with a prostitute), Father Murphy (sexually abused countless deaf children), W. V. Grant (a faith healer who was exposed for using magic tricks to fool his followers), Father Thomas Laughlin (molested underage boys), Monsignor William Lynn (covered up countless cases of priest molestations and rapes by moving priests to new parishes), Benny Hinn (televangelist and faith healer exposed on *Dateline NBC*), Bishop James Hunter (arrested for selling drugs), Terry Hornbuckle (drugged and raped women in his congregation), Anthony Martinez-Garduno (sold meth and "date rape" drugs at his church), Ryan Jay Muehlhauser (sexually assaulted two homosexual men while allegedly attempting to turn them straight during a counseling session about their sexual orientation), Oscar Perez (sexually assaulted boys in his congregation).

13. Occasionally I'm told that no person of "true faith" would ever do anything immoral. This is a version of British philosopher Antony Flew's "No True Scotsman" fallacy: Imagine a Scotsman reading the morning paper. He sees an article about how a person from Scotland commits an act of brutality against an innocent. He responds, "No true Scotsman would ever do that." When reading the paper the next morning, he sees an article about a person

from Scotland who does something even more horrific. He repeats, "No true Scotsman would ever do that."

This is one of the few instances when I don't generate an example of a person of faith who is immoral. If I generate the example it could be met with, "Well, no person of *true* faith would ever do that." It's better to have subjects generate their own examples to avoid this fallacy.

14. American philosopher Matt McCormick offers a variant of this that he calls, "The Defeasibility Test" (McCormick, 2011). It's worth carefully reading. ("What would it take for you to abandon your faith?" is the first question I ask people interested in debating me.)

McCormick writes, "Are there any considerations, arguments, evidence, or reasons, even hypothetically that could possibly lead me to change my mind about God? Is it even a remotely possible outcome that in carefully and thoughtfully reflecting on the broadest and most even body of evidence that I can grasp, that I would come to think that my current view about God is mistaken? That is to say, is my belief defeasible? If the answer is no, then we're done. There is nothing informative, constructive, or interesting to be found in your contribution to dialogue. Anything you have to say amounts to sophistry. We can't take your input any more seriously than the lawyer who is a master of casuistry and who can provide rhetorically masterful defenses of every side of an issue. She's not interested in the truth, only in scoring debate points or the construction of elaborate rhetorical castles (that float on air)."

I briefly discussed a version of the Defeasibility Test in my 2012 talk at the Freedom From Religion Foundation's (FFRF) national convention.

15. On *Real Time with Bill Maher*, Maher has a humorous response to what it would take for him to believe: Jesus Christ coming down from the sky during the halftime show at the Super Bowl and turning nachos into bread and fish.

16. If I have a little more time, I simplify the following idea: Both the faithful and atheists lend their beliefs to identical propositions (2+2=4, apples fall from trees in a downward direction, the Earth goes around the sun, etc.).

The faithful, however, also lend their beliefs to an additional number of propositions (bathing in the Ganges River can wash away sins, or Bahá'u'lláh was a messenger from God). What atheists believe is a subset of what (most) of the faithful believe. Obvious exceptions include the claims of creationists and other antiscientists, but in most cases, there's nothing that an atheist believes that a religious person doesn't also believe. The faithful just lend their beliefs to additional propositions.

17. What *you* think is a good reason to motivate someone to action may not constitute a good reason for your subject. Conversely, what your subject thinks is a good reason may not be a good reason for you.

A few years ago I stopped for gas late at night at a twenty-four-hour gas station. A young woman who was obviously on drugs approached me. She had open pus sores across her face and a cigarette hanging out of her mouth. She blurted out, "Can I have a ride? I really need a ride." I responded by lifting up my shirt. (I have a large scar on my stomach from surgery.) I said, "I would give you a ride, but the last time I gave a woman a ride my wife stabbed me." She looked at me and nodded as if this made perfect sense. Then she walked to the next car. To her, this really did make perfect sense. This is an example of "meeting people where they are."

Here's another example: A friend of mine called me because her son wanted to get a large tattoo of a decapitated Jesus on his back. She wanted me to talk him out of it. When I called him on the phone he said to me, "Pete, I know my mom asked you to call me. It's not gonna work." I immediately responded by asking him if he was still smoking pot. He said, "Yeah, what of it?" I said, "Well have you ever considered the fact that you'd be an international criminal, wanted by law enforcement?" He said, "Dude, I think about that shit all the time." I replied, "Okay, so let's say they're after you, the cops, the FBI, do you think it would make it more or less likely to identify you if you had a large tattoo of a decapitated Jesus on your back?" He never got the tattoo. Meet people "where they are."

18. Socrates said that a man doesn't want what he thinks that he doesn't lack (*Symposium* 200a-b; *Lysis* 221d). That is, if one doesn't think that one lacks a big nose, one doesn't want a big nose. Similarly, if one thinks one has the truth, one stops looking.

19. In the field of addiction, for example, the recent thinking is that an individual is not in a state of denial, but in a precontemplative state. I've heard speakers point out that even people who suffer from severe forms of alcoholism regularly, routinely, spontaneously choose to quit drinking and then just quit drinking. This happens every year among a large number (maybe a minority but still a large number) of alcoholics. Even seemingly incorrigible alcoholics who appear to be in the deepest state of denial spontaneously remit. In the transtheoretical model, this means that they were not in denial, but that they were precontemplative. (This is also how the Motivational Interviewers would frame the state of the individual.)

CHAPTER 5

ENTER SOCRATES

10th Grader: "Do you think we should be allowed to get stoned?"

Pete: "I dunno, what do you think?"

10th Grader: "I think we should be allowed to get stoned if we want to."

Pete: "Hmm, why do you think that?"

10th Grader: "Because we should have a right to do what we want to do."

Pete: "What do you mean by 'right'?"

10th Grader: "I mean something I should not have to earn, like, I should just get to do it, you know what I mean?"

Pete: "I think so. So you mean you think you should have the right to do anything you want to do?"

10th Grader: "No, not anything, if it harms people we shouldn't have that right."

Pete: "And does smoking pot harm anyone?"

10th Grader: "No."

Pete: "No?"

10th Grader: "No."

Pete: "Nobody?"

10th Grader: "No."

Pete: "What about yourself? Does it harm yourself?"

10th Grader: "What do you mean?"

Pete: "I mean is it physically injurious to you? Does it harm your body?"

10th Grader: "Maybe a little bit, but not that much."

Pete: "But it does harm you, no?"

10th Grader: "Yeah, I suppose so. But . . ."

Pete: "So if it harms you, you shouldn't have the right to do it, no?"

10th Grader: "But a lotta stuff harms me and I'm allowed to do those things."

Pete: "But we are not talking about 'a lot of stuff' we are talking about the right to do something that harms you—your position holds that you should not be allowed to do that either."

10th Grader: "So you think we should not have the right to get stoned?"

Pete: "I don't know, but it's not about what I think, it's about what you think. And you seem to think that you should be allowed to do something that harms you and not be allowed to do something that harms you. Does that make sense to you?"

10th Grader: "Not really"

—Peter Boghossian, "The Socratic Method (or, Having a Right to Get Stoned)"

"Often as a consequence of sustained Socratic dialogue, one realizes that one did not know something that one thought one knew."

—Peter Boghossian, "Socratic Pedagogy"

The purpose of this chapter is to demonstrate how to use the Socratic method as a conversational intervention to liberate people of their faith. The Socratic method may sound complicated, but essentially it's asking questions and getting answers.

The Street Epistemologist can reason with unreasonable people—for more than twenty years I've made a career of doing just that. But you'll need more than the broad strategies discussed in chapter 4 to reason someone out of the kind of beliefs they didn't reason themselves into. Beyond faith-based beliefs, examples of other false beliefs include the groundless popular belief that driving a red car increases the likelihood that you'll get a speeding ticket, or the untrue folk wisdom that going outside without a jacket will cause you to catch a cold, or the superstition that walking under a ladder is bad luck. In this section, I'll explain the primary tool that I use to help free people who are doxastically trapped.

The Socratic method is a powerful, no cost, dialectical intervention that can help people reason away their faith. Effectively used, the Socratic method can create moments of doxastic openness—moments when individuals become aware that their reasoning is in error. In these instances people become less certain, less sure, less confident, and correspondingly more open to alternative hypotheses and explanations. People become aware of their own ignorance. The Socratic method is like putting a tool into the hands of a believer who ultimately uses that tool to dismantle the scaffold of their own (false) belief.

Socrates used his method as a guide to help people show *themselves* they didn't know what they thought they knew.[1] He exposed untrue beliefs, developed a sense of disquiet in his interlocutors, and elicited contradictions by asking pointed questions in an unthreatening way. These conversations forced people to substantively evaluate, and in many cases ultimately change, their beliefs. And this was all accomplished merely by asking a question, listening to the answer, then asking another question, listening to that answer, etc.

This chapter begins with an explanation of the stages of the Socratic method, followed by a detailed sampling of successful and unsuccessful Socratic interventions I've had over the years. Finally, I guide readers through Socratic techniques along with the supplementary treatment methods described in chapter 4.

STAGES

The Socratic method has five stages: (1) wonder; (2) hypothesis; (3) elenchus, (4) accepting or revising the hypothesis; (5) acting accordingly (Dye, 1996). I'll now briefly explain these stages and then show how they inform actual faith interventions.

Stage 1: Wonder

The Socratic method begins in wonder. Someone wonders something: "What is justice?" or "Is there intelligent life on other planets?" or "Does karma govern the cycle of cause and effect?" etc. Wondering takes propositional format—words are used to capture one's thoughts—and are thus expressed as questions. Simply put: from wonder a hypothesis emerges. (See appendix B for the Socratic questions used in my study to increase prison inmates' critical thinking and reasoning ability.)

Stage 2: Hypothesis

Hypotheses are speculative responses to questions posed in stage 1. They're tentative answers to the object of wonder. For example, one possible response to the question, "Is there intelligent life on other planets?" would be, "Yes, there must be. The universe is just too large for there not to be." Another response could be a simple, "No."[2]

Stage 3: Elenchus (Q&A)

The elenchus, or question and answer, is the heart of the Socratic method. In the elenchus, which is essentially a logical refutation, Socrates uses counterexamples to challenge the hypothesis. The purpose of the counterexample is to call the hypothesis into question and ultimately show that it's false.

Continuing with our previous example:

Person A: "Is there intelligent life on other planets?" [Note: Stage of wonder]

Person B: "Yes, there must be. I think the universe is just too large for there not to be." [Note: Stage of hypothesis]

Socratic Interlocutor: "Well, to paraphrase Carl Sagan, 'We could be the first; someone had to be the first and it could be us.'" [Note: Stage of counterexample and beginning of the elenchus, which causes the epiphany of ignorance]

In the elenchus, the Socratic facilitator generates one or more ways that the hypothesis could be false. That is, what conditions *could* be in place that would make the hypothesis untrue? Definitively stating there's no life on other planets is not a counterexample because it simply states that the hypothesis *is* wrong, it doesn't state how it *could* be wrong. This may seem like an issue of style, but in fact the interchange is critical to the process, because without a dialogue there can be no intervention. Simply put: both parties enter into an open discussion.

Using the example of life on other planets, one condition to make the hypothesis false would be if we were the first intelligent life forms to arise. If it is the case that we're the first intelligent life forms to emerge, then by definition this means there is currently no intelligent life on other planets. This is a successful counterexample because it calls the hypothesis into question—that is, it's one viable explanation for why there could be no other intelligent life forms in the universe.

Another condition that would call the hypothesis into question might be, "Just as it could be that we're the first intelligent life form to have arisen, so too could it be that we're the last intelligent life form." This is a counterexample because it notes a possible condition that could make the hypothesis false. It is possible the universe was, at one point, teeming with intelligent life but perhaps there's a "Great Filter" that either prevents or makes it exceedingly difficult for intelligent life to sustain itself (Hanson, 1998). The Great Filter possibility,[3] or the possibility we're the first intelligent life form to arise, calls the hypothesis into question.

A hypothesis is never proven to be true. After a hypothesis survives repeated iterations in the elenchus, this only means that to date it has withstood a process of falsification. For example, through a window by a lake, you've seen one million white swans; nevertheless, this doesn't mean all swans are white. No matter how many swans you've seen, this does not make the hypothesis that all swans are white true, it only means the hypothesis hasn't been shown to be false (yet).

A single counterexample can kill a hypothesis, yet even millions of confirming instances don't change the status of the hypothesis. (There's an asymmetry between confirmation and disconfirmation.) For example, let's look at the hypothesis, "All swans are white." Yet, one day, standing in your yard is a black swan. In this instance, the hypothesis was shown to be false, independent of your experience of seeing a multitude of white swans.

Regardless of the content of one's beliefs, that is, whether or not one believes in reincarnation, talking serpents, or that Tom Cruise is God, all but the most severely delusional individuals will recognize some constitutive, fundamental mistakes in reasoning, like contradictions (a thing cannot be both X and not X) and inconsistency (incompatibility with other claims). The elenchus is a simple yet effective way to undermine a hypothesis by eliciting contradictions and inconsistencies in one's reasoning, and thus engendering aporia. A classic aporia, or puzzlement, being, "Everything I say is a lie."

Stage 4: Accept or Revise Hypothesis

In stage 4, the hypothesis is either accepted as provisionally true, or it's rejected. If it's accepted as true then this ends the elenchus and immediately begins stage 5. If it's rejected then another hypothesis is given and the elenchus begins again.

If the interlocutor cannot overcome the argument made in the elenchus, then she is forced to revise her hypothesis. In our present example, if she cannot rebut the claim that we could be the first intelligent life to have arisen, then she needs to revise the original hypothesis, which was, "Yes, there must be." She could, for example, offer a new hypothesis, "Almost definitely," or she could offer no new hypothesis and state that she no longer knows with certainty.

If the arguments that emerge from the elenchus cannot refute the hypothesis, then the hypothesis stands. It's vital to reiterate that if the hypothesis stands this does *not* mean one has found eternal truth. This simply means the hypothesis is accepted as provisionally true.

Stage 5: Act Accordingly

As a consequence of the Socratic method, one would ideally act upon the results of one's inquiry. Acting could be anything from changing one's belief to taking a specific action. Stage 5 has less to do with the implementation of the method, and more to do with the consequences of one's examination.

ACTUAL SOCRATIC INTERVENTIONS

I'll now show how the stages of the Socratic method can come into play when administering Socratic treatments. I'll examine actual conversations I've had with a broad spectrum of people in a wide variety of contexts and explain, statement by statement, techniques referenced in chapter 4. I've included a range of treatment outcomes, from immediately successful to completely unsuccessful.

I note the failures here because most interventions aimed at removing faith are not an initial success. Sometimes, even after years of treatment, the faith virus is not separated from its host. Initial, comprehensive success is rare. I conduct multiple Socratic interventions *daily*, and as much as I try to help people shed faith, very rarely has someone abandoned their faith on the spot. What is common—and promising—is that people experience glimpses of doxastic openness as a direct consequence of Socratic discourse. Some of these moments are captured in the conversations below. (Remember that the goal of each intervention is to move the subject one step along the transtheoretical model, for example, from precontemplative to contemplative, or from action to preparation.)

Finally, experiencing failures are important in your practice as a Street Epistemologist. There is perhaps more to learn from unsuccessful interventions than from successful ones—we learn from our failures, not from our successes. Some of the conversations detailed below may help to shed light on specific instances of doxastic closure, some may give readers insight into how they could improve upon and tailor the intervention given their particular skill set, and others still can be seen as a snippet in the context of long-term treatment.

Intervention 1: Doxastic Openness

I had the following late-night discussion with a young man (YM) at a local gym. I was on a treadmill when he began walking on the treadmill next to me. A few minutes later he asked me about my MMA (mixed martial arts) T-shirt. From there the conversation turned to superstition in the martial arts, to many popular but false beliefs, and ultimately to religion. About ten minutes into our discussion he told me Jesus Christ came into his life.

> *YM*: He [Jesus Christ] touched me. At that moment my life was forever changed.

This statement, "He touched me," is the hypothesis. It is the statement I targeted for refutation. Note that at no point in this intervention do I deny the feelings he experienced. To do so would be counterproductive because we're all infallible in terms of our tastes and feelings. What I target for refutation is the source or cause of these feelings and the resultant faith it engendered.

> *PB*: That's really interesting. Can you tell me about that?

I asked this question for two reasons. Primarily, I needed to make sure I understood the *exact* nature of the claim. I was virtually certain I did understand, but needed to be positive. It's a good idea to ask someone to repeat or restate their claim. In Covey's *7 Habits of Highly Effective People*, this is habit 5, "Seek First to Understand Then to Be Understood" (Covey, 2004). Secondarily, I framed this in terms of a question because I wanted to make him more receptive to answering. I admitted my ignorance and asked him to help me understand. That is, I did not say, "Please tell me about that," as this phrasing can be interpreted as a command with the word "please" stuck in front of it.

Framing questions this way makes people feel like they have the option to not answer. I've found subjects are usually more receptive to continuing treatment when questions are framed as just that—questions—and when you show your interest in a conversation by asking follow-up questions.

YM told me of his experiences, what he'd gone through in his life, and what he felt.

> *PB*: That's really interesting. But I have a question. How do you know the thing you felt was caused by Jesus?

Four points to note: (1) Use of the passive voice doesn't make Jesus the actor in the sentence as it would with the active voice, "How do you know Jesus caused the thing you felt?" If you construct your statement with the passive voice, the subject may be more likely to be open to alternative causes. (Active voice: Mary tuned a violin. Passive voice: A violin was tuned by Mary.) (2) Because this is a question, YM can give individual responses that can then be broken down and targeted for refutation. This is important because there may be specific moments in the intervention when the subject is too doxastically entrenched in a particular hypothesis. When this occurs, an alternative line of questioning may help advance the conversation. In other words, one may also find additional fertile ground for creating doxastic openness when the list of conversational topics expands. (3) I've found that questions, as opposed to statements, tend to be less threatening as people feel they have the freedom to answer as they like. For example, the declarative statement, "That wasn't Jesus. That feeling was produced by the complex interplay of your own neurobiology and culture. Experiencing Jesus never happens to indigenous peoples who are cut off from the world. That alone should tell you you're delusional," does not act to increase the subject's doxastic openness (Kim, 1979, p. 203), but rather furthers doxastic entrenchment by creating threatening or adversarial relationships. (4) This question resets the Socratic conversation, beginning again in wonder. YM would then offer a hypothesis that could be targeted.

YM basically went on to say he "just knew" it was Jesus and he felt it was true in his heart.

> *PB*: That's interesting. But a lot of people feel some religious belief in their hearts, Buddhists, Muslims, Mormons, people who think the Emperor of Japan is divine. But they can't all be correct. Right?

I specifically avoided the word "you." For example, I did not say, "So how do you know your belief is true?" This can be threatening, as it may be perceived as creating an uncomfortable environment by placing the focus on the subject personally as opposed to the hypothesis. In discussions of faith in particular, it's crucial the Socratic clinician differentiate between people and propositions (Boghossian, 2002a). Faith is a deeply personal experience for people, and the more faith as an epistemology can be separated from faith as an identity, the easier the transition from stage 3 (elenchus) to stage 5 (action). Cultivating togetherness and not stressing differences continues to move the conversation forward.

I was attempting to open YM up to alternative ways of conceptualizing his experience—providing a more objective way for him to view the cause of his feelings.

The conversation went back and forth a few times, with YM reiterating that he just felt it to be true.

> *PB*: So what do you think accounts for the fact that different people have religious experiences that they're convinced are true?

Again, this is posed in terms of a question, resetting the Socratic method back to stage 1 (wonder). At this point rapport has been established and YM does not feel threatened (Clark, 1992; Horvath & Luborsky, 1993;

Szimhart, 2009, p. 260). The use of the word "you" is again avoided, so as to allow the subject the possibility of escaping from his own situated experience. To create a framework where the faith being discussed is essentially treated as someone else's faith benefits the discourse, because getting too personal about something so intimate can be very threatening.

YM: I don't know.

Bingo! A glimmer of doxastic openness. YM partially removes himself from the equation. The faith virus has received its first vaccination.

PB: Yeah, I don't know either.

I immediately modeled the behavior of openness and uncertainty that I'm attempting to engender in the subject. "I don't know" is a deceptively powerful statement. It also leads the subject to think, correctly, that you don't have all of the answers and that not having all the answers is okay. And it is okay, not just for me to not have all the answers, but for anyone and everyone including the subject.

(Long pause)

A pregnant pause is a very useful, nonthreatening technique, typically used in sales, to get the result you want. Often the uncomfortable silence will be filled by an answer; regardless, it allows the discourse to move forward, but if the dialectical space isn't filled you can continue at your leisure.

PB: So people who deeply and genuinely feel these experiences—these religious experiences—do you think they understand that they might not be caused by what they think they're caused by?

I had this conversation years ago. Today, I would no longer ask such a leading question. Instead, I'd more carefully construct a framework and ask other questions about which he'd form additional hypotheses that I'd then continue to target for refutation. One effect of this constant targeting and undermining is to create a chowder of epistemic uncertainty—with individual propositions floating untethered from their cognitive foundation. By targeting virtually every proposition that populates his worldview, I'd be able to undermine his confidence in what he holds as true. Once this is accomplished, the specific belief caused by the faith virus—in this case Jesus Christ revealing himself—can then be dialectically isolated, made hollow, and extirpated.

I jumped ahead because of his age, but also because I saw an opportunity to drive a wedge into his belief system—separating the faith virus from his other cognitions—and frankly because I was less experienced.

> *YM*: Some probably do. Some don't.

This statement is a hypothesis. It seems rather obvious and there was no point in targeting it for refutation. Also, by not targeting reasonable hypotheses at this juncture, the subject may feel he has just enough to grasp onto so he's not drowning in uncertainty.

> *PB*: Yeah, that's probably right. But you've thought about the feelings you had not being caused by Jesus. Right?

> (Long pause)

Again, note the passive voice.

> *YM*: No.

I was somewhat surprised by this answer. I thought ego alone might have led him to answer in the affirmative.

> *PB*: So is it possible that the feelings you had were not caused by Jesus?

> (Long pause)

I repeated the question.

> *YM*: I don't know.

Jackpot! He went from certainty to uncertainty—from absolute confidence to doubt; from precontemplation to contemplation; from thinking he experienced Jesus to being unsure. This particular intervention had ended. However, I was acutely aware of the danger he would face when he returned to his faith community. I was concerned he'd be pulled back into his faith delusions by loved ones or by clergy. For the next few weeks I made late night visits to the gym to look for him. I wanted to administer a follow-up treatment and see how he was doing. Unfortunately, I never saw him again. I've always regretted not giving him my phone number.

Intervention 2: Unsuccessful

The following is a conversation I had the morning of July 16, 2012, with a friend of the family. I've been engaging her on the topic of faith for more than five years, but to no avail.

> *PB*: So tell me, in one sentence, why, after all of our conversations, do you still retain your faith?
>
> (Long pause)
>
> *PB*: You don't have to answer now, you can tell me later.
>
> *HD*: Okay. Let me think about it.
>
> (Very short pause)
>
> *PB*: Okay, what's your answer?
>
> (Laughter)
>
> *HD*: Because it gives me comfort. It's ingrained in me.

This is the hypothesis: "It gives me comfort. It's ingrained in me." It's what's targeted for refutation in the elenchus.

A little humor, if it's sincere and well met, goes a long way to cementing the therapeutic alliance. Humor is an incredibly effective and underused dialectical technique, probably underused because there are so many ways it can backfire. But when successful almost nothing is more effective in advancing rapport.

PB: Do you think slave owners were granted comfort knowing that they'd have others to till fields for them?

An admittedly over-the-top counterexample, but in the context of our relationship it was appropriate. I'd tried various intervention strategies and they'd all been unsuccessful. Consequently, I often experiment in our conversations. Street Epistemologists are flexible and are encouraged to experiment and develop their own script and style. It's important for your growth and for the development of the techniques to experiment and develop your own ideas and strategies.

HD: Oh, Peter. Those two things aren't alike at all.

PB: You're right, but my point is that not all things that give you comfort are morally good, or even good for you, right? Like the homeless alcoholic near the underpass who clings to his bottle.

My immediate goal was obvious: to get her to acknowledge that not all things that give one comfort are good. I again used a rather extreme example in the hope this would increase the likelihood she'd accept my counterexample, thus undermining the hypothesis.

HD: I'm not harming anyone. I'm not one of these people who pushes my beliefs on others.

PB: Do you think you're harming yourself?

This question was popularized by German philosopher Immanuel Kant (1724–1804). It's also a question I frequently use with those who hold their views less tenaciously. Sometimes this question can create just enough cognitive space to make one aware of possible contradictions in one's reasoning. It does this by forcing people to reflect on a new line of inquiry (justice toward oneself) and then seeing if the belief in question is a form of injustice toward oneself.

This question is also effective on a much broader level: I often use it when asking people about epistemological systems, "Do you think using a bad way of reasoning, a way of reasoning that takes one away from reality, is a form of injustice toward yourself?" This is also very Socratic—thinking in terms of harm to yourself or society as a measuring stick.

HD: What do you mean?

PB: I mean do you think having a belief because it's comfortable and not because it's true is a form of harm to yourself?

HD: I never said it wasn't true.

She might not have explicitly stated that her faith beliefs weren't true, but if she believed they were true then in response to, "why, after all of our conversations, do you still retain your faith?" she would have said, "Because it's true." Because this was not her first response, my suspicion was that her verbal behavior didn't align with her beliefs.

PB: Are the beliefs in your faith true?

HD: I don't know Peter. They make me feel good, and you seem to want to take that away from me.

I knew she wouldn't claim her faith beliefs were true, only because we've had similar discussions before. I never allow people to steer these discussions from *faith is true* to *faith is beneficial* (comforting) unless they explicitly acknowledge that faith is not a reliable guide to reality. In this case, however, I was targeting "it gives me comfort" for refutation, as I genuinely do think she receives comfort from her faith.

PB: I don't want to take away your comfort HD. I just don't understand how much you could be comforted by something you know isn't true. Did you ever watch professional wrestling with Vince McMahon?

Now, I'm setting the stage for the counterexample—I'm attempting to undermine the hypothesis: faith gives her comfort. I also wanted to bring more levity into the conversation, in the hope that this would act to lubricate the discussion and make her beliefs more likely to become unstuck.

HD: No, but my husband used to.

PB: Well, maybe you can explain something to me. I've never understood how people can root for a "wrestler" [finger quotation marks] when they know the outcome is rigged. When you know who's going to win, you know the match is fixed, I just don't get rooting for someone in that context.

HD: It makes people feel good.

PB: Yeah, that's what I don't get. How so?

HD: Because people want someone they like to win.

PB: I guess that's kinda like faith. You know it's false but you subscribe to it anyway because it makes you feel good?

I inserted the word "false" here hoping she would just resign herself and accept that her faith beliefs are actually false. I wanted her to wonder, "Should one subscribe to a belief because it makes one feel good?"

(Long pause)

PB: What if I told you that you could feel good because of something that actually worked? Something that was real. Reason makes you feel good. It makes me feel better than eating bacon. [laughter] It makes me feel awesome to know that I can solve problems based on something real. What would it take for you to open yourself up to that gift?

Here I used specific language from the cult exiting literature. There's a body of research that analyzed factors influencing why people had fallen prey to cults. The phrase "open yourself up" and the word "gift" are frequently used to indoctrinate people into faith systems. These terms may also be effective in nudging people toward embracing reason.

HD: I'm fine just the way I am.

It appears the intervention was not effective. However, one can never really be sure what long-term effect a treatment will have. I will continue to engage HD on the subject of faith and will continue to try to help her by experimenting with different dialectical strategies. I remain hopeful HD will eventually abandon her faith.

Intervention 3: Ineffective

The following Socratic discussion is from a research study I conducted with prison inmates at a nearby prison (Boghossian, 2010). The purpose of the study was to improve subjects' critical thinking and moral reasoning abilities, and to increase their desistance to crime.

The subject, Subject 6, had been incarcerated for approximately nine months and was a recent born-again Christian. I did not have institutional review board (IRB) approval to help the subjects abandon their faith,[4] so I did not continue the particular line of questioning. If I did persist, I would have targeted specific beliefs about what he conceptualized to be the historical Jesus. His doxastic closure about specific propositions was too entrenched—as often occurs in the initial stages after one catches the faith virus. There was some room in this conversation to create an openness with ancillary beliefs, so that's what I attempted.

Subject 6: You made a comment about Jesus needing to be clever.

Researcher (PB): I was asking, was Jesus clever?

I reset the conversation to wonder. I made sure he offered the hypothesis that I would then target for refutation. When administering Socratic treatments, make sure to offer as few hypotheses as possible. If you get stuck and are unsure how to proceed, reset the conversation back to wonder. For example, you could say, "Do you think Jesus needed to be clever?"

Subject 6: He chose to die. He was God incarnate. His purpose was to be the sacrificial lamb for all sinners.

These are all hypotheses, all potential targets for refutation. I choose sacrifice for no other reason than that I find this concept interesting. Generally speaking, if you select something you find interesting or about which you have a particular knowledge, pursue that line of inquiry—it has a greater chance to be effective, or at the very least, engaging and educational—thus benefiting your own intellectual curiosity.

> *Researcher*: Okay, so would you consider Him a greater man for having made that sacrifice?

There was no questioning the divinity of Christ at this point in the treatment (because I did not have IRB permission to do so). The subject was clearly in the precontemplative stage. The goal, then, was to elicit doxastic openness in other areas of his cognitive life. I again went back to the idea of sacrifice.

> *Subject 6*: Absolutely.

It's easier to elicit contradictions from responses that indicate certainty as opposed to ambiguity. Certainty requires overwhelming warrant—in other words, one needs an ironclad justification before one can claim one knows something as an absolute truth. Showing someone doesn't have the necessary justification to warrant belief in a claim in which they're certain is fairly easy. With subjects who are not suffering from severe doxastic pathologies, it makes for an effortless elenchus: all one has to do is find some condition that could possibly hold that undermines the truth potential for the belief in question. (For example: "All Asians are good at math." To undermine this hypothesis all one would need is a single example of an Asian who is not good at math. However, refuting, "Most Asians are good at math," is considerably more difficult.)

> *Researcher*: Okay, so what if the lesser men around Him were actually clever and prevented Him from achieving that mission?

> *Subject 6*: The lesser men didn't want Him to achieve His purpose.

> *Researcher*: Yeah, but if the lesser men, who were clever, prevented Him from achieving His purpose, then couldn't ya say that the virtue that He should have had was cleverness because that would have enabled Him to achieve His purpose? I mean it couldn't have been a sacrifice unless He chose it, and in order for Him to have chosen it, He had to have the possibility of choosing otherwise. Therefore He could have not chosen it and failed.

> *Subject 6*: He achieved His purpose.

This response indicates he's prehope. The subject is suffering from a severe form of doxastic closure. The more closed the subject is about certain beliefs, the further up the belief chain—the higher in the house, to use our foundationalist metaphor from chapter 4—one must go. Ideally, one would find a belief in which the subject placed a reasonable degree of confidence, and then administer a Socratic treatment targeting that specific belief. The hope is that because the foundational belief is too entrenched, the way to loosen the foundational belief is through the ceiling boards in the attic. Once the attic is demolished, one can destroy the top floors of the house and work one's way down to the foundation.

Researcher: Could He have failed, or was He destined?

Subject 6: He could have failed. He had a choice.

Researcher: So then He might have needed cleverness to increase the likelihood of success.

Subject 6: Go back and read Matthew, Mark, Luke, and John.

Researcher: That doesn't answer the question.

Some Socratic conversations feel unsatisfying and even frustrating. This was one such example. I've found that when people are coming out of lows—for example, recently incarcerated prison inmates or drug addicts in the very early stage of recovery—it's very difficult to dislodge the faith virus. I've also found that many people have a type of fundamentalism in their actions and thoughts in the early stages of faith adoption (and addiction recovery), particularly if faith is adopted because of a personal tragedy.

Intervention 4: Immediate Success

The following intervention took place with a security guard (SG) at a university where I taught night classes. SG and I had made small talk a few times, but we never had a substantive conversation. He was a soft-spoken and kind young man. I liked him.

One day I overheard SG telling someone about training for his upcoming missionary work. He was a Mormon and evidently he was learning how to convert others.

> *PB*: So what's your best line? I mean, what's the line you're gonna use that will convince them? You can try it on me if you want. Maybe you'll convince me.

> (Self-conscious laughter)

> *SG*: Okay. So look around you. How did this get here? This had to have a cause, right? All of this.

The question, "How did this get here?" is a statement of wonder (stage 1). The answer he gave to his own question was, "It had to have a cause." This is his hypothesis. In this example he supplied both wonder and a hypothesis. I moved straight to the elenchus and gave him a counterexample.

> *PB*: Well, what if it was always here?

> *SG*: What do you mean?

> *PB*: Well, you assume that nothing is the default. What if the default was something. In other words, what if there was always something stretching back into infinity.

> *SG*: What do you mean?

I wasn't sure if his question was a genuine glimpse of doxastic openness, or if he couldn't comprehend a universe that stretched back into infinity. Accordingly, at this point I rephrased the question to convey openness and to reinforce the safe environment for our discussion.

> *PB*: What do you mean what do I mean? You assume the universe had to have a beginning. What if there was no beginning?

> (Pause)

> *SG*: I never thought of that.

I was extremely surprised by this comment. He was about to try to convert others and yet he had not even thought of the most basic objection to his worldview? I was also shocked this point of doxastic openness came so early in the conversation. At this juncture I wanted to make sure he didn't feel stupid, and I also wanted to make sure I drove home stage 5 (act accordingly). My goal was not just to help him to question his faith, but also ultimately to detach him from the structure supporting and sustaining his faulty epistemology—the Mormon Church.

> *PB*: Well, I think about this stuff a lot, so don't feel bad. Plus this is what I do for a living. So if it's possible that the universe always existed, what would that mean to you?

I reset the conversation to wonder. I also wanted him to draw his own conclusion, and perhaps even impose the method upon himself. In other words, SG would use the same method of questioning upon himself that I'd been using on him, so I waited for him to see the opportunity to talk himself out of his beliefs. The obvious conclusion was that if the universe always existed then God didn't create it. It's a short intellectual step from God not creating the universe to God not existing—but SG didn't see that yet. I continued.

> *SG*: I'm not sure.

> *PB*: Well, let's think through it together.

> (Pause)

> *PB*: So the main argument for God was, "Look around you. How did this get here?" But we know there's another possible explanation for what there is. So if the universe always existed, what would that mean?

Here I use the word "we" to confer upon the subject the feeling that he is not alone, that we are equals, and that we as humans are all facing the same ultimate questions.

> (Pause)

> *SG*: I'm not sure.

I would have normally taken more time with this process, but I was already running late for class. Still, I had to seize the opportunity.

In my rush, I made a mistake by leading the subject too much. It would have been better to give him more cognitive space to come to his own conclusions and thus increase the likelihood of a successful transition to stage 5 (act accordingly). This is because he would have been more likely to accept the conclusion if he arrived at it of his own accord, as discussed earlier.

> *PB*: Well, if the universe always existed then it wasn't created. If it wasn't caused what would that mean?
>
> (Pause)
>
> *SG*: That there's no God?

I tried to hide my joy, show my approval, and acknowledge our success.

> *PB*: Yup. That's what it would mean.

He looked horrified and scared. Even though late for class, I proceeded to provide him with the resources he needed to escape from the Mormon Church. Specifically, I furnished him with contacts and resources he could use for support. I made sure to let him know he wasn't alone. I also specifically explained why it's crucial to not succumb to the "just pray about it" line that I was certain he'd be subject to once he started voicing doubts. (Asking people to "just pray about it" pushes them into a form of confirmation bias where the very act of prayer means they've already bought back into the system they just escaped.)

This was a successful intervention. It was successful because the conversation was brief and because he came to the conclusion on his own with minimal prodding. When I left him that night he told me he was "freaked out." I don't know if SG ever completed stage 5 and left the church. I never saw him after that.

CHAPTER SUMMARY

Socratic interventions are easy to administer, no-cost treatments that can engender doxastic openness and even separate faith from its host. The main way this happens is by helping expose contradictions and inconsistencies in subjects' reasoning processes.

When administering Socratic treatments, keep the following in mind:

- Be aware of the stages of the method. Don't transition from one stage to another stage until you've exhausted everything you need to do in that particular stage. Don't rush.

- When appropriate, incorporate strategies noted in chapter 4: be attentive to context, don't develop adversarial relationships or negative tones, "roll with it," divorce belief from morality, focus on epistemology and not metaphysics, target faith not religion, and model the behavior you want the subject to emulate. Develop a safe space for discussion, almost a camaraderie.

At the conclusion of some interventions, subjects will be confused or even scared. In chapter 6, I'll discuss how to deal with this and what goes in faith's place.

DIG DEEPER

Articles

Peter Boghossian, "How Socratic Pedagogy Works" (Boghossian, 2003)

Peter Boghossian, "Socratic Pedagogy: Perplexity, Humiliation, Shame and a Broken Egg" (Boghossian, 2011b)

Books

Guy P. Harrison, *50 Simple Questions for Every Christian* (Harrison, 2013)

Platonic Dialogues

Plato, *Euthyphro*

Plato, *Meno* (focus on the discussion with Meno's slave)

Plato, *Republic* (particularly Books I, II, and III)

NOTES

1. Socrates was the protagonist in Plato's dialogues. The majority of scholars think he never wrote anything. Socrates also never referred to his teaching method as "the Socratic method." Subsequent scholars termed his method of teaching—by asking questions instead of telling—the Socratic method.

2. In the context of a Socratic intervention, and only in the context of a Socratic intervention, do I use the words "hypothesis" and "belief" interchangeably.

3. Virtually everyone has wondered whether or not there's intelligent life in the universe. Why haven't extraterrestrials made contact with us? One way to conceptualize this question is with the Drake Equation. The Drake Equation estimates the number of intelligent, technologically capable civilizations in the universe: $N = R^* \cdot f_p \cdot n_e \cdot f_l \cdot f_i \cdot f_c \cdot L$

   Where,

   N = The number of communicating civilizations in the Milky Way

   R^* = The number and rate of star formation

   f_p = The fraction of those stars with planets

   n_e = The number of planets per star with an environment suitable for life

   f_l = The fraction of planets on which life develops

   f_i = The fraction of planets on which intelligent life develops

   f_c = The fraction of civilizations that develop technology (that release detectable signs of their existence into space)

   L = The length of time such civilizations release detectable signals into space

   By plugging in best estimates for the variables, one can guestimate the number of intelligent, technology-producing life forms in the Milky Way. Even by conservative estimates the number is larger than 1.

Why then have we not witnessed evidence of intelligent extraterrestrial life? (This question is made even more curious when one factors in American inventor Ray Kurzweil's idea of exponential technological growth, with mere centuries translating into unimaginable technological differences among civilizations.)

One answer to this is that there's something wrong with our model of the universe. There's something we don't understand, or something we've considered to be a remote possibility that's an actuality. For example, we could be brains in a vat (à la *The Matrix*), or as Swedish philosopher Nick Bostrom has posited, we could be living in a holographic simulation (Bostrom, 2003). Alternatively, there could be some kind of "Great Filter," that is, a kind of "probability barrier" that life must pass through (Hanson, 1998).

Hanson (1998) provides a "best-guess evolutionary path to an explosion which leads to visible colonization of most of the visible universe." He writes:

1. The right star system (including organics)

2. Reproductive something (e.g., RNA)

3. Simple (prokaryotic) single-cell life

4. Complex (archaeatic & eukaryotic) single-cell life

5. Sexual reproduction

6. Multicell life

7. Tool-using animals with big brains

8. Where we are now

9. Colonization explosion

The Great Filter hypothesis states that one or more of these steps must be "*very* improbable" (Hanson, 1998). If it wasn't improbable, then humanity would have already witnessed evidence of intelligent, extraterrestrial life, perhaps in the form of von Neumann probes (self-replicating spacecraft that draw raw material from stars, planets, gas giants, etc.) or spaceships or even signals.

Fortunately, as Bostrom argues, failure of contact is actually good news for humanity, as this means that the Great Filter likely lies behind and not in front of us (Bostrom, 2008). That is, if it's more difficult for life to arise in the initial stages, then it may be easier for life to become spacefaring in the latter stages. No news of intelligent life is good news—it bodes well for our future.

4. There's a glaring problem with knowing that the strategy of using the Socratic method to help people overcome faith works: there are no studies to support the effectiveness of this approach. In fact, there are *no studies at all* documenting the use of the Socratic method as an intervention to alleviate people from their faith.

    Here's why: in order to conduct a study that uses human subjects (people), the researcher *must* submit approval through an IRB. IRBs are independent ethics review boards, usually associated with universities, that grant approval for studies that use humans as subjects in experiments. Their purpose is to protect research subjects from abuses.

    It would be impossible to receive approval for a study that would help people overcome faith.

    Proposing this sort of study would be considered not just far too controversial, but also abusive and damaging to subjects. *No researcher could ever receive IRB approval for such a study.*

    This means that one can attempt to use the Socratic method to help others to abandon their faith and then blog about it, or tell one's friends about their failures and successes, or use it in the classroom as a pedagogical intervention. (I've helped countless people abandon their faith and acquire reliable paths to knowledge.) Without IRB approval, no peer-reviewed journals would accept such a study and no university would allow faculty to conduct research on human subjects. Consequently, the effectiveness of Socratic techniques in helping people abandon their faith is not, at this present time, documented.

    Fortunately, there is solid evidence that Socratic techniques can elicit behavioral changes outside the realm of faith. Much of my previous research focused on using the Socratic method to help prison inmates desist from criminal behavior (Boghossian, 2004; Boghossian, 2006a; Boghossian, 2010) and explained the mechanics of the Socratic method (Boghossian, 2002a, 2002b, 2003, 2012). My current research focuses on using the Socratic method to help diabetics in the Diabetes Clinic at Oregon Health Science University improve treatment compliance by generating counterexamples to clarify their thought process and reach their health-related goals. Others have also conducted studies on the effectiveness of using the Socratic method to change cognitions (Froján-Parga, Calero-Elvira, & Montaño-Fidalgo, 2011) and improve critical thinking and reasoning (Boghossian, 2004). Furthermore, somewhat similar cognitive behavioral interventions have an extensive basis in the corrections, addiction, and psychological literature, though again not for the purpose of liberating people of their faith.

The current body of literature is highly suggestive, though not conclusive, that the Socratic method can be used as a self-imposed corrective mechanism that helps people fix flaws in their reasoning. We know what the Socratic method does, how it works, its preliminary successes, etc. What's not been documented in the peer-reviewed literature is the Socratic method's use as a treatment for faith. Based upon a related body of literature in regard to the effectiveness of the Socratic method, and based upon literature detailing the success of questioning to deprogram members of religious cults (Dubrow-Eichel, 1989, pp. 43–49, 195), it's reasonable to infer that Socratic interventions are a reliable treatment for faith. However, because of popular perceptions of faith as a virtue, concerns over threats to religious liberties (Robbins & Anthony, 1982, p. 292), and the ethics (IRB) involved in conducting studies with the explicit aim of helping people abandon their faith, there is no research on the effectiveness of the proposed intervention.

CHAPTER 6

AFTER THE FALL

On Oct 14, 2012, at 11:26 AM, Katie Z. wrote:

I just stopped believing in God. It's an unbelievable feeling. Are there any books you can recommend? I'm not ready for anything sarcastic or ribbing. Not yet. But I do need some direction. I just feel lost. Anything you can suggest will help. Thank you.

On Oct 22, 2012, at 5:40 PM, Peter Boghossian <pgb@pdx.edu> wrote:

I've always thought that what's important is to be a person who values reason and rationality, and not to be an atheist. Atheism is a conclusion one comes to after a sincere, honest evaluation of the evidence. Here's the evidence for the existence of God: Nothing. There is no evidence for God's existence.

This may not be the advice you want to hear, but in my opinion the most important thing is to be comfortable with ignorance. I still struggle with this. Religion offers answers. When you embrace reason and make the decision to be rational, reasonable, thoughtful, and honest when examining your life, you will quickly come to the conclusion that you don't have all of the answers. How do we teach people to be comfortable with uncertainty? I don't have an answer that will satisfy everyone. I do know that the *attitude* of being comfortable with uncertainty is key, but as to the road to get to this place in your life, well, I'm still thinking about it. I don't know. I don't have the answers. As long as you maintain a sincerity with regard to belief, and an honesty with yourself, and truly examine your own life, then this alone may help you to be comfortable with not knowing. But I doubt it. I only know that I know nothing. That is my only certainty.

The Muslims will tell you to repeat the name of Allah until you come to believe. The Christians will tell you to open your heart to Jesus to find true belief. These are easy answers that bend you in the direction of your initial starting point. This isn't the case with reason. When you form beliefs on the basis of evidence, no conclusion will be guaranteed. Everything will be up for grabs. There's no book that can teach you how to do this; it is not just a skill set, it is an attitude.

So, my suggestions: Be genuine and sincere with yourself and with others. Everything else will take care of itself. I'm sorry I can't offer you more than this.

I'm free to chat. Anytime.

pete

This chapter is brief because of a lack of peer-reviewed literature on the subject, and because my primary focus is to help people abandon their faith and not to offer them a "plan of recovery." Those who have come to terms with doubt have most often spent years in recovery—intellect was their guide, honesty and a hunger to know their motivation, and the discovery of new courage their therapy. Unlike God's spokespersons— the rabbi, the priest, the imam—I would never presume to tell someone which path is best for them. That kind of paternalism and arrogance are the behaviors that contribute to people turning their backs on religion.[1]

One of my roles is to provide support information to those who recover from faith. Beyond this, I wouldn't presume to tell Street Epistemologists there is something you should or shouldn't tell your clients. There are just too many variables (personal history, faith tradition, education, cultural heritage, psychological disposition, relationships, life context, etc.) for universal dos and don'ts.[2]

This chapter contains post-treatment advice, followed by broad goals to help create a culture in which people value those dispositions crucial to allowing reason and rationality to flourish. It ends with two brief dialogues.

EMBRACE THE VAST SKEPTICAL COMMUNITY ONLINE AND IN YOUR NEIGHBORHOOD

You've created a cognitive space, exposed a flawed epistemology, helped someone on a journey out of their faith, now what?

After an intervention, don't leave the subject hanging. Be prepared to provide names, contact information, and resources that can help. Initially the abandonment of faith can be both liberating and traumatic, especially when one "comes out" to unsupportive friends and family. Those who have abandoned their faith need to know there are support groups ready to help them. Always be prepared to furnish resources at the end of your intervention, and also have that information on hand just in case you run into a subject at a later time. I keep phone numbers and Web addresses of local resources (Center for Inquiry–Portland, Humanists of Greater Portland, Meetups, and the Portland State University FreeThinkers) on cards in my wallet.

If you have time, try and make yourself available for post-treatment relationships. I invite people to "friend" me on Facebook where they'll at least have online support. I also invite the formerly faithful to lunch or dinner, to office hours, and even to my jiu jitsu class—I've become friendly with many people I've helped.

Another advantage in forming personal relationships is that you can introduce people to new communities and new friends who use reliable epistemologies. Forming new relationships is important because these interactions mitigate the risk of recidivating and falling back into faith communities. Disrupting one's interpersonal milieu by providing supportive relationships and communities has the potential to cement new values and new, more reliable epistemologies—this is especially crucial in early stages (precontemplation, contemplation, preparation) when one begins to question one's faith.[3]

INSTITUTIONALIZING THE VALUE OF WONDER

"We live in a society where people are uncomfortable with not knowing. Children aren't taught to say 'I don't know,' and honesty in this form is rarely modeled for them. They too often see adults avoiding questions and fabricating answers, out of either embarrassment or fear, and this comes at a price. To solve the world's most challenging problems, we need innovative minds that are inspired in the presence of uncertainty. Let's support parents and educators who are raising the next generation of creative thinkers."

—Annaka Harris (*Secular News Daily*, 2012)

Faith has fallen. What goes in its place? Wonder.

Wonder, open-mindedness, the disposition of being comfortable with not knowing, uncertainty, a skeptical and scientific-minded attitude, and the genuine desire to know what's true—these are the attributes of a liberated mind. Let's observe, let's document, let's carefully describe, and let's be open to discomforting conclusions. Inquiry and wonder must replace dogmatism and certainty. The long-term goal is to create conditions that turn the dispositions of inquiring and wondering into culturally trumpeted virtues.[4]

One of the most disappointing realizations for an unseasoned Street Epistemologist is understanding the degree to which wonder and inquiry are prisoner to social values. Like the boy in James Agee's tragic novel, *A Death in the Family*, who is robbed of curiosity and hope, often reason and wonder are extinguished by pernicious forces in society (Agee, 2009, pp. 54–55). Interrupting the relationship between wonder and those institutions and forces that put down free inquiry will require the creation of a potent social and intellectual movement—a New Enlightenment— that will enable individuals to adopt the disposition toward reason en masse.

In chapter 9, I suggest that we borrow tools from the civil rights movement to nudge people away from certain values and dispositions and toward the use of reliable epistemologies.

When Wonder Isn't Enough

In the span of two weeks, my mother had a heart attack, renal failure, sepsis, and a mass discovered in her uterus. The mass turned out to be cancer, which spread to her bowels and bones. A dynamic, vibrant, generous, irreverent, and unbelievably funny and loving woman suffered a slow, painful end. On October 27, 2012, she died at home, surrounded by those who deeply loved and respected her.[5]

My mother was raised Catholic, though she was not particularly religious, or at least she never showed me that side of herself. She never went to church or, as far as I knew, never prayed or spoke of faith in a Catholic God. Yet when she went into heart surgery she clutched a small statue of baby Jesus on a manger. During her hospital stay, she asked my father to bring it to her, which he did every single day.

I don't think my mother was scared of death. I do know she lived for her grandchildren and she desperately wanted to see them grow up. Even aside from all of the pain she experienced in her final months, knowing she'd never see the children again was by far the most agonizing thing of all.

When I reflect back, and think about my mother making the sign of the cross with the small figure of Jesus, I know offering her wonder was not enough. Not nearly enough. She needed something else . . . maybe the news that her grandchildren were safe and doing well . . . maybe to know that my dad and I were with her, holding her hand, and that we loved her so completely. Or maybe something else entirely?

What can we offer people like my mother in their most trying moments? I've thought about this question for quite some time, and the answer is as disconcerting as it is disparaging. Perhaps nothing. Once one has been indoctrinated and infected by faith, there may be nothing we can offer those in need that would grant them the same psychological and emotional comfort offered by their misplaced trust in the unknowable.

However, at the same time we know we're all going to die. Though a life without certainty can engender upon some a level of despair, there is hope in the idea that every human being is now equal in death. The human species is made stronger by the fact that in the end we're all going to die.

Faith's greatest appeal may be solace—comfort and peace of mind in impossibly difficult times. Even the reward of seventy-two virgins in the afterlife falls short of the promise of eternal bliss with loved ones.[6] What comfort does reality-based reasoning offer someone suffering or facing death? I don't know. During these difficult times, if we can offer anything at all, it is our physical presence. Being at my mom's deathbed and holding her hand was both incredibly difficult and lovely, and I knew that simply being there helped ease her suffering. When I asked if I could sit on the edge of her bed and hold her hand, she mumbled, "Yeah, sure," and then smiled. Those were the last words she ever said to me.

I'm aware that my lack of action goes against the thesis of this book, but I was unable to even engage my mother about her faith in the last days of her life.

The Next Generation and the Revaluation of Values

Our hopes rest on the next generation. We need a targeted, comprehensive campaign, in the K–12 school system across multiple scholastic disciplines, in summer camps, in libraries, in discussions with the faithful in front of their children, on TV and radio, in Internet chat rooms, and any and everywhere we can reach children. The thrust of our message must be that there are things we don't know and it's okay to not know— even in death. Not claiming to know something you don't know isn't a character flaw, it is a virtue.

Helping people, especially children, to be comfortable with not knowing, yet at the same time encouraging the development of curiosity, of wonder, and of a zest to explore the world, is a crucial and indispensable undertaking. New books and lines of literature about how to make children comfortable with not knowing and how to develop reliable epistemologies must be written, widely circulated, and read ubiquitously. To start we must create the *value* of being comfortable with uncertainty, particularly with regard to life's ultimate questions. In other words, not only do we need to devalue an existing paradigm (faith), we also need to revalue an underappreciated one (reason).

Among the valuable lessons I learned from teaching prison inmates is that books alone aren't enough. We need to get a message to children who can't read, who would never open a book, and particularly to those in sheltered religious communities. These are often the greatest challenges—reaching the otherwise unreachable: The pastor's daughter, the youth who's recruited to be an altar boy, the children who commiserate about being in Sunday school (then, in awe, falsely attribute the church's architectural splendor to Jesus and not to the skilled laborers who painstakingly constructed it), teenagers in alcohol and drug twelve-step recovery programs, kids in Islamic and Hasidic youth programs, and economically disadvantaged children who have no access to reading material and are stuck in a failed school. The vulnerable, the indoctrinated, and the hardest to reach children are where we should place the lion's share of our efforts.[78]

Intervention

I ran into one of my former students (FS) while waiting in line at a popular sushi restaurant. He had taken two of my philosophy classes, but I didn't recognize him as my classes have between 70 and 130 students. He was with his girlfriend (GF), who looked wholesome and in her mid-twenties and who wore out-of-place cowboy boots. I was typing on my phone when he enthusiastically greeted me.

FS: Pete! Pete! What are you doing here? Oh my God! Pete!

PB: Hey man.

FS: Do you know who I am?

PB: Nope.

FS: That's cool. I was in your Critical Thinking class, and your Science and Pseudoscience class.

PB: Right on. How'd those classes go for you?

(We chatted for a few minutes. FS introduced me to his girlfriend. Then he told me he abandoned his faith and it had become an issue in their relationship.)

PB: You two must really love each other.

GF: We do.

PB: Well that's great. And you've obviously listened to each other and really discussed FS's embrace of reason, right?

GF: Yeah. But . . .

PB: Go ahead, it's okay.

(Long pause)

PB: If you're comfortable I'm all ears. If not it's all good.

(Pause)

GF: But I'm scared for him. For my family. For us, you know. It's been a really hard time.

PB: Yeah. I can totally understand that. Life after faith can be scary.

(Long pause)

PB: What scares you the most?

GF: Well . . . well, that he won't go to heaven. I know that must sound silly to you. But it makes me sad.

PB: It doesn't sound silly at all. I totally understand that's how you feel and that that's how you were raised.

FS: Yeah.

PB: So you think that because he doesn't believe in heaven he won't go there?

GF: No, but, but because he doesn't believe in Jesus.

PB: Is FS a good man? Does he treat others well. Is he kind? Is he sincere?

FS: Yes!

(Laughter)

GF: Of course he is.

PB: But you'd like more? You'd like him to be good *and* to believe in Jesus?

GF: Yeah, I would.

PB: If someone's bad but they believe in Jesus do you think they'll go to heaven?

GF: If they believe, yes.

PB: So if heaven is your goal, then it's more important to believe in Jesus than it is to be a good person? I ask because I'm trying to figure out how you're thinking about it.

GF: Well the way you get to heaven is through Jesus. If you believe in Jesus that will make you good.

PB: Really? A lot of people believe in Jesus but they're not good. Or do you think they're just pretending?

GF: I don't know. Maybe they're just pretending.

PB: Yeah, I'm sympathetic to that view. There's way too much pretending going on. So I'm curious, if you could choose only one, FS being good or FS believing in Jesus, which would you choose?

GF: Both.

(Laughter)

PB: But let's just say you can't have both.

(Brief silence)

GF: Good.

PB: Then you already have what's really important to you.

GF: Yeah, I guess so. I just want more. For him.

PB: Wanting more is probably part of the human condition. I'm curious, you obviously consider yourself to be a good person, right?

GF: Yeah.

PB: Would you be good if you didn't believe in Jesus?

GF: What do you mean?

PB: I mean if you didn't believe Jesus was the Son of God, if you came to the conclusion that this was just a fairytale, would you still act the way you do or would you do bad stuff? Would you be mean, vindictive, petty, you know, do bad stuff?

GF: I never thought about it before.

PB: Let's just say at some point, maybe tomorrow or the next day, you decided that the whole Jesus, heaven, devil thing was just a story, a myth, and so you stopped believing. Would you continue to be good?

GF: I don't know. Honestly, I think I'd be scared.

PB: Scared of what? Death? Not going to heaven?

GF: Yeah. Not going to heaven. Death. Yeah. All of it.

PB: Of not seeing the people you love, like FS?

GF: Yeah. I guess of nothing. You know?

PB: You mean of there being nothing after you die?

GF: Yeah, sure. Of course.

PB: I don't want to put words in your mouth. I'm just trying to understand.

GF: I know. What do you think?

PB: It's not really about what I think, it's about what you think.

GF: I know. But I want to know what you think.

PB: What I think about what?

GF: What you think about this discussion. About what I've been saying. About this.

(Gesturing at FS)

PB: Well, I think you're both good people. I think you're sincere and that you're trying to do the right thing. I think you really love each other, and that matters—a lot. I also think you've been indoctrinated into a set of beliefs. I think if you were raised in another part of the world, like Saudi Arabia, you'd be a sincere Muslim. I don't think that Jesus Christ is the Son of God, and deep down I think you really question whether or not that's true, and that you have for some time now. I think you like the idea of believing in something, and you like to think of yourself as the type of person who holds this belief. I think that you have a real possibility of letting go of that belief and making your own way. I know you can do that. And I also think you're at a point in your life when you're ready to. That's what I think.

(Long pause)

FS: Wow. Dude.

PB [to GF]: What do you think about what I think?

(Pause)

GF: Well . . . well. Maybe. I don't know.

PB: It's okay not to know. I think you're ready to take your sincerity and honesty and apply that to your beliefs. Just be really, really honest with *yourself.* Ask yourself if you really believe someone rose from the dead or walked on water. Ask yourself if you or if [FS] needs to believe that to be good. Really ask yourself.

(Long pause)

GF: Okay, okay.

(We hugged each other.)

DIG DEEPER

Books

Seth Andrews, *Deconverted: A Journey from Religion to Reason* (Andrews, 2012)

Jerry DeWitt and Ethan Brown, *Hope after Faith: An Ex-Pastor's Journey from Belief to Atheism* (DeWitt & Brown, 2013)

John W. Loftus, *Why I Became an Atheist: Personal Reflections and Additional Arguments* (especially chapter 20) (Loftus, 2008)

Marlene Winell, *Leaving the Fold* (Winell, 1993)

Online Resources

The Clergy Project (http://clergyproject.org): "The Clergy Project is a confidential online community for active and former clergy who do not hold supernatural beliefs. The Clergy Project launched on March 21st, 2011. . . . Currently, the community's 390 plus members use it to network and discuss what it's like being an unbelieving leader in a religious community. The Clergy Project's goal is to support members as they move beyond faith."

John W. Loftus, "Advice to People Who Leave the Fold," http://debunkingchristianity.blogspot.com/2009/07/advice-to-people-who-leave-fold.html

RationalWiki, "RationalWiki Atheism FAQ for the Newly Deconverted," http://rationalwiki.org/wiki/RationalWiki_Atheism_FAQ_for_the_Newly_Deconverted

Recovering from Religion (http://recoveringfromreligion.org/pages/home): "Recovering from Religion is a nonprofit organization dedicated to providing multi-dimensional support and encouragement to individuals leaving their religious affiliations through the establishment, development, training, and educational support of local groups nationwide."

The Secular Therapist Project (http://seculartherapy.org/index.php): "In my work with the secular community I have heard many stories from people who consulted a mental health professional only to find out after several sessions that the professional was spiritual or religious or had new age ideas. Investigating, I soon learned that it is quite difficult to find a therapist that is actually secular or will only use evidence based methods with a client. Secular therapists don't advertise that they are humanist or atheist because that might alienate the churches and ministers who often make referrals to them. It might also drive off religious clients. Too many people have told me that they simply cannot find a therapist in their community who is not religious. On the other hand, I know that there are thousands of secular therapists, so how do we get these clients together with therapists. That is the task that Han Hills and I decided to tackle in 2011. We went live with the site in April of 2012 and are seeing clients and therapists finding each other and hopefully engaging in productive, life enhancing work."

NOTES

1. My parents' generation, and presumably the generation before them, went out of their way to insist that they knew what was best for their children. Even my own progressive parents maintained this attitude. It is my hope that the children my wife and I are raising will not be hobbled by the same sense of certainty that was so rife in previous generations. Indeed, I think there's a more egalitarian relationship between children and parents now than at any time in the recent past.

2. It is my sincere hope that a field of academic study can develop around issues related to recovery from religion and faith, including how to raise skeptical children. Furthermore, innovative and gratifying careers can be based upon developing inoculation and containment strategies that promote the value of belief on the basis of reason and evidence, as opposed to believing on the

basis of anything else. This is a pristine area ripe for study.

3.   It may be worth looking at the literature on grief, specifically, Swiss-American psychiatrist Elisabeth Kübler-Ross's views on grief (Kübler-Ross & Kessler, 2005). I've just started incorporating her richer understanding of loss, as applied to faith, to deepen and enrich my interventions.

4.   Our objective should be to create people who have learned key lessons from Socrates, Nietzsche, and the Four Horsemen—people who understand the dangers inherent in faulty reasoning processes, certainty, and religiosity. We need to create a society that holds not pretending to know things one doesn't know as a virtue, as opposed to the contemporary view that holding a belief with certainty makes one a better person.

5.   Nevada, where my parents lived and my mother died, does not have a Death with Dignity law. The faithful have extinguished hope that my mother, and others who are dying slow, painful deaths, can pass gracefully at a time of their choosing. As of 2013, only Oregon and Washington have Death with Dignity laws, and even those laws are highly restrictive.

Tragically, the primary reason that terminal patients enduring tremendous pain are unable to quickly and painlessly end their lives, but are instead forced to endure days, weeks, or months of misery and suffering, is intertwined with the same false certainty created by faith. It's a toxic problem when people believe the demands of their faith tradition apply to people who do not share their faith. This is evidenced by the Catholic Church's campaign against Death with Dignity measures.

6.   Perhaps my predilection is just a product of my liberal sexual culture. If I had been denied sex from adolescence, then seventy-two virgins would likely be more appealing.

7.   I've been working closely with my students at Portland State University, Ryan Marquez, Anna Wilson, Renee Barnett, Kai Pak, Steve Helms, and others, to get critical thinking into the public high schools. For more than a year we worked diligently, facing a myriad of challenges. Unfortunately, our project is on hold (primarily because of budget cuts), but the materials that the students presented to school administrators will be made available and

licensed under Creative Commons (http://creativecommons.org/). Anyone who wishes to duplicate our proposed program will have access to all of the student and instructor materials once it becomes available. It is our sincere hope that readers will take up this project, duplicate, and improve upon our program in their local high schools.

8. My reasons for arguing that resources should be disproportionately devoted to those at greater risk are rooted in criminal justice literature. Though counterintuitive, the evidence is clear: when low-risk inmates receive treatment in prisons, or in the community, their recidivism actually goes *up*. Lower-risk inmates are not "broken" to begin with, but putting them in treatment they do not need tells them they are broken, makes them angry, and mixes them with higher-risk inmates who are broken and who negatively influence other people.

In one study, high-risk offenders averaged a 92 percent recidivism rate under minimal treatment conditions, but their rate *dropped* to 25 percent under intensive treatment conditions. The lower-risk offenders, on the other hand, averaged 12 percent recidivism under minimal treatment conditions, but their rate *increased* to 29 percent under intensive treatment conditions (Andrews & Friesen, 1987). Many meta-analyses have confirmed this counterintuitive pattern of higher-level offenders getting better with the right kind of treatment and lower-level offenders actually getting worse (Andrews, et al., 1990).

By putting lower-risk people in prison we also take them away from all the things that make them low risk—supportive wives and children, meaningful jobs, pro-social friends, etc. Higher-risk inmates are broken and when they receive the right treatment their recidivism goes down. This is called the "risk principle." It tells prison administrators who they should focus their scarce treatment resources on—the higher-risk inmates. The "need principle" tells administrators what they need to focus on once they know who requires the most help.

Many need areas such as mental health, poverty, and self-esteem are not predictive of crime. Most people who are poor and have low self-esteem, and most people who are suffering from clinical depression, do not commit crimes. Other need areas, known as "criminogenic need," are highly predictive of crime. For example, individuals who have antisocial attitudes, values, and beliefs, antisocial friends, antisocial personalities (traits of impulsivity, low self-control, and narcissism), or substance abuse problems, are highly likely to commit crime and need help with these areas of their life. The risk and the need principles are just two of several, counterintuitive principles of effective correctional programming (Andrews, et al., 1990; Bogue, Diebel, & O'Connor, 2008; Bonta & Andrews, 2010; McNeil, Raynor, & Trotter, 2010).

CHAPTER 7

ANTI-APOLOGETICS 101

Sam Harris observed that there are only three defenses offered in response to critiques of religion (Harris, 2007b): (1) Religion is true; (2) Religion is useful; (3) Atheism is somehow corrosive of society or other values.

The same is the case with faith (though some defenses of faith hinge on redefining the word "faith," or upon offering deepities). There are basically only eleven defenses of faith. Most of these defenses fall into one of Harris's three categories regarding religion: true, useful, or socially consequential.

In this chapter I'll break down common defenses of faith into Harris's categories, and note my preferred responses to each.[1] I note quotations at the beginning of most defenses to situate context for the response.

FAITH IS TRUE

1. "Why is there something rather than nothing? You have faith that there was no Creator."

"Bear in mind that an atheist believes that all these miraculous coincidences took place by chance. But he doesn't just believe that man and woman came into being without a Creator, but that all of creation did—amazing flowers, massive trees, succulent fruits, beautiful birds, the animal kingdom, the sea, fish, natural laws, etc. His faith is much greater than mine."

—Ray Comfort, *You Can Lead an Atheist to Evidence, but You Can't Make Him Think* (2009, p. 2)

This is the best argument I've heard for the existence of God. It's the trump card played by believers. However, it doesn't work.

There are several related ways to respond to why there's something rather than nothing: "Why assume nothing is the default?" This is a question that has no answer. As prolific German philosopher Adolf Grünbaum states, "Why be astonished at being at all? To marvel at existence is to assume that nothingness is somehow more natural, more restful. But why? The ancients started with matter, not the void; perhaps nothingness is stranger than being" (Holt, 2012).

Similarly, "How do you know the universe didn't always exist?" Even if appeals are made to the Big Bang, one can never know either that reality is one endless time loop with Big Bangs strung together for eternity, or that à la American theoretical physicist Brian Greene, we're part of a larger multiverse with an infinite number of Big Bangs constantly occurring.

Why isn't there nothing rather than something? On what basis can one claim nothing is the default position for existence?[2] Couldn't something be the default position, with nothing being the truly extraordinary thing? And even if we do accept by fiat, given our limited knowledge, that something rather than nothing is extraordinary, does that give license to make up answers as to why this is the case? It begs the question: is it better to pretend we know an answer to something we don't actually know, or is it better to simply be honest and say, "I don't know?"

The possibility that the universe always existed cannot be ruled out.[3] This by definition casts doubt on a creator. No faith is needed to posit that the universe may have always existed.

2. *"You can't prove there's not a God."*

> "I think that St. Paul is the great faith statement. Paul doesn't need to prove it, he just tells you his experience, and that's what it is: 'It's my experience, and I don't need to prove it to anybody and you can't disprove it!' Now if the church had only stuck with that position, I think that we'd be a lot better off. This business of trying to find proof, of trying to figure out what happened to Jesus's body—all of that is irrelevant to the life of faith. In a sense the belief in the resurrection is the final—I was going to say test of faith, but it's not that—it is the final experience of faith.
>
> I believe that Jesus was crucified, died, and rose again. That for me is a final expression of faith. I cannot prove any of that, but without that, anything else is meaningless. Paul says this better than anybody I know: 'If Christ has not been raised, then your faith has been in vain' (I Corinthians 15:14). That is a marvelous passage, and I think that sums it up. I cannot prove to you that Christ has risen, but without that resurrection experience, without my experience of the resurrection, there's no meaning to anything. We may as well throw it all out. When I would hear that part as a child, I used to say that it was one of the most fallacious arguments I'd ever heard! Because Paul goes on from there and says, 'But in fact Christ has been raised from the dead.' So he hasn't proved anything at all, except his faith, and I find that very moving."
>
> —Verna Dozier, *Confronted by God: The Essential Verna Dozier* (2006, p. 18)

I try to have patience when I hear this. What's perpetually surprising about this defense is that I hear it from people all over the intellectual and educational spectrum. The basic idea is that because you can't prove that there's not a God, then God must exist. Of all of the defenses of faith, it is most difficult to comprehend how someone could actually offer this as a legitimate defense for faith or for belief in God.

To rebut this, I talk about little blue creatures living inside Venus.[4] Clearly one cannot prove there are no little blue men living inside Venus. I then ask the question directly, "Do you believe there are little blue men living inside the planet Venus?" There are basically three answers for this: yes, no, or I don't know.

If they say "yes," then I change the color to yellow. I continue to change the color until they admit that not all the men I've described can physically live inside the planet. I then repeat the question and ask if they believe there are little blue men living inside Venus.

If they say "no," I reply, "Why not? You can't prove it not to be true." Most people will get the point and then say there's something different about God. That is, this line of argument works against everything *except* God. (Here I'm reminded of defenders of Anselm's argument for the existence of God. Every time someone would bring up an objection, they'd state that the argument only works with God.) When the respondent says there is something special about God that makes this argument not work, then I always press them to know what's different about God. I've yet to hear a coherent answer to this question.

If they respond, "I don't know," to the question of little blue men living inside Venus, I ask them why they don't take the same stance with God and say, "I don't know."

Finally, I ask, "What evidence could I give you that would prove God doesn't exist? Can you please give me a specific example of exactly what that evidence would look like?" Because it's not possible to have a justified belief in God due to the fact that there's insufficient evidence to warrant this belief, very few people have been able to cogently answer the question.[5] I then use the discussion as a springboard to suggest that they don't believe in God on the basis of the evidence. From here it's a rocky but clear path to, "One ought not believe in something for which there's insufficient evidence."

3. "I don't have enough faith to be an atheist."

> "Dawkins voices distress at an imagined opponent who 'can't see' the evidence or 'refuses to look at it because it contradicts his holy book,' but he has his own holy book of whose truth he has been persuaded,

and it is within its light that he proceeds and looks forward in hope (his word) to a future stage of enlightenment he does not now experience but of which he is fully confident. Both in the vocabulary they share—'hope,' 'belief,' 'undoubtedly,' 'there will come a time'—and the reasoning they engage in, Harris and Dawkins perfectly exemplify the definition of faith found in Hebrews 11, 'the substance of things hoped for, the evidence of things not seen.'"

—Stanley Fish, "Atheism and Evidence" (2007)

"And basing on the evidence that exists in this postmodern scientific world, which system of beliefs now requires more faith, the atheistic belief that life and the universe began by chance or the theistic belief that we are here because there is a Supernatural Being who put us and the universe in place? The point is, both systems of belief require faith, but the atheistic belief requires more faith in light of the evidence."

—Don Sausa, *The Jesus Tomb: Is It Fact or Fiction? Scholars Chime In* (2007, p. 9)

I have personally heard this objection innumerous times—mostly from those who are more fundamentalist in their orientation. My suspicion is that people who have genuine doubts about their faith but want to demonstrate or voice strong verbal support for their faith (not necessarily to others but for themselves) make this statement.

This defense is problematic for several reasons. First, what amount of "faith" is required for someone's nonbelief in the Norse god Thor? Or, are most people Thor atheists? Does nonbelief in Thor require effort? Do people need to congregate and sing songs together to reinforce their nonbelief in Thor? Anyone who says, "I don't have enough faith to be an atheist," doesn't understand what the word "atheist" means, or is simply insincere.

Second, one possible reason this defense has gained such traction is the starting point. The faithful start with defaulting to God; in other words, the faithful look at the world around them and say, "God." I happen to be on a plane now, and when I look around I see clouds, seats, people, my laptop, but I don't see an invisible, unifying metaphysical and supernatural element. I see objects. It is unclear to me why one's default would be God.

Borrowing from a term first used by pastor and French theologian John Calvin, contemporary American Christian apologist Alvin Plantinga tries to answer questions of defaulting to God with the Sensus Divinitatis or "God sensor" (Plantinga, 2000). Basically, Plantinga's answer is that some people have a built-in sense of the divine—something within them senses God in the same way that we have eyes that sense things in the visual realm.

One of the main problems with the God sensor argument is that just as some people allegedly claim to sense God, other people can allegedly claim to sense other imagined entities. This common rebuttal is referred to as "the Great Pumpkin" objection. In American cartoonist Charles M. Schulz's comic strip *Peanuts*, Linus believes there's a Great Pumpkin who arises from the pumpkin patch to reward well-behaved children. If the theist can claim that her sensation of God is immediate, why can't anyone who genuinely feels an imagined entity claim that entity is real? (This argument can become very complicated, and as a general rule I'd suggest avoiding it whenever possible. Focus instead on the fact that one's confidence in a sensation does not map onto its accuracy—just because people feel in their hearts the Emperor of Japan is divine, does not make the Emperor of Japan divine.)

When responding to, "I don't have enough faith to be an atheist," I begin by clearly defining the words "faith" and "atheist." I can't imagine how these two definitions could align so as to make this statement sensible.

4. "My faith is true for me."

"My faith is true for me" is rarely heard among more sophisticated believers and almost never heard among fundamentalists.

It is very difficult to explain why this claim is fallacious because often the type of person who makes this statement does not have the intellectual or educational wherewithal to understand more thoughtful, substantive responses. (The exceptions are the youthful solipsists, the postmodernists, and the epistemological and cognitive relativists.)

The statement, "My faith is true for me," means the faith-based beliefs one holds are true for the speaker and not necessarily for other people. The utterer of this statement is not making claims about faith beliefs being universally true—that is, true for all people.

Here's my response: does your faith tradition include statements of fact about the world? For example, humans are thetans trapped on Earth in physical bodies, Jesus walked on water, the ability to fly can result from fasting (Jacobsen, 2011), or the Garden of Eden is in Jackson County, Missouri.

If your faith tradition includes no empirical statements, then it's unclear what your faith tradition entails. However, if your faith tradition makes empirical claims (and *all* faith claims that fall within the domain of religion make empirical claims), then what you're saying is that your belief is true for you, regardless of how the world actually is. Since the world is the way it is regardless of our beliefs or of the epistemology we use to know the world, "my faith is true for me" is a nonsensical statement. One can have faith that if one jumps out of a twenty-story window one will polymorph into an eagle and fly to safety. This doesn't make it the case.

What one is really saying when one states, "My faith is true for me," is, "I prefer my delusions, and I wish to remain with them in spite of the evidence."

5. "Science can't explain quantum mechanics."

This line is tossed out in conversations when all else has failed in a desperate attempt to fortify the fiefdom of faith. As frequently as I've heard this, and asked people exactly what they mean, I'm not even sure how this could be a defense of faith. Quantum mechanics is science, discovered through the tools of science, and is verifiable and testable within science.

The attempt to draw fire away from the discussion may be why I've never read this defense of faith in peer-reviewed literature. It also doesn't fall into one of Harris's categories. It is not another version of the God of the gaps argument, and is not precisely a deepity.[6]

I think this statement may be a way of saying that we can't really be certain of anything. On one level, this is a feeble attempt to undermine reason by stating that there are some mysteries even our best and brightest can't grasp—thus giving the faithful license to pretend to know things they don't know.

On an even more pedestrian level, I've often heard this deployed as a justification for miracles. That is, quantum instability leaks into the visible realm—what Dawkins calls the Middle Kingdom, or what British philosopher J. L. Austin termed the realm of "medium-sized dry goods" (Dawkins, 2005)—and could be responsible for a whole host of bizarre occurrences, like the sea parting or people being spontaneously healed.

In the latter case, the response to this is that quantum weirdness does not lend itself to a specific faith tradition. That is, if somehow what was happening in the quantum realm seeped into the Middle Kingdom and caused unexplained phenomena (and there is no evidence it has) this wouldn't be relegated to a single faith tradition. Quantum weirdness didn't cause *only* the alleged miracles in the Koran (or the Bible)—but if someone claimed to know this is how the phenomena manifested, I'd ask how they knew this and to produce the evidence. (For practice, you can also argue that quantum states do manifest, but only in [insert any faith tradition other than your interlocutor's].)

In the former case, I'm not sure how a lack of understanding about subatomic particles translates into the need for faith. Because we don't yet and might never entirely understand how the universe is ordered and operates in the realm of the very, very small, this does not translate into needing to use an unreliable epistemology.

6. *"You have faith in science."*

"But if faith in God requires independent scientific confirmation, what about the colossal faith our new atheists place in science itself?"

—John Haught, *God and the New Atheism* (2008, p. 45)

"Whether they admit to it or not, scientists have faith. It is, obviously, a rational faith that stems from their trust in the scientific method to reveal natural truth. But it is faith nonetheless. Scientists have faith that, based upon past successes, the scientific method will uncover natural truths yet to be discovered. They conduct experiments and make observations without knowing if they will discover something truly new, but they trust that if anything has yet to be discovered in the natural world, science will discover it. That's faith, and it's faith that mirrors the rational faith of religious individuals; one that is based on past successes, rationality, and personal experience."

—Peter Doumit, *A Unification of Science and Religion* (2010, p. 24)

"Scientists have to believe in the validity of materialism. They have to say, 'For my work, I need to assume the hypothesis that everything is materialistic!' which is a statement of faith."

—Anne Foerst, "Do Androids Dream of Bread and Wine?" (2001, p. 197)

"What incredible faith an individual must have to trust that science is true and the Bible, Heaven and Hell, and the risen Lord Jesus Christ is a myth."

—Floyd McElveen, *Faith of an Atheist* (2009, p. 11)

This is usually a "late game" line, offered after faith has been demolished and exposed as fraudulent. People say this because they want to show some parity in belief: they have faith in X and you have faith in Y. You both have faith, but in different things. I've also found that people make this statement because they're afraid of being seen as stupid or ignorant, so they want to leave the conversation and save face.

Science is the antithesis of faith. Science is a process that contains multiple and redundant checks, balances, and safeguards against human bias. Science has a built-in corrective mechanism—hypothesis testing— that weeds out false claims.

Claims that come about as a result of a scientific process are held as tentatively true by scientists—unlike claims of faith that are held as eternally true. Related to this, claims that come about as the result of a scientific process are falsifiable, that is, there is a way to show the claims are false. This is not the case with most faith claims. For example, there's no way to falsify the claim that the Norse god Loki was able to assume other forms.

Scientists also try to prove claims false (falsification), unlike faith leaders who unequivocally state that their faith claims are true. Related to the bizarre notion that there's a vast conspiracy among scientists to suppress certain lines of research, if a scientist can demonstrate that a popular scientific claim is false, she can become famous, get tenure, publish her results, earn more money, and become respected by her peers. Moreover, the more prominent the defeated hypothesis, the greater the reward. If a preacher states that the claims of his faith tradition are false, he's excommunicated, defrocked, or otherwise forced to abandon his position.

Science is a *method* of advancing our understanding. It is a process we can use to bring us closer to the truth and to weed out false claims. Science is the best way we've currently found to explain and understand how the universe works. It should be jettisoned if something better (more explanatory, more predictive, more parsimonious, etc.) comes along (Schick & Vaughn, 2008).

7. *"You have faith your partner loves you."*

> *Dawkins*: We only need to use the word "faith" when there isn't any evidence.

> *Lennox*: No not at all, I presume you've got faith in your wife? Is there any evidence for that? Or would you base it—

Dawkins: Yes, plenty of evidence.

Lennox: Hmmm.

Dawkins: Let's generalize it, never mind about my wife . . .

. . .

Dawkins: . . . Let's say that in general, how do we know that somebody loves us? Okay—

Lennox: Yes.

Dawkins: Um, you can use the word faith for that, if you like, but it's not, it's not the right use of the word—

Lennox: Oh, it is.

Dawkins: Because, because you know why, you know your wife loves you because of all sorts of little signs. . . . That's the evidence.

Lennox: Yes, that's right.

Dawkins: That's evidence. That's perfectly good evidence. That's not faith.

Lennox: Yes it is.

In 2007, Dawkins was asked this question in a debate with British philosopher John Lennox (Dawkins, 2007). Dawkins eventually replied it's "not the right use of the word." Lennox responded, "Oh, it is." It's not.

"You have faith your partner loves you" tends to be an "early game" response, given before faith has been razed. It's similar to, "You have faith in science," but not as lofty. It's a more colloquial way of saying that in everyday events you use faith to navigate reality.

Comparing that for which we have abundant evidence (the actions of a real person) to a faith claim, which by definition is that for which we lack evidence (like the existence of an undetectable creator of the universe), is not analogous. The idea that my wife probably loves me is not a radical hypothesis. The idea that there is a being who created the universe, inseminated a woman, and gave birth to a son who rose from the dead, is an extraordinary, radical claim.[7] Equating an extraordinary claim with a mundane one, and then suggesting they "both require faith," is disanalogous.

FAITH IS USEFUL

8. *"My faith is beneficial for me."*

> "I rely on my faith to help me cope with my diabetes. Prayer is a huge part of my diabetes care and control. I accept the fact that I can do nothing on my own. My faith in God's love, grace, and providence really helps pull me through. I don't know why I have diabetes but I know that I have a mission to accomplish with this condition in my life. For me, that focus and faith is essential to my peace of mind."
>
> —Nicole Johnson, *Living with Diabetes* (2001, p. 185)

> "It was faith that restored my sense of purpose and self-confidence. My faith gave me back my joy and enthusiasm for life."
>
> —Ali and Ali, *The Soul of a Butterfly* (2004, p. 147)

> "My faith gives me hope. I say 'my faith' because say if at the end of all this there was nothing, my faith would still have sustained me. It helps keep me grounded and focused. It keeps me optimistic. It gives me joy. It drives me. I believe in something much larger and more powerful and omnipresent than myself. I know it's God that keeps me going."
>
> —Sugar Turner and Tracy Bachrach Ehlers, *Sugar's Life in the Hood* (2003, p. 215)

I never allow the conversation to devolve into the merits of faith until my interlocutor has explicitly admitted that faith is an unreliable path to the truth. Almost invariably discussion about the alleged benefits of faith are red herrings, distracting one from the main issue—whether or not faith can reliably help one to arrive at the truth.

In your work as a Street Epistemologist, once you've started engaging the faithful in dialectical interventions, you'll notice conversations about the merits of faith will have no clear demarcation. Someone won't say, "Okay, you're correct, faith is a failed epistemology and thus highly unlikely to get one to the truth. However, having faith is of tremendous benefit both to the faithful and to society."

Conversations about whether or not faith is beneficial should only take place *after* your interlocutor *explicitly* states that faith is an unreliable path to truth. Once you ask people to acknowledge this, you'll almost never enter into a conversation about the benefits of faith.

If you do, however, find yourself in this position, I'd ask how an unreliable reasoning process can benefit someone. I'd also ask how an unreliable and potentially unrevisable faulty process of reasoning can benefit an entire group of people.

One of the problems with the benefit argument is that people can be mistaken about what's in their own interest. On an individual level, heroin addicts, alcoholics, and people in abusive relationships will, at various times, claim these states of affairs are beneficial. And in the realm of religious faith, people are often mistaken about what's in their interest—for example, decisions about personal relationships that are not sanctioned by the faith (my grandfather, who converted to Catholicism, was prohibited by the Catholic Church from walking my mother down the aisle at her wedding because my parents were married in an Apostolic Church), refraining from engaging in homosexual relationships, staying in a deeply unhappy and emotionally harmful marriage due to prohibitions on divorce, physically harmful self-flagellation or extreme fasting, etc.

On a macro level, the Taliban believe imprisoning half their population and beating them is not only in their interest but also their duty: *The more people who share a faulty process of reasoning the greater the magnification of potential harm.* Premodern history is littered with cultures that have navigated themselves to extinction in part due to faith.[8]

Finally, and perhaps most importantly, all or virtually all of the studies you'll hear people cite about the alleged benefits of belief communities have nothing to do with faith, and everything to do with religion, community, social networks, social support, etc.[9]

It could be that the variables in these studies being tested are social cohesion and group reciprocity. Faith would need to be teased out and isolated before any benefits could be shown. To my knowledge, no study has isolated faith as a variable and shown its positive results.

9. "Life has no meaning without faith."

> "Without faith, life becomes worthless and meaningless, and failure or death is the outcome."
>
> — Herminio Gamponia, *Great Prescriptions to a Better You* (2010, pp. 67–68)
>
> "Without hope or faith life becomes meaningless; an empty charade to be played out before an unseeing and unhearing audience."
>
> —Lewis Solomon, *From Athens to America* (2006, p. 1)

This is a remarkably common statement, although I'm not sure how this is a defense of faith. This is a statement about the consequences of faith as opposed to whether or not one's faith latches onto truth. Many people allege that their lives would be meaningless and that they'd have no life purpose without faith.[10]

If life has no meaning for someone unless they pretend to know something they don't know, then I would strongly and sincerely urge extensive therapy and counseling. This is particularly true if feelings of meaninglessness and lack of purpose lead to depression, which is a serious illness. Absent a mental disorder, or head trauma, there is no reason an adult should feel life is meaningless without maintaining some form of delusion.

When I hear someone say, "Life has no meaning without faith," I suggest possible sources of meaning one could find in one's life: children, music, art, poetry, charity, reading, hobbies, simply trying to make the world a better place, small acts of kindness, etc. I usually try to tailor the source of meaning to the person with whom I'm speaking. I also talk about our daughter who was adopted from China as a "waiting child." I discuss the meaning and joy she's brought into our lives.

The overwhelming majority of people will acknowledge that they can find sources of meaning in their lives. For those who don't, I sincerely recommend seeking professional psychological services.

10. "Why take away faith if it helps get people through the day?"

This is a common line among blue-collar liberals who've not been indoctrinated by leftist academic values.[11] I've never really understood how removing a bad way to reason will make it difficult to get through the day. If anything, it would seem that correcting someone's reasoning would significantly increase their chances of getting through the day. With reliable forms of reasoning comes the capability of crafting conditions that enable people to navigate life's obstacles. By using a more reliable form of reasoning, people are more capable of bringing about conditions that enable them to flourish.

Another interpretation of this statement is that it's the contents of one's beliefs that help people cope. For example, if one believes a recently deceased loved one has gone to the Happy Hunting Ground (a belief found among certain Native American tribes) where the wild game is in abundance, this makes it easier to deal with that person's passing. However, if one used sound methods of reasoning one would produce better results and feel more in control of one's life than unreflectively buying into a commonly held belief about what happens after death. One would thus rely less on the content of one's beliefs and more on the process one uses to arrive at one's beliefs.

To argue that people need faith is to abandon hope, and to condescend and accuse the faithful of being incapable of understanding the importance of reason and rationality. There are better and worse ways to come to terms with death, to find strength during times of crisis, to make meaning and purpose in our lives, to interpret our sense of awe and wonder, and to contribute to human well-being—and the faithful are completely capable of understanding and achieving this.

ATHEISM IS CORROSIVE

11. *"Without faith, society would devolve morally."*

> "I think a world without faith would be a world on the path to tragedy and disaster, I really believe that."
>
> —*Tony Blair* (as quoted in Hallowell, May 15, 2012)

> "Last century we tried Godlessness on a grand scale and the effects were devastating: Nazism, Stalinism, Pol Pot-ery, mass murder, abortion and broken relationships—all promoted by state-imposed atheism . . . the illusion that we can build a better life without God."
>
> —Anglican Archbishop Peter Jensen (as quoted in Stefanelli, 2012b)

This tends to be a late-game line, with Stalin and Hitler always included, sometimes followed by Pol Pot, Mussolini, and the Kims thrown in for good measure. The basic idea is that without objective standards of right and wrong, not only do ordinary people descend into savages, but vicious dictatorships are also inevitable.

"Without faith, society would devolve morally," is an empirical claim. It's a claim about the world. It's also false. To respond, one need only survey religiosity and livability indices among various societies. Scandinavia has the lowest rate of religious belief in the world, yet on virtually all measures of well-being Scandinavian countries top every index (for more on this, see American sociologist Phil Zuckerman's work).

I usually hear this defense from Christians. One response I offer is, "Saudi Arabia." (For a one-word response, try "Iran.") Saudi Arabia has one of the most devout, adherent populations on the planet, yet its citizens lack basic freedoms and are subject to the tyranny of religious police.

Finally, people use the Stalin/Hitler card in an attempt to argue that the worst dictatorships in recent times have had atheists at their helm (Hitler was more likely a deist if not a theist).[12] However, even granting this argument's assumption, these men didn't act like they did because they were atheists. That is, their nonbelief in a deity didn't dictate particular actions they took. (This would be akin to arguing that Pol Pot—who was a bad man—didn't believe in leprechauns, you don't believe in leprechauns, therefore you're as bad as Pol Pot.) Their systems were horrific precisely because they resembled faith-based systems where suspending warrant for belief is required (as is the wholesale adoption of an ideology, like Communism, Nazism, Fascism, etc.).[13]

MISCELLANEOUS

The following are less common defenses of faith, along with my preferred responses:

*   *Defense*: "Atheism is just another religion. You have faith in atheism."

    Response: "Atheism is a conclusion one comes to as a result of being rational and honest. Atheism is a conclusion that's based on the best available evidence for the existence of God—which is that there is none. Atheism is not a religion. Atheism is not a belief. Atheism is, basically, the lack of belief in God(s). Atheists follow no creeds or doctrines. They engage in no particular set of behaviors."

*   *Defense*: "Much of modern science and practical mathematics is based upon mere 'native preference,' not on any rational proof. Faith is the same." (For an interesting glimpse into this read French mathematician Henri Poincaré's *Science and Hypothesis*, written over one hundred years ago but still pertinent.)

    Response: "Science has a built-in corrective mechanism that faith does not have. There's been convergence across all fields of science on virtually all scientific theories since the eighteenth century. At any point in the future, do you ever think there will be convergence on specific faith propositions? I don't, because those propositions are arbitrary."

- *Defense*: "You should never say such things. You'll offend people and they'll think you're a jerk."

  Response: "What people believe, and how they act, matter. They particularly matter in a democracy where people have a certain amount of influence over the lives of their fellow citizens. My intent is not to be a jerk. I don't buy into the notion that criticizing an idea makes me a bad person. A criticism of an idea is not the same as a criticism of a person. We are not our ideas. *Ideas don't deserve dignity; people deserve dignity.* I'm criticizing an idea because that idea is not true, and the fact that people think it is true has dangerous consequences."

- *Defense*: "You're just talking about blind faith. My faith is not blind."

  Response: "There is no need to modify the word 'faith' with the word 'blind.' All faith is blind. All faith is belief on the basis of insufficient evidence. That's what makes it faith. If one had evidence, one wouldn't need faith, one would merely present the evidence."

- *Defense*: "Atheism and secular humanism are as much a religion—and require as much faith—as any religion. Atheists and secular humanists love to equivocate on religious issues—claiming they are not religious and are free of religious bias—but they are no less religious or faithful than anyone else. They are not aware of their own faith and are blind to their biases. There is a saying: 'There are *no* nonreligious people, only false Gods.'"

  Response: "Confusing atheism with secular humanism demonstrates a fundamental misunderstanding as to what the terms mean. Secular humanism is a philosophy and a set of ideals; atheism is simply the lack of belief in a God or Gods. There is no dogma attached to nonbelief in a divine Shiva the Destroyer. And, as to the saying—it's silly. To assert that people are incapable of letting go of belief in mythological fairytales without attaching themselves to some other form of worship is narrow-minded, condescending, pessimistic, and without evidential merit."

INTERVENTIONS

I'll now show how I've used these responses in two brief informal, dialectical interventions. The purpose of the interventions was to change targeted beliefs held by my interlocutors.

The first intervention was with a colleague (JM) I bumped into on the street. The second intervention was with a friend of a friend (KP) at a party; we were discussing philosophy and faith. Both conversations begin in medias res.

Intervention 1

JM: What you seem to want to do is to take away everyone's faith.

PB: Yeah. Why is that a problem?

JM: Well what the hell do you think? I mean what do you *really* think?

PB: It's not about what I think, it's about what you think. Why is that a problem?

JM: I'm not one of your students. Don't answer a question with a question.

PB: Okay. Here's what I really think. I think I should be given some type of community service award for devoting my life to helping people learn to reason effectively. Now could you please answer my question? Why is helping people to abandon their faith a bad thing?

JM: Because for the most part these are good, decent people. You're taking good, kind, Christian people and you're taking away something that they rely on.

PB: Do you think the thing that they rely upon [faith], do you think that will lead them to the truth?

JM: Of course not. No sane person could. But it [faith] not only makes them feel good, it also keeps them in check. What do you think would happen if you and X [a colleague] had your way?

PB: What do you think would happen?

JM: You know what would happen, that's why you're asking me what would happen. They'd be murdering and raping and who only knows what else.

PB: So you mean that by taking away a bad way of reasoning the natural consequence is that people become murderers?

JM: The reason that a lot of people don't rape and murder in the first place is because of religion.

PB: Well what about Scandinavia?

JM: You people love to talk about Scandinavia.

PB: Well?

JM: Well that's not the same.

PB: The same as what?

JM: The conditions there are not the same as the conditions here, and you know it.

PB: I have no idea what you're talking about. What do you mean?

JM: You know exactly what I mean. I mean they're not analogous, and you're making them analogous.

PB: You mean if all other variables were held constant and the Scandinavians became more faithful, the murder and rape rates would drop?

(Sigh and a long pause)

JM: You're impossible.

PB: So are you willing to change your mind and agree that helping to rid large numbers of people from an unreliable process of reasoning will not have a detrimental effect on the society?

(Sigh)

PB: Well?

(Sigh)

Intervention 2

KP: Do you trust your wife?

PB: To do what? To fly a plane, no. To diagnose a basic medical condition, yes. [My wife is a board certified physician and professor of medicine.]

KP: Well, I mean, you have faith in your wife.

PB: Well that's not the same as trusting my wife, right? Trust and faith are not the same.

KP: Well, yeah, I mean, you do have faith in your wife, right?

PB: No, actually, no. I don't have faith in my wife. I trust my wife to do or not do certain things. I trust her to not abuse our children. I trust her to not pull a Lorena Bobbitt on me. But that has nothing to do with faith. Why do you ask?

KP: I'm asking because you said that faith is always bad, you know. And I think that you have faith.

PB: What do I have faith in?

KP: Well, lots of stuff. [Motioning to my wife] Your wife. When you flick a switch the light will go on—

PB: I have no faith. My life is joyfully devoid of faith.

(Mutual laughter)

PB: I don't have faith that the light will go on when I flick a switch. I know it will both because of past experience and because of the scientific process that enabled that to occur in the first place. Why do you think that has anything to do with faith, or with unwarranted belief?

KP: Because you don't know the light will go on.

PB: That's true. The light could be burned out—

KP: So you do have faith that the light isn't burned out.

PB: No. I *hope* the light isn't burned out, but it's always possible it is. That's hope, that's not faith. I don't believe it's burned out unless I see it's burned out. And if it is burned out, then I'll just replace it. And I know that replacing it will likely work because of my history with replacing bulbs. So I don't need faith. Faith isn't required at all. Or am I missing something? Is my reasoning in error?

(Pause)

KP: No, I guess not.

PB: So, can we agree that when it comes to my wife, or to flicking a light switch, we don't need faith?

(Long pause)

KP: Yeah, I guess so.

PB: Cool. So we now need to extend this further and talk about why we don't need—shouldn't have—faith at all. Faith, just say no.

(Laughter)

DIG DEEPER

Books

Christopher Hitchens, *The Missionary Position: Mother Teresa in Theory and Practice* (Hitchens, 1995)

Christopher Hitchens, *The Portable Atheist: Essential Readings for the Nonbeliever* (Hitchens, 2007)

Victor Stenger, *The Fallacy of Fine-Tuning: Why the Universe Is Not Designed for Us* (Stenger, 2011)

Victor Stenger, *God and the Atom* (Stenger, 2013)

Phil Zuckerman, "Why Are Danes and Swedes So Irreligious?" (Zuckerman, 2009)

Video

"Is God Necessary for Morality?" William Lane Craig versus (American philosopher) Shelly Kagan Debate, http://www.youtube.com/watch?hl=en&client=mv-google&gl=US&v=SiJnCQuPiuo&nomobile=1

NOTES

1. To move beyond arguments in support of faith and focus on arguments in support of God's existence, I highly recommend American author Guy P. Harrison's accessible and clear *50 Reasons People Give for Believing in a God* (Harrison, 2008). I use this text in my Atheism class at Portland State University. I'd also recommend American mathematician John Allen Paulos's *Irreligion: A Mathematician Explains Why the Arguments for God Just Don't Add Up* (Paulos, 2008). In this brief book, Paulos rebuts classical and contemporary arguments for God's existence.

2. I usually avoid Lawrence Krauss's argument that nothingness is unstable and that sooner or later something springs from nothing (Krauss, 2012). First, this argument bumps up against the limits of my conceptual understanding. Second, I don't have anywhere near the grasp of theoretical physics I'd need to argue this position. Unless you have an intimate familiarity with the physics behind these ideas, I'd suggest not using this line of argument.

   Krauss's book, *A Universe from Nothing: Why There Is Something Rather than Nothing*, is important. However, the lines of thought contained here are much better in the context of a debate than for a Street Epistemologist.

3. This is also the deathblow to the Kalām cosmological argument, which has recently become the darling of Christian apologists. The Kalām argument goes like this:

   Premise: Among that which exists, everything that has a beginning has a cause.

   Premise: The universe has a beginning.

   Conclusion: The universe has a cause.

4. This is a version of the British philosopher Bertrand Russell's (1872–1970)

teapot. Russell claims that there's a small teapot, undetectable by telescopes, in an elliptical orbit between Earth and Mars. If you can't disprove that such a teapot exists, do you believe it does exist? Personally, I've not had as much success with Russell's teapot as I have with the example here. Perhaps it's because people can't wrap their mind around an object that we cannot detect floating in space, or because it's easier to elicit a contradiction with an increasing number of substances found within a contained space. If you find Russell's teapot to be more effective than my example, then use what's most effective.

5. When one does attempt to provide "evidence" for God's existence, the usual suspects emerge, the most common of which are fine-tuning and complexity. Basically, the fine-tuning argument states that God(s) calibrated initial conditions in the universe to make it possible for life to emerge. Physicist Victor Stenger completely dismantles this in his superbly readable book, *The Fallacy of Fine-Tuning: Why the Universe Is Not Designed for Us* (Stenger, 2011).

    The idea behind the complexity argument, sometimes called the "watchmaker argument," is that just as the inner workings of a watch are too complicated to have arisen on their own, so too are the workings of the universe. The universe is just too complicated to have come into existence without a designer. Dawkins and others have addressed this idea in detail.

    My response, which I offer as an intervention to disabuse people of unwarranted belief, I owe to a colleague; I ask about tornados: "Have you ever seen a tornado? Do you think that God has his finger on a button and just designs these incredibly intricate natural phenomena?" The idea is that complexity can emerge as a natural result of a system and not as designed or orchestrated by an entity.

6. The "God of the gaps" argument is the believer's appeal to God as an explanation for whatever phenomenon we cannot explain scientifically. For example, if the scientific understanding of the day cannot explain lightning bolts, the believer will say, "God did it." Once we can scientifically explain the mechanism behind lightning, the believer will move on to another phenomenon and attribute God as the cause of that phenomenon. The argument is referred to as the "God of the gaps," because as our scientific

knowledge expands the gaps close, and there are fewer and fewer places (phenomena) that can be attributed to being caused by God.

Currently, intelligent design (ID) is a type of God of the gaps argument. The idea behind ID is basically, "You don't know how life was formed and sustained, so it was God that formed life and sustains life." Questions about origin of life present another God of the gaps–type argument, "You don't know the process by which living organisms naturally arise from nonliving matter; therefore the cause was God."

7. It initially surprised me when people asked why I thought this was an extraordinary claim. It no longer surprises me as I've become numb from being asked so frequently. If rising from the dead was an everyday occurrence, and it was not just commonplace but expected that one would rise from the dead, then *not* rising from the dead would be extraordinary. We don't live in a universe in which people rise from the dead either regularly or at all. Therefore, the claim that someone rose from the dead is a remarkable claim.

When I state that rising from the dead is a remarkable claim that demands extraordinary evidence, I'm told that the Bible is a not just a reliable source of evidence, but that it's also extraordinary evidence and thus constitutes sufficient justification to warrant belief. Here's my response: "Suppose you heard a story about a woman who could walk through walls. Let's also suppose that you were an investigator charged with figuring out if this was true. What would you do?" Basically, I encourage the person who believes the claims in the Bible are true, to use the same standards of evidence they'd use as a modern-day investigator: What are the names of the witnesses? Where did they live? Are they reputable? How many people witnessed this? Did you interview them directly? How do you know they were credible? What was their relation to the individual in question?

If a seasoned Street Epistemologist asks these questions, many people will acknowledge that the Bible is not a reliable source that can justify belief in these extraordinary claims. The conversation will usually come back to having faith, which can then be targeted as an unreliable epistemology.

However, in my interventions, instead of continuing the discussion about the resurrection of Jesus and the evidence that supports this claim, I talk about Muhammad riding to heaven on a winged horse. Specifically, I ask why they don't believe that proposition on the basis of faith, especially given that there's *overwhelming* evidence that Muhammad was an historical figure. Conceptually distancing oneself from a faith tradition often helps the subject examine what constitutes extraordinary evidence for an extraordinary claim. (This is a variation on John W. Loftus's idea of the outsider test for faith.)

8. Examples include the Anasazi, Easter Islanders, Mayan, and Norse Greenlanders. Among the reasons the Norse outpost in Greenland failed, for example, was because Norse religious teachings prohibited eating shellfish and other common, locally available foodstuffs. In short, religious dietary prohibitions (like Jews' and Muslims' prohibitions on pork) were the difference between success and failure.

9. A brief but thorough summary, which unfortunately has no references, is Tom Bartlett's "Dusting Off God" (Bartlett, 2012).

10. What the faithful want, and what they claim to know, is that the universe comes prepackaged with abstract qualities such as meaning and purpose. One problem with believing that the universe has these abstract qualities as built-in properties is that it abrogates our duty to create meaning in our lives.

    In Viktor Frankl's *Man's Search for Meaning*, Frankl discusses meaning that he and his fellow prisoners found when interned in Auschwitz. This book had a profound effect on my understanding of how we seek meaning in our lives. It helped me understand how radically contextual meaning is, how we create our own meaning and purpose, and how we can find meaning in every instant of our lives.

11. The academic left tend to take a more pitiful view of the faithful while simultaneously becoming upset in response to questioning a person's faith. They view attacks on faith as a type of intellectual hegemony and epistemological colonialism (see chapter 8).

12. I often hear the simplistic, reductionist claim that there is a kind of equation between atheism and Nazism—for example, statements like, "Atheism leads to Hitler/Nazism." There have been any number of similar claims made in

various quarters: Nazism was an inevitable product of Darwin, or of Luther, or of the Versailles Treaty, or of Wagner's operas, or of Nietzsche, or of Hegel. All of these break down under the obvious objection that there were plenty of atheists, Darwinists, Lutherans, objectors to the Versailles Treaty, Wagnerites, Nietzscheans, and Hegelians who did not become Nazis. These are all vacuous arguments from a historiographical perspective.

Was Adolph Hitler an atheist? Hitler cannot be called a churchgoing Christian, but neither can he be used as an example of an atheist. Hardly the product of an anti-Christian childhood and upbringing, he attended Mass with his devout mother and was a choirboy, which he quite enjoyed. Indeed, the majesty and pageantry of the Church heavily influenced the staging in Nazi rallies and rituals.

Born and raised a Roman Catholic, Hitler remained a nominal Catholic for the rest of his life. He never officially renounced the Church or his membership in it, but he was hostile to the Church's impulses of caring for the weak, infirm, and mentally handicapped, whom he wished to destroy. But this did not lead Hitler to outlaw Christianity.

Hitler never doubted the divinity of Jesus of Nazareth, just his Jewishness, convinced that he was actually an Aryan! The portraits of a fair-haired, blue-eyed Jesus that grace so many American homes would have doubtless met with Hitler's approval.

What follows are specific examples rebutting the claim that Hitler was an atheist:

- When Party Secretary Martin Bormann closed a convent where Eva Braun's aunt was a nun, Hitler reversed the order, telling Bormann such measures did more harm than good.

- Hitler allowed the German Army to have Catholic and Protestant chaplains in the field. All troops wore a belt buckle embossed with the German eagle clutching a swastika surrounded by the inscription "*Gott mitt uns*"—God is with us.

- Hitler lamented the influence of the Bible, "that Jewish artifact," on German Christians. In endless monologues to those around him, Hitler never once professed to be an atheist or unbeliever in the Abrahamic

God of Islam, Judaism, and Christianity. Of the three, he had the greatest admiration for Islam, particularly its military tradition.

- Survivor of over two-dozen assassination plots and attempts, Hitler credited "Divine Providence" and "Almighty God" for saving him to complete his Great Mission. On the eve of the invasion of the Soviet Union and his war of extermination and conquest, Hitler ended his address to his troops with the words, "Almighty God Bless Our Arms!"

- The first foreign policy coup of Nazi Germany was the "Concordat with the Vatican," allowing the Church independence and Catholic schools to remain open in exchange for staying out of politics. It was a major recognition and early legitimization of the regime. The Church also "welcomed the way" when Operation Barbarossa—the campaign against the Godless Soviet Union—was launched. Hitler, SS chief Heinrich Himmler, and architect of the Holocaust Reinhard Heydrich, nominal Catholics all, were never excommunicated by the Holy See. To this very day they remain Catholics of good standing in the eyes of the one true Church.

- As to restricting church attendance, as it has been claimed, Hitler said, "If my mother were alive today, she would doubtless be a churchgoer and I would not want to hinder her." When overzealous Nazi Party officials removed crucifixes from classroom walls in Bavaria, Hitler personally reversed the order and had them rehung.

Some of the myths surrounding Hitler's atheism can be attributed to an inaccurate and poorly translated version of *Table Talk*. *Table Talk* is a book of transcribed conversations that Hitler had with those close to him. Some versions of this text that were translated from German to other languages contained fabricated statements not found in the original German manuscript.

Ian Kershaw, Alan Bullock, and other biographers of Hitler present Hitler and Nazism in general as, on balance, anticlerical. But this has to be understood as a political response that may not have anything to say about Hitler's religious views or lack thereof. Hitler respected or even feared the Catholic Church as a potential rival (institutionally vis-à-vis the Nazi Party or the German state). Alongside Socialist or Communist labor union members, and of course Jews, practicing Catholics were the demographic least likely to support the Nazi Party in the years during which there were still free elections. Probably for this very reason Hitler was eager to make deals with Catholic authorities (quasi going above the head of the Catholic population as a whole) when it suited his purposes.

Protestants were much more likely to support Nazism, and for that reason Hitler regarded the Protestant churches as more malleable (he also held them in contempt). However, Hitler's attempt to co-opt the Protestant churches did not in the end work out too well; it generated in response the creation of the so-called Confessing Church, which became one of the centers of Nazi resistance: Barth, Niemöller, Bonhoeffer, etc. Perhaps, too, there are echoes of the cultural prejudices of his small-town Austrian upbringing, both in regard to the Catholic hierarchy and in regard to (predominantly north German/Prussian) Protestants.

13. Communist dogma and religion are both ideological systems that demand belief. They have no self-correcting mechanism. (With regard to Communist indoctrination, think of Marxist ideological training; with regard to religious indoctrination, think of the Catholic Catechism.) Atheism is based on skepticism rather than dogma and does not limit wonder.

CHAPTER 8

FAITH AND THE ACADEMY

Colleges and universities could do far more to combat faith, poor thinking, epistemological relativism, and bad reasoning. In this chapter I explain why they don't and what can be done to address these issues. I'll also guide readers through the template I use to disabuse people of epistemological relativism (that is, any way to come to knowledge is just as good as any other).

Employing universities in the struggle against faith is a cornerstone in the larger strategy to combat faith, promote reason and rationality, and create skeptics. Many university graduates will become the next generation of leaders and policymakers. We need to train educators not just to teach students how to think critically, but also how to nudge attitudes about faith on their downward spiral.

This chapter, which contains three separate sections, is a clarion call to educational administrators, academicians, educators, and more importantly, student activists. The first section, "Contemporary Academic Leftism: How Criticizing Bad Thinking Became Immoral," describes the problem; the second section, "Faith-Based Claims in the Classroom," offers a specific solution to part of the problem; the third section, "Beyond Relativism," offers a roadmap for educators and Street Epistemologists to disabuse people of epistemological relativism.

CONTEMPORARY ACADEMIC LEFTISM:
HOW CRITICIZING BAD THINKING BECAME IMMORAL

"The confusion between ideas and people when it comes to tolerance creates an environment where reason and rationality cannot be used to differentiate between good and bad ideas. When we refuse to admit that our preferences don't determine reality, we create an environment where reality cannot be improved."

—Matt Thornton, community activist

In this section, I'll explain how the dominant incarnation of (academic) liberalism—which I term "contemporary academic leftism"—turns epistemological critique into moral taboo. To make this argument, I begin with a brief genealogy of liberalism; segue with an explanation of parasitic values that have latched onto liberalism; continue with a discussion of Islam and Islamophobia; then end with the effect of the perversion of contemporary liberalism on feminism and faith.

Classical and Social Liberalism

Liberalism is a creation of the seventeenth century, fathered by British philosopher John Locke (1632–1704). For Locke, liberalism means limited government, the rule of law, due process, liberty, freedom of religion, freedom of speech, freedom of the press, freedom of assembly, separation of church and state, and separation of government powers into branches that oversee each other's authority.

Locke's classical liberalism evolved over time and became social liberalism—a creation of the nineteenth century—whose father is another British thinker, Thomas Hill Green (1836–1882). Green wrote about positive freedom, described human beings as fundamentally good, and argued for a social and economic order devoted to promoting the common good.

In the twentieth century, social liberalism evolved further still, with its dominant strain becoming contemporary academic leftism.[1] This current manifestation of liberalism is a skeleton of former incarnations and is best described not by what it is, but by the parasitic ideologies that have given that skeleton its corrupted form: relativism, subjectivity, tolerance, diversity, multiculturalism, respect for difference, and inclusion.[2] These invasive values betray classical and social liberalism's history of standing for basic freedoms and fighting all forms of tyranny.

Historically, there's nothing intrinsic to liberalism that necessarily weds it to the ideologies currently piggybacking on it. The fact that there is no necessary connection between the classical forms of liberalism and the values that currently fall within the sphere of contemporary academic leftism is reason for hope—hope that contemporary academic leftism can be decoupled from these external, invasive values, which undermine the emancipatory hope offered by classical and social liberalism, to return liberalism to its historical and intended roots.

Invasive Values and Preferences

It's difficult to tease out and differentiate the values and ideologies piggybacking on liberalism, but cultural relativism is one starting point.

Contemporary academic leftists have broadly adopted the mantle of cultural relativism and promote cultural relativism *as a value*. (I've yet to meet a conservative who's a cultural relativist.) The basic idea behind cultural relativism is that because everyone is always judging a culture from their own particular, situated cultural viewpoint, it's therefore impossible to make reliable judgments about other cultures and cultural practices. This means that cultures and cultural practices cannot be judged. For example, people in Brazil eat avocados with sugar and with sweet foods (like avocado smoothies) and in the United States we eat avocados with salt and with salty foods (like guacamole). These are cultural practices and thus neither correct nor incorrect.

The alleged inability to make reliable judgments about cultural practices has been illegitimately translated into a *moral* value. That is, the shift has been made from, "We *cannot* make judgments about cultural practices" to, "We *should* not make judgments about cultural practices." Notice the spurious move here, from the impossibility of a rational critique of a cultural preference, to the *immorality* of making a judgment about a cultural preference.

Relativism and the immorality of critique were then extended from the cultural to the epistemic realm—that is, from an impossibility of making reliable judgments about cultural preferences, to an immorality in making reliable judgments about systems of knowing the world. And just as there's no single, privileged cultural vantage point from which one can make objective judgments, by this reasoning, there's also no privileged epistemic viewpoint from which one can make objective epistemic judgments.

Epistemic relativism is either coupled with the idea that any process one uses to form beliefs is either just as good as any other process—a kind of epistemic egalitarianism—or with the idea that processes cannot be judged because one process is always judged by another process. In the latter case, there would thus be no basis for a reliable epistemological comparison.

For example, let's say people in society A prefer to use the Koran to come to knowledge and to understand reality, while people in society B prefer to use the scientific method. For the epistemological relativist these are just different ways to know the world. If a person uses the scientific method in an attempt to lawfully align his beliefs with reality, then he'd judge any other process—like using the Koran—to be not just inferior, but foolish. By extension, the same is true for the person who starts with the Koran. If one starts with the premises that the Koran is a perfect book and it is the best way to understand reality, then by this standard any other process will be judged to be inferior and misguided.

Epistemic relativism both led to, and was concurrent with, the turn toward subjectivity (also called the subjective turn).[3] That is, we went from thinking in terms of an objectively knowable world to a subjectively knowable world. In a subjectively knowable world, whatever is true for me is true. In an objectively knowable world, there actually exists something to which one can lawfully align one's beliefs—some shared, stable reality, or to use philosophical parlance, a communal, fixed, mind-independent metaphysic (Boghossian, 2006b, 2012a). In other words, think of objectivity like this: if everyone—including you—were to disappear, the universe would continue to be what it is. What is, is, independent of your beliefs. But in a world in which subjectivity is given primacy, there are no objective truths—what's true is just true for you.

Epistemic systems are thus reduced to preferences. That is, those people, in that culture, prefer to use process A to form beliefs (divination, astrology, consulting the sacred text), while others prefer to use process B (hypothesis and experiment, falsification, scientific method). Epistemic systems become like pizza toppings—matters of taste that are not subject to truth or falsity.[4]

Multiculturalism

The idea that epistemic systems are subjective and merely preferences is connected to, and paved the way for, multiculturalism. Here's where things get tricky and where we need to clarify terms.

"Multiculturalism" is a term frequently heard in academia. (Canadians started using the term in official policies in the 1970s.) The fundamental idea behind multiculturalism is that different cultures can and ought to peacefully coexist. Initially, multiculturalism was a strategic way of bringing people together into a larger, inclusive culture that consisted of many distinct groups. Multiculturalism—as the term is used in academia today—means something very different.[5]

The umbrella of multiculturalism has been extended to cover other kinds of coexistence—like the coexistence of cognitive and epistemic systems. And just as different cultures and races can harmoniously coexist when they're not, for example, attacked, so too can different epistemic systems harmoniously coexist when they're not attacked.

Now we're starting to see how classical liberalism has morphed into an ideology that undermines the emancipatory potential of critical rationality. *Contemporary academic leftism turned the rational analysis of criticizing a process one uses to know reality from an epistemological critique into a moral taboo.*

What I'm about to write may confound those inculcated in the academic zeitgeist: a criticism of a *process* (like the process of understanding the age of Earth through reading ancient texts), or a criticism of a cultural practice (like using the metric system or making women cover themselves), or a criticism of a religious text (like the Book of Mormon or The Urantia Book), is not the same as a criticism of a *person*.[6] Nor is it the same as criticism of a *race of people*. Multiculturalism contributed to this confusion by extending immutable properties of people—like race, gender, sexual orientation, religion—to all epistemic systems, cultural ways of knowing, faith traditions, local mythologies, etc.

Yet another tenet of contemporary academic leftism is the belief, the value, that *ideas have dignity*. When one believes dignity is a property of ideas and not just a property of people, then criticizing an idea becomes akin to criticizing a person. In other words, morally, just as one shouldn't criticize physical attributes common among sub-Saharan Africans, or among Scandinavians, so too one should not criticize ideas, faith traditions, and so forth.

Granting ideas dignity has two consequences. The first consequence is that criticizing faith traditions becomes viewed as a form of hate speech—like saying the "N" word. This kind of political correctness further buttresses faith from dialectical criticism. Most people won't criticize faith out of fear people will think not only that they're bad people, but also that they're mean-spirited, angry, bigoted, prejudiced, insensitive, hateful people.

The second consequence is the *medicalization* of individuals based on their criticisms. This is done by attaching the suffix "o-phobia" to someone who criticizes, for example, beliefs within the Islamic faith-tradition. (Note the parallelism in the terms: Islamophobe, homophobe, faithophobe.) The implicit message is that rational analysis and criticism are indicative of a mental disorder.

Labeling someone who criticizes ideas, in whatever domain, as driven by fear, or by some other pathological condition—in effect as mentally unbalanced—is a complete betrayal of the core ideas of classical and social liberalism, that is, of the right of every person to live by his own lights, be free, pursue happiness, and enjoy the right of self-expression. (There are people of different faiths and different races who experience genuine instances of discrimination and hatred. Conflating the categories of ideas and people, and medicalizing rational criticism, both demeans the experience of people who suffer from discrimination and simultaneously tosses away a root liberty: the freedom to rationally analyze and critique.)

Tolerance and Islam

Tolerance is another liberal value, and by the same line of thinking, has been perverted into another value that undermines reason.[7] Tolerance only works when there's reciprocity. That is, tolerance doesn't handle intolerance very well. When tolerance—and the protection offered by toleration—are extended from people and cantilevered out to ideas, we end up protecting intolerance, antiscience views, irrationality, and all other forms of rank bias. We see examples of this in old Europe, with liberal democracies neutered in dealing with Islamic radicals.

And then there's social tolerance. Many societies that enshrine faith-based processes are truly, profoundly intolerant: intolerant of homosexuals, intolerant of women's rights, intolerant of minority rights, intolerant of other faith traditions, intolerant of freedom of speech, intolerant of freedom of assembly, intolerant of freedom of religion, etc.[8] Leftism, and the values I've just discussed that piggyback on it, have extended the value of tolerance to social, cultural, and epistemic practices. For example, recently in Afghanistan there were mass protests and killings at the alleged desecration of the Koran (Partlow & Londono, 2011; Sieff, 2012), and in the wider Islamic world there were riots because of cartoons of the Muslim prophet Muhammad published by the Danish newspaper *Jyllands-Posten*.

More recently, in reaction to the film, *The Innocence of Muslims*, there were violent protests in Libya, Egypt, Indonesia, and even Australia. In the West, these acts were interpreted through the lens of tolerance. Academic leftists saw the problem as coming from our society—that is, that our society, the United States in particular, needs to be more sensitive, more tolerant, and more understanding of the values, and the faiths, of other cultures (Davis, 2012; Falk, 2012; Williams, 2012). But the societies in which protest killings occurred are perhaps the least tolerant societies on Earth.

The people in these societies did not rampage because we are not tolerant enough, or because they are asking for more tolerance. Mass hysteria occurred when people went on a rampage because their sacred text was desecrated by those who do not value it as a path to knowledge or truth.[9] Yet many leftists interpreted this behavior as a call for more tolerance on our part—and many even publicly advocated censorship (Malik, 2012).

There's something else that's disturbing about rampaging in the streets. Many leftists hold the idea that someone who does not live in one of these societies would only become upset at this behavior because they don't understand these cultures and their epistemic systems. If people just understood other cultures then they wouldn't be upset. Here, the idea is that there's something intrinsic to one's understanding that prevents one from seeing the matter clearly—as opposed to seeing something actually wrong with rampaging in the streets and killing people because religious sensitivities have been offended—and by extension something actually wrong with faith-based epistemic systems.[10]

My own view is that people are not disturbed because they don't understand why people rampage in the street, but *because they do understand* why people rampage in the street.

Leftists, Feminists, and Resuscitating Classical Liberalism

Today's leftists cannot detect moral and epistemic imbalance because the invasive values piggybacking classical and social liberalism have robbed them of the opportunity and capability of making moral and epistemic judgments. What is going on in higher education today is the paradigmatic example of well-educated leftists withholding judgment, teaching others to do the same, and even somehow feeling sanctimonious as a result—as opposed to, just making well-reasoned matter-of-fact judgments.

Most educators in American institutions today are academic leftists of the kind I've described—and even academicians who have not bought into this ideology wholesale have trouble sorting out the difference between respecting the value of the individual and making a critical judgment of an epistemology (Gross & Simmons, 2007; Jaschik, 2012; Kurtz, 2005; Rothman, Lichter, & Nevitte, 2005; Tobin & Weinberg, 2006). An unfortunate consequence of this is that many professors teach students to withhold judgments, especially moral judgments.[11] Withholding epistemological critique is wrong and needs to end. What educators should be teaching students is how to make better, more discerning judgments: how to discern reliable ways of reasoning from unreliable ways of reasoning.

I would be remiss if I did not mention the failure of contemporary academic feminism. Feminism is currently married to, or rather cohabitating with, academic leftism. Consequently, feminism has absorbed the same exogenous values that liberalism absorbed. Thus, there has been a tragic, catastrophic, and almost wholesale failure of contemporary academic feminism to speak out against the unbridled, ruthless misogyny of the Taliban, the horrific and wide-scale domestic violence suffered by women in Papua New Guinea, the sexual and physical violence common among Aboriginal women and girls in Australia, and the list goes on, and on, and on.

If one were to abstract feminism from values like tolerance, diversity, multiculturalism as applied to the realm of ideas, etc., what would the results be? Would American feminists be more likely or less likely to criticize the treatment of women in other cultures? The answer is obvious. Feminism's silence can be understood because it's been tainted by a litany of invasive values such as multiculturalism and relativism.

Faith

Contemporary academic leftism is also faith's unwitting ally. Contemporary academic leftists have bullied criticisms of faith off the table.[12]

Multiculturalism and associated ideologies grant "diverse" epistemologies—especially faith processes—immunity from criticism. Multiculturalism buttresses faith-based processes from criticism by conflating race with culture, and by making attacks on faith and reasoning processes ethically synonymous with attacks on race, gender, and other immutable characteristics. Rational critiques thus become immoral actions.[13]

Belying classical and social liberalism, contemporary academic leftism transforms the speech act of criticizing faith and faith claims into a moral problem—even a moral failure. Criticizing faith becomes unethical, immoral, hurtful, unnecessary, and unkind. By extension, individuals who offer these criticisms are themselves seen to be immoral, intolerant, divisive, cruel, and even hateful. This is an illegitimate and wrongheaded move.[14]

Faith is not an immutable characteristic; people leave and switch faith traditions. It is not like gender or ethnicity. There's even a word, "apostasy," for people who have left a particular faith tradition.[15] In some parts of the world the punishment for this is death (United States Department of State, Bureau of Democracy, Human Rights and Labor, 2011a).[16]

Shows of deference to the practice of murdering people who leave a faith tradition is a grotesquely misplaced use of the value of "tolerance" that Enlightenment thinkers trumpeted during the time of John Locke and Thomas Hill Green. This isn't tolerance, but rather ideological blindness and moral cowardice.

Hope

Contemporary academic leftism has created a cascading social, moral, and epistemological catastrophe. It has undermined reason and rationality and created conditions for faith, religion, superstition, pseudoscience, and faulty epistemologies of all stripes to flourish. It is directly responsible for an entire generation of students disengaging their capacity for critical rationality—*and consequently believing they're better people as a result.*

I hope contemporary leftism will revert back to liberalism and be decoupled from relativism, subjectivity, multiculturalism, and the muddled thinking that emerges from extending dignity from people to ideas. Harris, Hitchens, Dennett, and others have eloquently articulated the limits of new liberalism and the urgency to resuscitate classical and social liberalism so that it can again become a vibrant and effective change agent.

FAITH-BASED CLAIMS IN THE CLASSROOM

"When one pretends to know things one doesn't know in science, one gets laughed at."

—Matt Thornton, community activist

All thirty students in your introductory philosophy class studied diligently for their midterm.[17] After all the exams are submitted, you inform your students that you'll grade their tests using a Ouija board—that is, you'll place your fingers on the planchette and spirits will divine their ideal grade.

What reaction would this evoke? Anger? Perplexity? Bemusement?

There will, of course, be two groups of students who think that this is a fantastic idea: those expecting a poor grade will hope that a roll of the dice might yield a passing grade, and the small few who actually believe the Ouija board as a reliable mechanism for producing fair grades. Everyone else will be astounded and will likely say so.

This situation is similar to one in which professors find themselves when critiquing students' reasoning, except that the current academic climate prevents us from saying so. This climate has made educators petrified to call into question a specific unreliable reasoning process—not just any unreliable process. Faith-based beliefs occupy a unique, coveted role protected by a cultural, social, and intellectual sheath of impenetrability.

In the soft sciences (sociology, philosophy, anthropology, etc.), if a student states that she believes a proposition because it comports with her faith tradition, that statement—and the process that gave rise to it— is treated as if it's a legitimate knowledge claim based upon unassailable logic. It is taken for granted that faith-based claims are invulnerable to criticism and immune from further questioning.

This intellectual rigor mortis is not allowed to occur across all disciplines. Again, in the soft sciences, questioning a student's belief-forming mechanism is taboo, but in the hard sciences (mathematics, chemistry, biology, etc.) challenging claims and questioning reasoning processes are *intrinsic to what it means to teach students to reason effectively.*

To render what using faith would look like as a justification in the hard sciences, let's look at a hypothetical, in-class discussion between a biology professor and her student:

>*Professor:* [X] happens when the influenza virus infects a cell.
>
>*Student:* Well, that's not my theory.
>
>*Professor:* What is your theory?
>
>*Student:* [Y] happens.
>
>*Professor:* Why do you think that?
>
>*Student:* I have faith that my theory is correct.

This one word, "faith," is the end to rational discourse.

In the soft sciences, educators pretend that rational dialogue has not been interrupted. Invoking faith as a justification for one's conclusions is treated as protected and even privileged speech. The default position is to grant the believer moral respect and social legitimacy.

This needs to end. Correcting students' reasoning processes, and granting faith-based responses no countenance, needs to be the academic, cultural, and pedagogical norm across *all* academic disciplines.

Faith is a process of attempting to know the world that will *decrease* the likelihood of coming to true conclusions, or in philosophical parlance, using faith will not yield warranted belief. One way we know this is that different faith traditions make competing claims and these claims cannot all be correct—yet they can all be false.

Unfortunately, both in and out of the academy, faith is not merely viewed as a specious epistemology. Faith is cemented to an implicit, underlying moral edifice that grants it moral currency, and cultural and social legitimacy. What's particularly interesting is that the elevated moral stature of faith is not just operating in the minds of the faithful; in education it's become institutionalized in such a way that others, even those who don't use faith as an epistemology, are forced to buy into the sanctity of faith-based reasoning.

It is considered impolite, uncouth, offensive, coercive, abusive, and even antidemocratic for a professor to correct students' faith-based claims. Yet it is expected that a professor will point out and even reprimand students if they voice antiegalitarian or race-based claims. (This indicates that there's nothing in the professor-student power/authority relationship that makes calling students out on certain claims inherently coercive or abusive; rather, there are social, cultural, and even political factors at play as to which claims should be subject to scrutiny. This is an obvious double standard.)

Educators in the soft sciences should adopt a pedagogical stance identical to the stance that's essential in the hard sciences: Give faith-based justifications no countenance. Do not take faith claims seriously. Let the utterer know that faith is not an acceptable basis from which to draw a conclusion that can be relied upon. Invite students to present evidence, arguments, and reasons for their conclusions, but absent these tell students that their claims will not be taken seriously: Back to the Kid's Table.

Just as we know using a Ouija board is not a reliable process for assigning fair grades, educators should stand with the fact that faith-based claims are not an acceptable basis for drawing a reliable conclusion.

BEYOND RELATIVISM

Introduction

Cognitive, epistemological, and moral relativism are toxins that students trained in the humanities regularly consume in large doses. They're taught to withhold judgments on different epistemologies, cultural practices, and moral systems. Consequently, their ability to make critical evaluations has been severely damaged.

Before faith can be exposed as a faulty epistemology, it's vital to disabuse people of the relativist notion that any epistemology is either just as good as any other—a bizarre and contradictory "egalitarian relativism"—or that epistemologies are impossible to judge.

The purpose of this section is to teach readers how to disabuse others of epistemological relativism. First, I'll briefly describe the teaching experiences that pushed me to develop an antirelativism pedagogical template. Second, I'll explain the template educators and Street Epistemologists can use to help individuals overcome epistemological relativism (see appendix C).

"Well That's Just True for You"

When I started teaching critical thinking more than two decades ago, my attempts to undermine relativism were met with a common student refrain: "Well that's just true for you." Any argument I presented was either met with this mantra, or with a similar utterance, "You perceive through your own cultural lens," or "You can't escape your Western, hegemonic, imperialistic, white male, situated perspective." At first I was stymied by these responses. No matter what examples I presented, or what my reasoning was, I always met the same one-line "objections."

Over time—because of my experience teaching prison inmates, tens of thousands of students at colleges and universities throughout the country, and people on the street—I came to the conclusion that not only was this problem pervasive, but that it also made it *impossible* for me to teach people how to improve their reasoning. In order to reason well, one needs to be able to rule out competing or irrelevant alternatives. But one cannot do this if one believes that there's no way to make an objective judgment about those alternatives.

For example, if I want to determine if I should visit an N.D. (Doctor of Naturopathic Medicine) to try a type of alternative medicine, or if I should visit a board certified M.D. to receive treatment based upon the paradigm of scientific evidence, I need to be able to develop some mechanism that I can rely upon that will lead me to the best answer to the question: which is better for my health? If I start with the conclusion that these are just different systems of medicine, and cannot be judged by the same metric, then I lose all motivation to formulate the mechanism by which I make a judgment. There's no point in learning how to make more discerning judgments if what I'm judging cannot be judged, and if the mechanism by which I make these judgments is wholly subjective.

For an educator, combating relativism is priority one. I spend the first thirty to sixty minutes of every class in a broadly Socratic discussion wherein I adhere to the template located in appendix C. I've made this process both simple and easy to use in hope educators and Street Epistemologists can readily use this tool in any discussion.

Misconstruing Reality

Pedagogically, it is possible to undo some of the damage students have suffered from contemporary academic leftism in thirty to sixty minutes. Depending on class size—this can be difficult with classes of more than one hundred students because it's time consuming to field every student's question—using this template as a model should help students escape relativism within the hour. In the five years I've used this template, I've yet to have a single student who (as far as I know) has not been disabused of epistemological relativism.

Question 1: Is it possible that some people misconstrue reality? Most students will say "yes" or nod their heads. For those few who say "no," or who look unsure, I ask, "If Fred thinks that two plus two is eighteen, and Sue thinks it's forty-one, and if they both conceive of the operator in the same way, has someone misconstrued reality?" Not a single student will say "no."

Question 2: Do some people misconstrue reality? Question two moves from the possibility of misconstruing reality, to the fact that some individuals actually do misconstrue reality.

It's important at this stage that you do not provide examples—instead let students provide their own. Sadly, I had to figure this out on my own, but students relate more to examples given by other students, and much less to those given by the instructor. Fielding examples is usually the most time consuming of all of the stages; I spend about five to seven minutes eliciting and encouraging as many students as possible to contribute to this stage.

There may be a few students—typically anthropology majors as their field is steeped in relativist dogma—for which this is a problematic concept. In these cases I'll ask if anything is knowable, and then I'll ask them to provide examples of things that are knowable and unknowable. Tautologies like those found in math and language ("A bachelor is an unmarried man") are usually sufficient for students to agree that some things are knowable. If this doesn't work, then I bring up the fact that we're having a conversation and even for them to disagree means that on some level they know what I'm talking about, thus meaning some things are knowable. This will usually propel even the most ardent relativist to the next stage and the next set of questions.

Questions 3, 4, and statement 5: If one wants to know reality, is one process just as good as any other? So then are some processes bad? If so, this must mean some processes are good, or better. Now I provide my own examples.

I avoid discussing faith. If faith does come up, I'll say, "We'll talk about that later. For now, let's just find unreliable processes that we can all agree upon." I use blatantly unreliable processes like flipping coins and goat sacrifice. It's very easy to get students to agree that flipping coins is not a reliable basis upon which they should make decisions—heads I'll be a math major and tails I'll be a dance major. I also elicit other processes that students think are unreliable.

I segue into the next question by stating, "So if there are some processes that are bad, like flipping coins, that means that you can't rely upon them. But in order for some processes to be bad, that must mean that other processes are good. By good I mean that one can rely upon them. As 'bad' is a relational word, it doesn't make sense to speak of a process as bad unless there's a process that's good, right?"

For those students who don't think that "bad" is a relational word, I'll discuss other relational words, like "stupid" or "delicious." I'll ask, "For someone to be considered stupid, doesn't that mean there have to be people who are smart?" This is usually enough to carry the discussion forward. However, on rare occasions someone will get hung up on the word "bad." I'll explain that by a "bad process" I mean a process that takes one away from reality. If there's still confusion, I'll ask how they use the word "bad." Their definition will usually comport with how I use the word "bad," but if it does not, then I'll borrow a line from Sam Harris and tell them that not only am I not sure how they're using the word "bad," but I don't even think they know how they're using the word "bad." After a brief discussion about the word "bad," I proceed to the next stage, with questions 6 and 7.

Questions 6 and 7: Is there a way we can figure out which processes are good, and which are not? At this point, the foundation has been laid. Once we've discussed what we mean by "reliable," "good," and "bad," very few people maintain a type of relativism in terms of processes that take one toward or away from reality.

I ask students their ideas about how to discern good processes from bad processes. Regardless of their responses, I'll ask them how they know the selection criteria they invoke will enable them to discern what's a good process and what's a bad process. With very little prodding, students will come to the conclusion that processes that rely on reason and evidence are good, while all other processes are bad.

Suggestions

- Avoid leaving a stage until every student is in agreement. If there's a student who does not understand, spend more time in that stage. Use questions as an opportunity to help students. If the concepts are still unclear,[18] invite them to office hours to continue the discussion.

- During question 1, you may need to discuss objectivity versus subjectivity. As noted in chapter 2, I tell students to think about the distinction in terms of matters of taste—for example, red wine is better than white wine with lamb.

- In question 2, be sure to dole out praise when students generate examples of people misconstruing reality. Generally, praise is underused in advancing dialogue.

- Question 2 also presents an opportunity to help students understand that the number of people who lend their belief to a claim does not increase the likelihood that the claim is true. You can capture this idea by asking, "Does the number of people who misconstrue reality increase the likelihood that their beliefs are true? For example, if Joe thinks there's an alien in the courtyard, and he convinces Betty that this is true, does this increase the odds of there being an actual alien in the courtyard?"

INTERVENTIONS

Intervention 1

I never answer my office phone. The one time I did, I received a call from an upset parent (UP). His son was enrolled in my class, and he was upset that I questioned students' faith. I told him to come in during office hours so we could talk about it. (For better or worse, putting the onus of action on someone usually ends the discourse, as most people won't act beyond the initial contact.)

He was in my office within thirty minutes. UP, who was in his mid-50s and rugged but with soft hands and dyed black hair, looked around suspiciously as he sat down. Frowning, he spoke with a sense of urgency.

UP: I told you on the phone. You've crossed the line by asking questions about my son's faith—

PB: Okay, wait, please. First, what class is your son taking?

UP: Critical Thinking.

PB: Okay, thanks. And why do you think faith should be off the table?

UP: Because it's an abuse of your authority. You have no right to ask students. They're young and they'll believe what you tell them. [He went on for a few minutes, basically repeating himself. I listened.]

PB: Okay, so what should I talk about in a critical thinking class?

UP: Anything except that.

PB: Algebra?

UP: That's ridiculous. You know yourself you shouldn't talk about algebra.

PB: True, but I'm trying to establish a baseline—things I should and shouldn't talk about. Right? So I shouldn't talk about algebra. But, what about other faiths? What about Islam? Should I talk about Islam?

UP: No. There may be Islamics in the class. No. Definitely not.

PB: Should I talk about how people come to knowledge?

UP: Yes, yes, as long as you don't talk about faith.

PB: So just to be clear, I should talk about how people come to knowledge as long as it doesn't relate to faith? Is that your view? I don't want to put words in your mouth.

UP: Yes. That's correct.

PB: And what about Noah's Ark? Can I talk about that?

UP: What? What about it?

PB: Am I allowed to talk about how people know about the big boat and all of the species and such?

UP: No. No.

PB: What about the koala bear?

UP: What about the koala bear?

PB: Can I talk about how the koala bear went from the Ark to Australia?

UP: What are you talking about? What koala bear?

PB: You know those cute little fuzzy bears? They're called koala bears. They live in Australia. Have you ever been to the zoo?

UP: I know what a koala bear is, but why are you talking about koala bears?

PB: Because I want to know how the koala bear got to Australia and I want to know if you think I can talk about this?

UP: But, what does the koala bear have to do with anything?

PB: Well, once the koala bear got off of the Ark, how did it get to Australia?

UP: It migrated. Migrated. You know.

PB: But it only eats eucalyptus leaves, and there's no eucalyptus trees where the Ark allegedly landed. So how did the koala bear get to Australia?

UP: It used to eat other things.

PB: So it evolved?

(Long pause)

PB: So should I or shouldn't I talk about the koala bear?

UP: You shouldn't talk about it because you're really talking about faith and that's beyond your authority—

PB: Okay, so I'm just trying to clarify this for myself. I feel like I don't get it, but I really do want to understand your position. I can—

UP: The koala bear lives in Australia.

PB: Is that a question?

UP: No, I'm saying, the koala bear lives in Australia.

PB: Okay.

(Long pause)

UP: So you're saying that the koala bear couldn't get to Australia without those leaves?

PB: No, I'm not saying anything. I'm merely asking. How did the koala bear get to Australia if there's no eucalyptus where the Ark crashed?

(UP abruptly whips out his phone and makes a call. I sit back patiently. There's no answer. He leaves a message for his religious leader and repeats the question: how did koala bears get to Australia after Noah's Ark landed?)

PB: Okay, so when you don't know something you call someone to ask them, right?

UP: Yeah . . .

(UP then went into an unnecessary but confident explanation about the religious hierarchy in his church. I cut him off after two minutes.)

PB: So maybe if these issues are raised in class, when your son comes home, or if he doesn't live at home then when he sees you, maybe you could talk these questions over with him. Do you think that would help?

UP: No.

PB: No?

UP: Well, yes, but he shouldn't have questions.

PB: Everyone has questions. You have questions. You just called your pastor with questions.

UP: That's different.

PB: How come you're allowed to have questions but he shouldn't have questions?

(Long pause)

UP: He can have questions.

PB: Now really think about this before you answer, please. We're two dads in a room—I have two kids, and like you I love them very much and sincerely want the best for them. Do you really, really think your son's better off having no questions? Is that really the type of life you want for your son? Truly?

(Long pause)

UP: No.

PB: Agreed. I don't want that for my kids either.

(Pause)

PB: In your son's critical thinking class, that's what we do. I ask students to question everything. Everything. I ask questions. Just like I asked you questions today. I never tell you what to think. I asked you questions.

(We finished with a handshake and an understanding.)

Intervention 2

I had the following discussion with a female colleague. She was a psychologist, in her early 50s, and a devoted Christian (DC). She initiated the conversation after she overheard me state that I was an atheist.

DC: I just can't believe you reject Christ's love. Why would you do that?

PB: It's ridiculous. Why do you believe your superstition is true?

DC: The fool says in his heart there is no God.

PB: That doesn't answer my question. That's like saying the number nine is my magic lucky number in numerology.

DC: I really feel sorry for you. I really do. I—

PB: That still doesn't answer the question. Why is your superstition true?

DC: Well, there are so, so many reasons.

PB: Just gimme the top three. Better yet, just one.

DC: God loves you. Without Christ's love you'll be eternally damned.

PB: Okay, do you teach any students who are Jewish?

DC: I'd never ask a student about that, but I'm sure I have, after all I've been teaching a lot longer than you.

PB: How does it make you feel to teach a student who doesn't share your faith, knowing that they'll be eternally damned? After all, Christianity is not a religion that allows people from different faith traditions eternal reward.

DC: What do you mean?

PB: Well, if you're a Hindu, they believe that no faith tradition is exclusive, but that every person of faith deserves tolerance and can achieve salvation.

DC: I go beyond tolerance. I nurture all of my students. I wouldn't even be talking to you if I didn't care about you—your salvation.

PB: Is it more important to nurture your students or to teach them more reliable ways of thinking?

DC: I do both.

PB: But if you had to pick one?

DC: But I don't.

PB: Okay, is it more important to have a reliable way to come to truth, or to hold beliefs you're sure are true?

DC: My beliefs are true.

PB: How do you know that?

DC: I see it in my life everyday.

PB: Can you give me an example?

DC: It's all around us, everyday, all the time.

PB: What's all around you? You mean like trees and stuff?

DC: Yes, trees, but everything is God's creation. I see Him in my life everyday.

PB: Well, what do you mean by that?

DC: Your problem is that you won't open your heart and give God's love a chance to enter your heart.

PB: If one were willing to open one's heart to Jesus, would you be willing to become a Hindu? You'd still get to heaven.

DC: No. I wouldn't feel comfortable with any other religion.

PB: What does comfort have to do with it?

DC: I've given my life to Christ. I know His love and I know the feeling I have.

PB: Just so I understand, you've come to the truths of your beliefs because of the way they make you feel? Is that right?

DC: Yes, I feel His love everyday and it's made me a better person.

PB: Okay, but we were talking about truth, and the conversation shifted to the consequences of having faith, like making you feel a certain way. You said that there were so, so many reasons you know it's true, and I've yet to hear one.

DC: I just know it's true.

PB: Isn't it more honest to say: I really don't know if it's true or not, but I know it makes me feel good? Wouldn't that be a more genuine way to live your life?

DC: Possibly, but only if I didn't think it was true.

PB: But you can't provide any reasons for why you think your beliefs are true. About matters of fact, your feeling states don't make your beliefs true. If nothing else, then as a psychologist you can draw upon your years of professional experience and acknowledge that, right?

(Silence)

DIG DEEPER

Article

Peter Boghossian, "Should We Challenge Student Beliefs?" (Boghossian, 2011c)

Books

Paul Boghossian, *Fear of Knowledge: Against Relativism and Constructivism* (Boghossian, 2006c)[19]

Austin Dacey, *The Future of Blasphemy: Speaking of the Sacred in an Age of Human Rights* (Dacey, 2012)

Greg Lukianoff, *Unlearning Liberty: Campus Censorship and the End of American Debate* (Lukianoff, 2012)

Hemant Mehta, *The Young Atheist's Survival Guide: Helping Secular Students Thrive* (Mehta, 2012)

Alan Ryan, *The Making of Modern Liberalism* (Ryan 2012)

Online Resources

The James Randi Educational Foundation (JREF; http://www.randi. org/site/): "The James Randi Educational Foundation was founded in 1996 to help people defend themselves from paranormal and pseudoscientific claims. The JREF offers a still-unclaimed million-dollar reward for anyone who can produce evidence of paranormal abilities under controlled conditions. Through scholarships, workshops, and innovative resources for educators, the JREF works to inspire this investigative spirit in a new generation of critical thinkers."

FIRE (Foundation for Individual Rights in Education; http://thefire. org/): "The mission of FIRE is to defend and sustain individual rights at America's colleges and universities. These rights include freedom of speech, legal equality, due process, religious liberty, and sanctity of conscience—the essential qualities of individual liberty and dignity. FIRE's core mission is to protect the unprotected and to educate the public and communities of concerned Americans about the threats to these rights on our campuses and about the means to preserve them."

Secular Coalition for America (SCA; http://www.secular.org): "The Secular Coalition for America is a 501(c)(4) advocacy organization whose purpose is to amplify the diverse and growing voice of the nontheistic community in the United States. We are located in Washington, D.C. for ready access to government, activist partners and the media. Our staff lobbies U.S. Congress on issues of special concern to our constituency."

The Skeptics Society's Skeptical Studies Curriculum Resource Center (http://www.skeptic.com/skepticism-101/): "A comprehensive, free repository of resources for teaching students how to think skeptically. This Center contains an ever-growing selection of books, reading lists, course syllabi, in-class exercises, PowerPoint presentations, student projects, papers, and videos that you may download and use in your own classes." (My "Atheism," "Critical Thinking," and "Knowledge, Value and Rationality" course syllabi are also available here.)

NOTES

1. While classical liberalism emphasized freedom, social liberalism acknowledged that freedom is curtailed not only by authority but also by circumstance. In other words, social liberalism recognized that certain factors (race, gender, sexual orientation, religion) limit freedom, and thus many social liberals argued for government intervention (e.g., Civil Rights Act of 1964). Social liberals argued that an activist society is necessary to ensure a level playing field and implement the principles of classical liberalism.

   Contemporary academic leftism recognizes that another limitation to freedom is social attitude. Attitudes keep certain individuals from opportunities simply because they belong to a particular group. It's legitimate to request that others be aware of a social consensus that limits people's opportunities, and to attempt to break up that consensus. There is a difference, however, between prejudice against individuals on the basis of their social group (which is bad because this prejudice is directed at people) and cultural criticism (which is good because it is directed at ideas). American philosopher Austin Dacey (1972–) speaks eloquently about doing people a disservice when we don't speak up for them when they're being victimized by their own groups, and as an example he discusses suppression of free speech by Muslims against other Muslims.

2. These terms started out as insights of critical reflection—uncovering privilege where no one dared look before—but in their current mutated form they erode the ability for *critical* reflection and rational analysis by placing a stranglehold on the values they should represent.

3. Historically, philosophy has focused on truth. Contemporary philosophy instead focuses on meaning. Meaning is subjective—it's a turning away from the world and a turning toward our experience in the world and to the language we use to describe that experience. This is a radical change, a shift, a turn in our thinking—a turn away from objectivity, truth, mind-independent metaphysics, and toward narratives, personal experience, meaning, and subjectivity (Tassi, 1982).

In this interpretive framework, individual experience is privileged over a world that exists independently of the knower (Boghossian, 2011a, pp. 714–715). Interpreted through the primacy of subjectivity there can be no doxastic errors (errors of belief). This is because it is impossible to adjudicate a proposition's truth or falsity in the absence of an objective world. Without a world that exists apart from a subject, as British philosopher and scientist Francis Bacon (1561–1626) famously stated, it's impossible to "put nature to the question." That is, without an independent, objective world, there can be no corrective mechanism that would allow for a proposition to be either true or false. And because the world cannot referee a proposition's truth or falsity, all propositions acquire the status of matters of taste, even demonstrably empirical propositions like, "Men have one fewer rib than women" or "The Holocaust never happened."

Every proposition thus has the same epistemic status as propositions about personal preference, such as, "Cherry pie is disgusting" or "Led Zeppelin's 'Stairway to Heaven' is a beautiful song." Interpreted through a subjective lens, propositions may be true for one knower and false for another (Boghossian, under review).

4. Epistemic relativism extends relativism to matters of fact. The best refutation of relativism I've read is American psychologist Chris Swoyer's "True For" (Meiland & Krausz, 1982). In this brief, dense article, Swoyer completely dismantles the idea that something can be true for one person and false for another person.

   Often when relativism emerges in the context of an epistemological intervention, it's usually in the form of, "Well that's just true for you." When I hear this I ask my interlocutor where they'd go if they were sick, to the witch doctor or to a Western hospital? If they tell me they'd go to the witch doctor, or that it makes no difference, I tell them I don't think they're being sincere.

5. Multiculturalism has become a distorted form of pluralism. The term "pluralism" has many meanings. Understood in the current context, pluralism is the idea that minorities (race, gender, sexual orientation, religion) have legal rights (Lamb, 1981). Pluralism has intrinsic merit and is an indispensable component of civilized societies. Multiculturalism and pluralism (in the abstract) are trying to get at laudable social goals—they try

to work toward these goals from a description of differences in populations.

6. One can think of parenting in these terms. Good parents criticize the acts of children and not the child.

7. Too much tolerance entails abandoning critical judgment altogether.

8. Incredibly, liberals will state that this is the result of United States' foreign policy. However, the cause of the state of affairs is not at issue; what is at issue is the accuracy of my description of these societies.

9. Another way to think about this issue is that Muslim extremists went on rampages because Western societies didn't follow rules unilaterally imposed by them. The attempt to unilaterally impose such rules is, of course, itself intolerant. Still, many leftists—and even moderate liberals—interpret the "desecration" of the Koran as lack of tolerance. However, tolerance does not, cannot, and should not mean having to submit to rules of belief systems to which one does not ascribe.

10. A leftist could respond that this is an exploitation of the liberal impulse to empathy. In "Indignation Is Not Righteous," Longsine and I argue that the attempt to shield ideas from contemplation, discussion, investigation, or criticism should be recognized as logical fallacies (Longsine & Boghossian, 2012).

11. Contemporary academic leftists don't withhold making judgments entirely, as do cultural relativists. Rather, they withhold judgment to the degree that a *culture* seems foreign and/or alien, or to the extent that they perceive a culture to be misunderstood or victimized by the West. Islam currently occupies the top rung on the contemporary leftist hierarchy of beliefs and practices that should not be criticized.

Leftist academicians fervently judge elements in Western culture. For example, academic leftists take great pride in condemning Western institutions, Western financial systems, and Western corporations. One might see a leftist academic withhold judgment regarding a clitoridectomy in Northern Africa, but loudly decry a gender imbalance in the headcount of speakers at an academic conference.

12. I originally encountered this phrase in Australian philosopher Russell Blackford's (1954–) "Islam, Racists, and Legitimate Debate" (Blackford, 2012a). Blackford credits American philosopher Jean Kazez with this phrase.

   "Bullying ideas off the table" is particularly germane in the case of leftism and criticisms of Islam. Contemporary leftists are playing the hero role, morally equating criticisms of Islam (ideas) to, for example, internment of Japanese Americans (people) during World War II.

13. To enforce rights and protections of individuals and groups, many colleges have established departments and offices of "Diversity." These are offices in search of tasks. Often, these departments bypass traditional academic structures, are not housed within particular colleges, and report directly to the president. The fact that the university system has been set up to enable Diversity Offices to bypass traditional academic structures and report directly to the president shows the privilege, the esteem, and the seriousness with which this ideology is held.

14. British philosopher Gilbert Ryle (1900–1976) coined the phrase "category mistake" to refer to the ascription of a property to something that could not possibly possess that property. For example, "The chair is angry" or "The number 16 feels smooth."

15. A recommended and emotional read is Ibn Warraq's, *Leaving Islam: Apostates Speak Out* (Warraq, 2003). Warraq provides detailed accounts of people who decided to leave Islam. The narratives he describes are as lovely as they are disturbing.

16. The United States Department of State, Bureau of Democracy, Human Rights and Labor states, "In particular blasphemy and conversion from Islam, which is considered apostasy, are punishable by death in Afghanistan, Iran, Pakistan, and Saudi Arabia" (United States Department of State, 2011a). Apostasy is punishable by death elsewhere as well. In Mauritania's penal code, "Article 306 of the penal code outlaws apostasy. It states that any Muslim found guilty of the crime will be given the opportunity to repent within three days and if the person does not repent, the individual will be sentenced to death and the person's property will be confiscated by the Treasury" (United States Department of State, 2011b).

17. A version of this section was originally published in *The Philosophers'*
    Magazine (Boghossian, 2012).

18. Notice that I did not write, "If they still don't get it." When teaching, it's
    important to frame issues not in terms of student understanding, but in
    terms of your explanation. For example, I'll often say, "Am I being clear?"
    as opposed to, "Do you get it?" This places the burden of clarity on me,
    and students are more likely to volunteer and engage issues if they don't
    think that the instructor believes they have a problem understanding the
    material. Finally, I'll often say, "If this is unclear please let me know. You'll
    help me to be a better explainer."

19. About twice a month I'm asked if I'm related to Paul Boghossian. I'm
    friendly with, but not related to, Paul.

CHAPTER 9
CONTAINMENT PROTOCOLS

"Imagine that a religion is a virus with its own unique mix of properties.

Just as the HIV virus is different than a cold virus, both infect and take over the mechanisms of the body in ways that allow them to reproduce. Religions. . .

1. Infect people.

2. Create antibodies or defenses against other viruses.

3. Take over certain mental and physical functions and hide itself within the individual in such a way that it is not detectable by the individual.

4. Use specific methods for spreading the virus.

5. Program the host to replicate the virus.

Every religion is more or less effective in each of these areas."

—Darrel Ray, *The God Virus* (p. 23)

Just as the body is exposed to toxins so is the mind.

Faith is an unclassified cognitive illness disguised as a moral virtue. Each of us dreads the thought of becoming ill, and we take whatever measures necessary to regain our health. Not so with the faith virus. People infected by faith feel gratitude and appreciation for their affliction. But even beyond gratitude, part of the difficulty in dislodging the faith virus is, as Dennett has argued, that it's perceived as a moral virtue (Dennett, 2007). People infected with faith don't think of it as a malady, but as a gift, even a blessing.

It's disturbing that many people who have no faith are untroubled by the possibility of their own infection. The reasons for this are complex and possibly extend into the domain of neuroscience (Berns et al., 2012; McNamara, 2009; Newberg, 2006; Previc, 2006), but a large part of the problem is that faith is intertwined with morality. People infected by the faith virus believe having faith is important, and resolute belief in something—anything—is a virtue (Dennett, 2007; Dennett & LaScola, 2010).

This pervasive, remarkably resilient phenomenon—this meme—has gained such traction it's become an entrenched cultural value and held as an a priori truth: Believe in something. Stand up for what you believe. Belief is good. Belief is important. Faith makes us better people. A man of faith is a good man.

As a society we've made virtues of the importance of belief and standing up for our beliefs. Even the common phrase, "Stand up for what you believe in," has embedded within it something positive—a virtue to which one should aspire and a moral shortcoming should one fail.

Whether or not one should stand up for what one believes depends exclusively on what it is one believes and why one believes it. Having a firm belief is not a virtue. No reliable moral inferences can be made about an individual based on the strength of their conviction—passionate belief does not equate to being a good person. Moreover, "standing up for what you believe" and "believing in something" are values that doxastically entrench particular beliefs.

It's important we believe things that are true.[1] It's important there's some lawful correspondence between what we believe and the actual state of affairs. Only when our beliefs accurately correspond to reality are we able to mold external conditions that enable us to flourish. If we lose respect for the truth, we'll no longer seek it. Among the most disturbing and tragic things about those who've been infected with faith is that they stop seeking.

Street Epistemology is a vital and perhaps even necessary first step in the struggle against certainty, dogmatism, superstition, pseudoscience, and faith. But Street Epistemology alone may not be enough to move us toward a New Enlightenment and Age of Reason. We need to fundamentally change the way people think about and value faith, belief, and conviction, and develop and ultimately implement large-scale solutions to address these seemingly intractable problems.

The purpose of this chapter is to suggest potential changes and to propose ways that readers can contribute to the struggle for reason. The suggestions here are organized from the easiest to implement, to the complex and difficult. This list is not exhaustive.

1. Use the word "faith" only in a religious context.

The word "faith" is used as a synonym for words like "hope," "trust," and "confidence." This is *not* how the faithful use the word "faith" in religious contexts. For example, as discussed in chapter 2, "faith" is almost always tied to knowledge claims. That is, when the faithful say they have faith Jesus healed someone suffering from leprosy (Matthew 8:1–4; Mark 1:40–45; Luke 5:12–16) and someone suffering from paralysis (Matthew 9:1–8; Mark 2:1–12; Luke 5:17–26), they are not saying they *hope* he healed them. They are claiming he actually healed them.

Examples of the word "faith" in nonreligious contexts include: "I have faith you'll pass the test tomorrow," "You have faith in your spouse," "She has faith that the airplane will not crash." When the word "faith" is used in these ways it gives cover for "faith" to be used as a synonym for "hope," "trust," etc., in religious contexts. This is highly problematic, because when the faithful are pressed on the definition of faith (when they're shown they can't and don't really know Jesus performed these miracles), they usually retreat to the words "hope," "trust," and "confidence," abandoning knowledge and certainty.

It matters how we talk about things. It matters what words we use. Certain words trap us into a make-believe picture of life—one that is false and misleading. If you use the word "faith" in ordinary contexts you've opened the door to misinterpret your own experience, and you've given cover to claims from various faith traditions. I'm advocating for a change in language usage, primarily with the word "faith," but with other words and expressions as well.[2] I'm not a grammarian suggesting new rules for English usage. I'm not saying the word "faith" or expressions with the word "God" should be forbidden. I'm not the language police. I'm not arguing that it is wrong to use the word "faith" out of a religious context, or that there should be a linguistic moratorium on the use of the word "faith."[3] My goal is to be helpful, not dictatorial.

What I am arguing is that we need to be more careful and more thoughtful when we choose words to explain our feelings, to describe our plans for the future, to identify what we care about, and to represent what we're for and against. By being more mindful with our choice of words, we can also be more thoughtful in the way we think about the world, our responsibility to society, our advocacy for the things we care about, and our understanding of our own ability to influence change. We need to get over the hurdle that long-term, multicontext use of "faith" has created—we need to think about our language usage and be aware that we say things which are incongruent with the way we think about the world.

I'm also recommending a change in usage because too many people have become accustomed to the idea of being comfortable with a definite picture of a future they don't have good evidence to support. Instead, people need to be comfortable with not knowing the future, and consequently take an activist stance: if you care about the future and you want something to get done—then do it. You cannot know the future, so take action. Don't wait for things to happen. Don't pray. Don't have faith. Don't rely upon imagined entities. Act.

2. Stigmatize faith-based claims like racist claims.

> "People who harbor strong convictions without evidence belong at the margins of our societies, not in our halls of power."
>
> —Sam Harris, *The End of Faith* (2004)

One mid- to long-term containment objective is to stigmatize faith as a methodology and faith-based claims that emerge from that methodology—the way racist statements have been stigmatized. I've previously argued, along with Shermer and others, that we need to deploy the model used in the civil-rights movement. This is a three-stage process: first, it begins with publically branding as inappropriate the use of faith as an epistemology (this stage is beginning to occur); second, it will be unthinkable to use faith as a justification; third, people won't even think about using faith—faith, like the idea that slavery is acceptable, will just go away. We've also seen this in the women's rights movement, where discrimination pushed women toward equality. So too, in time, will faith give way to reason and a critical reflection that is unmediated by cultural values.

In the short term, one specific verbal technique to help contain faith-based justifications is through the "Adult Table" response. One can sit at the Adult Table if one has evidence in support of a position. Absent evidence, the claimant needs to go to the Kid's Table. For example, if one thinks homosexuals shouldn't be allowed to adopt children because they're more likely to beat them, this is an empirical claim and the tools of science can be used to ascertain whether or not this is true (it's not). Make empirically verifiable claims, even if the conclusions are ugly, and you get a voice in the conversation—you've earned the right to sit at the Adult Table. Wave an ancient text and expect others to cede to its authority, or claim faith as a justification for your beliefs—then you need to sit at the Kid's Table. Those at the Kid's Table can talk about anything they'd like, but they have no adult responsibilities and no voice in public policy.

The idea behind the Adult Table containment strategy is to first hold ourselves, and then others, epistemically responsible. It does justice to the faithful to treat them like responsible adults and hold them to the same standards of justification that we hold all rational agents. Buying into the hands-off position that silences criticism and allows the faithful to publicly air conclusions that result from a faith-based process is not just dangerous, but also leads the faithful to believe that they're entitled to have their delusions seriously entertained by other adults.

The Adult Table metaphor is best used with leaders of faith communities who are accustomed to deference. If you're fortunate enough to engage imams, mullahs, rabbis, pastors, ministers, clerics, swamis, gurus, chaplains, shamans, priests, witch doctors, or any other faith leaders, be blunt and direct when demanding evidence for their claims. Continued failure to produce evidence should be met with, "You are pretending to know things you don't know. Go to the Kid's Table, this is a conversation for adults."

3. *Parrhesia: Speaking truth in the face of danger.*

> "We fear clear, honest, blunt dialogue, but what we ought to fear are stupid and dangerous ideas, because while blunt and honest dialogue might be offensive to some, stupid and dangerous ideas can be fatal to all of us."
>
> —Matt Thornton, community activist

We live in a culture in which faith claims go unchallenged. Too often people cower before faith statements. We're so afraid to offend others we silence ourselves. This needs to end.

Among the consequences of self-imposed silence: faith-based claims making their way into the public square and onto the ballot; people becoming accustomed to not having their faith-beliefs challenged, and consequently assigning ever-higher confidence values to their beliefs; the faithful continuing to harbor the mistaken notion that faith makes them a better person.

One remedy for this is honesty and bluntness. Give the faithful the same dialectical and conversational reciprocity they give you. Be honest. Be direct. Be blunt. Be unapologetic. Don't complain, apologize, or mumble in the defense of reason. Don't tone it down or talk baby talk. Never say, "I'm sorry but . . ." or "Forgive me for saying . . ." or "You'll excuse me for mentioning . . ." Instead, tell people exactly what you think and why you think it. Take a punch and give a punch. Speak truth in the face of danger. Be a part of Team Parrhesia. Be a Street Epistemologist.

And don't worry about people not respecting you. You'll find people will respect you more, and not less, when you sincerely and directly confront their faith claims. Sincere, honest people are respected. People who are inauthentic and cower are not respected.

4. Stay informed.

Study. Read. Watch YouTube debates with the leading apologists. Listen to quality podcasts. Enroll in MOOCs (massively open online courses).[4] Stay informed.

If you haven't read their books already, I'd start with the Four Horsemen and Michael Shermer (I suggest beginning with Harris and Shermer and ending with Dawkins and Dennett). From there, read select Platonic dialogues (the *Republic*, the *Apology*, the *Euthyphro*, the *Gorgias*) and move to key works by Nietzsche (*The Dawn, Thus Spoke Zarathustra: A Book for All and for None, Beyond Good and Evil, On The Genealogy of Morality, Twilight of the Idols*, and *The Antichrist*).[5]

To prevent doxastic closure it's also important to read the work of noted apologists. The only two I'd suggest are Alvin Plantinga and William Lane Craig, though I'd urge you not to buy their books; their projects don't need your support. If you must buy one of their books buy it used and support a local bookstore, this way the author doesn't receive any royalties.

Finally, the "Dig Deeper" section at the end of most chapters has additional recommended reading.

5. Contribute.

Not everyone can become a Street Epistemologist. Some people don't have the disposition. Others don't have the inclination. Others still are held back by social fears or interpersonal anxieties.

If you don't become a Street Epistemologist, you can still make a contribution to reason and rationality. Find the unique contribution you can make and do it: if you're an attorney, volunteer your legal services; if you're a sound technician, volunteer on public access shows or help secular groups with their podcasts; if you like to entertain, then volunteer your house for potlucks in support of local freethinker groups; if you enjoy writing, then write editorials that identify and expose instances of unreason (print publications are starved for thoughtful letters); if you're an organizer, then create groups to raise money or help established, reputable organizations like the Center for Inquiry or the James Randi Educational Foundation; if you're more of a street activist, then picket events designed to spread faith;[6] if you don't have the time or the inclination to engage, then make a financial contribution to one of the secular legal organizations noted in the "Dig Deeper" section at the end of this chapter.

Be active. Get involved. Volunteer. Vote for candidates who support reason. Use your individual skill set and your voice to promote reason and combat unreason. Make a contribution.

6. Experiment and publicize.

Develop and test your own strategies to fight the faith virus. Consider publicizing your particular contribution in an appropriate medium: books, magazines, YouTube, fiction, documentaries, plays, editorials and letters to the editor, songs, art works, etc. Allow others to learn from your successes and from your failures. It's much better to act and fail spectacularly than to have never acted at all.

7. Form academic-community partnerships.

The high school and university systems should be used as reason and rationality incubation chambers. One of the ways to do this is through the formation of academic-community partnerships. Individual teachers, professors, and entire departments can reach out to organizations—like the Skeptics Society, the James Randi Educational Foundation, the Richard Dawkins Foundation for Reason and Science, the Center for Inquiry, the Secular Student Alliance, Project Reason, or other well-respected organizations—and ask how they could be of use in the promotion of reason, rationality, critical thinking, and the public understanding of science.

These partnerships can take many forms: online publishing of student papers on select topics, commenting on curricula, contributing research for journal articles, teaching critical thinking curriculum in the local school system, reviewing journal articles, and doing whatever else a community partner would find helpful. The purpose of the partnership is to help like-minded, nonprofit organizations extend their reach and better discharge their mandate to promote reason, rationality, and the public understanding of science.[7] Additionally, partnerships provide educators with an opportunity to promote reason, translate theory into practice, help their communities, and find and nurture students who want to pursue further study.

8. Treat faith as a public health crisis.

> "Biological virus strategies bear a remarkable resemblance to methods of religious propagation. Religious conversion seems to affect personality. In the viral paradigm, the God virus infects and takes over the critical thinking capacity of the individual with respect to his or her own religion, much as rabies affects specific parts of the central nervous system. A simple thought experiment reveals how the God virus works to dull critical thinking. The God virus infects an individual and then inoculates against other viruses. Vectors in biology carry a parasite, virus or pathogen from one reservoir to another. Religious vectors act in similar ways. Priests, imams, ministers, etc., carry the virus and infect

new people. The virus carefully directs resources toward it and creates taboos against giving to competing viruses. Sometimes vectors fail. The expense of developing a vector makes it imperative to protect it even in failure as in the case of priest pedophilia. Mutations are constantly produced. Occasionally one breaks out, as in the case of Martin Luther, to infect vulnerable people and cultures."

—Darrel Ray, *The God Virus* (2009, p. 32)

There are groups, institutions, and organizations actively promoting the spread of unreliable epistemologies (e.g., Alliance Defending Freedom, Alliance Defense Fund, American Center for Law and Justice, Christian Legal Society, Christian Law Association, National Legal Foundation, mega- and micro-churches, synagogues, mosques, temples, etc.). We need to view the spread of these unreliable processes, along with the institutions that promote them, as a public health crisis. The purpose of this section is not to explain what policies would look like or to describe particular interventions. Rather, I want to add my voice to the growing number of people who argue that we must reconceptualize faith as a virus of the mind (Brodie, 1996), and treat faith like other epidemiological crises: contain and eradicate.[8]

Just as society has established mechanisms to deal with contagions, pathogens, and infectious diseases that affect our water, air, and food supply (with objectives like ensuring that the commons are free of toxins and preventing the spread of diseases), there's also an urgent need for large-scale interventions in educational systems, houses of worship, and other institutions that promote failed epistemologies.

However, there are serious ethical, constitutional, and free speech issues that prevent the development and institutionalization of large-scale epistemological interventions. Given these constitutional and basic rights issues, instead of epistemologically sanitizing organizations, interventions need to be designed that counter the spread of these virulent epistemologies (not the conclusions that follow from these epistemologies, but the epistemologies themselves). Such interventions should promote, laud, and even glamorize reliable epistemologies.[9] That is, an inoculation and containment strategy should promote the *value* of believing on the basis of evidence. The specifics of how this could be accomplished are subjects for further study.

I want to be clear that I'm not advocating making faith illegal, in the same way racism cannot be made illegal. I advocate conceptualizing the faith problem from a public health perspective and designing interventions based upon this model.

9. Financially cripple purveyors of faulty epistemologies.

A key containment protocol is to financially cripple any institution that propagates a faulty epistemology, starting with the most egregious perpetrators: religious institutions.[10] Ultimately, the tax-exempt status of religious organizations must be removed, particularly those exemptions that are not granted to other nonprofits. (In the United States this is probably *at least* twelve years away.)[11]

Once these organizations are financially compromised, their reach and power will be greatly diminished. Here are two of the better and more politically viable, medium-term (five to ten years) goals to financially cripple faith-based institutions:

- Eliminate the "exemption from federal taxes for most of the money they [clergy] spend on housing, which typically represents roughly a third of their compensation" (Henriques, 2006a). It must be noted that this same tax exemption "is not available to the staff at secular nonprofit organizations whose scale and charitable aims compare to those of religious ministries like Pastor Warren's church, or to poorly paid inner-city teachers and day care workers who also serve their communities. . . . Nor do people at secular nonprofit organizations engaged in humanitarian work" (Henriques, 2006a).

- Revoke pension law exemptions granted to religious institutions. "Religious employers are exempt from Erisa, the federal pension law that establishes disclosure requirements and conflict-of-interest restrictions for employee pension plans. That exemption has given rise to several cases in which workers at religious hospitals found that their pensions had vanished because of practices that would not have been allowed under Erisa's rules" (Henriques, 2009b).

Both of these measures would deal a serious financial blow to religious institutions, and also restrict their ability to proselytize.

Religious institutions will not easily give up their positions of favoritism, but as faith is devalued, time and the law will demand each church, mosque, temple, and synagogue pay taxes. Among those leading the way toward this fundamental change is the Freedom From Religion Foundation (FFRF): http://ffrf.org/. Lending your support to the FFRF will help to facilitate needed legal changes to contain the faith contagion.[12]

10. Create skeptical (atheist) children.

"Virtually all religions rely upon early childhood indoctrination as the prime infection strategy."

—Darrel Ray, *The God Virus* (2009, p. 23)

"My son told me that in his rebellious phase he's going to become a fundamentalist."

—Peter Boghossian

Much has been written about how to raise a child Catholic or Muslim or Mormon or Baha'i. There is no scholarship on how to raise a child to not pretend to know things she doesn't know. In this section I offer my own ideas: drawing from opinions and personal correspondence with notable atheists, reverse engineering literature on raising children in a faith tradition, and broadly surveying research relating to brain development and the process of belief formation in children.

It may seem odd: raise a child so she doesn't hold preposterous metaphysical beliefs. Strange indeed, but also vital. In a society in which the overwhelming majority of people are faithful, and in a culture that frowns upon atheism and even condemns atheists, how is growing up with a skeptical mind-set accomplished?

Let me start by saying that creating religiously skeptical children is probably quite simple. The fact that children tend to track their parents' religious beliefs is good news for atheist readers (Acock & Bengtson, 1980; Erikson, 1992, pp. 141–148; Hoge, Petrillo, & Smith, 1982; Iannaccone 1990, p. 309; Myers, 1996). Many children from religious households abandon and do not regain their faith. And, if trends of belief in God continue to plummet, both social acceptance of atheism and the number of atheists will continue to rise ("The Global Religious Landscape," 2012). This bodes well for our children and for the future.

There are no formulas guaranteed to create an atheist child, but raising a child as a critical thinker, a skeptic, a humanist, or a free thinker will most likely immunize her against delusional thinking and pretending to know things she doesn't know. While these are all related and interdependent, teaching children the importance of adopting a skeptical mind-set, and how to think skeptically, may be the most important of all educational values (Luce, Callanan, & Smilovic, 2013). Atheism is skepticism applied to a specific extraordinary claim, and children should be taught to apply skepticism to claims in general—not just faith and extraordinary metaphysical claims.

It's more important to develop the attitudinal *disposition* to be skeptical than it is to develop the critical thinking skill set. If you can cultivate a skeptical disposition, then it will be more likely your children will not succumb to the faith virus. Anyone can develop a critical thinking skill set—it's like learning to ride a bike—but without the attitudinal component one will not act upon the results of the inquiry—one will never actually ride a bike. In other words, if you brought the skill set to bear on an issue, but were unwilling to change your mind based upon the results, then there was no purpose of inquiring in the first place. It was a cognitive kangaroo court.

These dispositions and skill sets are primarily achieved through modeling. There's interesting educational, correctional, and psychological literature on pro-social modeling; that is, act the way you want others—particularly your children—to act. For example, if you want your children to read, don't read to them but have them watch you read. If you don't want your children to pretend to know things they don't know, don't pretend to know things you don't know. Model the behavior you want them to adopt.

Also, be careful about being too strident. Speak bluntly but model doxastic openness: tell your children you're always willing to listen to the evidence for specific faith claims (faith healing, people speaking in dead languages they've never heard, reincarnation, etc.). Then genuinely listen. Help them evaluate claims by focusing on the *process* used to come to conclusions. For example, focus less on reincarnation and more on how one knows people are reincarnated. For example, is the process used to select the successor to the Dalai Lama one which can be relied upon?

Exposure to different faith traditions may also act as a prophylactic against unwarranted belief. Making something "an other," mysterious or wondrous, may push children toward the very things you want them to avoid. Instead, read different religious texts with your children, attend religious services with them, be eager and ready to help them answer any questions they may have (and not just about faith and religion). Don't make religion a forbidden fruit: acknowledge and read religious literature with your children, model the behavior you want them to emulate, genuinely listen, and gently encourage mutual examination of each other's reasoning processes.

11. *Remove religious exemption for delusion from the DSM.*

The *Diagnostic and Statistical Manual of Mental Disorders* (DSM), published by the American Psychiatric Association (APA), is the single most important text used by clinicians. It is *the* diagnostic rulebook.[13] Currently, the DSM grants religious delusions an exemption from classification as a mental illness. The following is the DSM-IV's definition of delusion:

> "A false belief based on incorrect inference about external reality that is firmly sustained despite what almost everyone else believes and despite what constitutes incontrovertible and obvious proof or evidence to

the contrary. *The belief is not one ordinarily accepted by other members of the person's culture or subculture (e.g. it is not an article of religious faith).* When a false belief involves a value judgment, it is regarded as a delusion only when the judgment is so extreme as to defy credibility. Delusional conviction occurs on a continuum and can sometimes be inferred from an individual's behavior. It is often difficult to distinguish between a delusion and an overvalued idea (in which case the individual has an unreasonable belief or idea but does not hold it as firmly as is the case with a delusion)" (italics mine) (2000, p. 765).

It is *crucial* that the religious exemption for delusion be removed from the DSM. Once religious delusions are integrated into the DSM, entirely new categories of research and treatment into the problem of faith can be created. These will include removal of existing ethical barriers, changing treatments covered by insurance, including faith-based special education programs in the schools, helping children who have been indoctrinated into a faith tradition, and legitimizing interventions designed to rid subjects of the faith affliction.

Removing the exemption that classifies a phenomenon as an officially recognized psychiatric disorder legitimizes research designed to cure the disorder. These classifications also enable researchers to assess their treatments and to continue to build upon what works. Of course there will be institutional and social barriers discouraging research into controversial areas, but with this one change *the* major barrier—receiving approval from the IRB to disabuse human subjects of faith—would be *instantly* overcome.

There is perhaps no greater contribution one could make to contain and perhaps even cure faith than removing the exemption that prohibits classifying religious delusions as mental illness. The removal of religious exemptions from the DSM would enable academicians and clinicians to bring considerable resources to bear on the problem of treating faith, as well as on the ethical issues surrounding faith-based interventions. In the long term, once these treatments and this body of research is refined, results could then be used to inform public health policies designed to contain and ultimately eradicate faith.

INTERVENTION

On October 25, 2011, at Portland State University, I delivered a lecture for Sigma Xi: The Scientific Research Society. Sigma Xi is an organization composed of professional researchers and academicians. This particular meeting was an interdisciplinary event attended by approximately two hundred science leaders throughout Oregon.

The original title of my lecture was, "Jesus, Muhammad, the Tooth Fairy, and Other Evil Creatures." However, the organizer of the event politely asked me to tone down the title. I submitted the following, which was accepted without question: "Jesus, Mother Teresa, the Tooth Fairy, and Other Evil Creatures."

After my talk, during the question and answer, an academician in the audience (AA) raised his hand.

AA: I'm very offended by what you've said here tonight.

(The room goes silent.)

PB: Your offense means nothing to me. If you have arguments or evidence I'd like to hear what you have to say. You saying that you're offended carries no weight. Nor should it.

AA: My wife was healed by Jesus Christ.

PB: How do you know that? People get sick and recover from illnesses all the time. What would make you think that your god had anything to do with it?

AA: She was suffering from an incurable illness.

This is an example of Kazez's "bullying ideas off of the table." AA wanted to shut down the discourse, presumably because he didn't think these issues should be discussed in public. And, in fact, not only did the room go silent, but I also saw virtually everybody hunch down as if they were trying to disappear.

Subsequent to this two attendees approached me to say that my not being cowed by his behavior was a seminal event in their lives. They'd never seen anyone stand up and voice their public opposition to a privileged faith-based claim. One young woman even told me that seeing me confront AA changed her life. She said it gave her hope.

DIG DEEPER

Themes Related to Parenting:

Books for Children

In the realm of children's books that meet the criteria of instilling a sense of awe, wonder, and comfort with not knowing, three books standout. Each of these books starts children on an anti-dogmatic path to wisdom:

Richard Dawkins and Dave McKean, *The Magic of Reality: How We Know What's Really True* (Dawkins & McKean, 2011)

Annaka Harris, *I Wonder* (Harris, forthcoming)

Stephen Law, *Really, Really Big Questions* (Law, 2012)

Books on Raising Skeptical (Atheist) Children

Dale McGowan, *Raising Freethinkers: A Practical Guide for Parenting Beyond Belief* (McGowan, 2007)

Dale McGowan, *Parenting Beyond Belief: On Raising Ethical, Caring Kids Without Religion* (McGowan, 2009)

Entertainment for Teens

Baba Brinkman (http://www.bababrinkman.com/): "Baba Brinkman is a Canadian rap artist, writer, actor, and tree planter. He is best known for his award-winning hip-hop theater shows, including *The Rap Guide to Evolution* and *The Canterbury Tales Remixed*, which interpret the works of Darwin and Chaucer for a modern audience."

Online Resource

Atheist Parents (http://www.atheistparents.org/index.php): "We are dedicated to helping parents worldwide to raise well-educated, thoughtful, ethical, socially responsible, environmentally aware, and most importantly, godless children."

Secular Camps

Camp Quest (http://www.campquest.org/): "Camp Quest provides an educational adventure shaped by fun, friends and freethought, featuring science, natural wonder and humanist values."

Camp Inquiry (http://www.campinquiry.org/): "This is a place where kids can be themselves. We work toward helping youth confront the challenges of living a non-theistic, skeptical, and secular lifestyle in a world dominated by religious belief and pseudoscience. Grounded on the conviction that kids can begin establishing habits of the good and ethical life early on, Camp Inquiry adopts a three-part focus: The arts and sciences, the skeptical perspective, and ethical character development comprise an integrated approach to this 'Age of Discovery.' Campers, counselors, and teachers will address key issues around individual identity, forging trusting relationships, establishing a sense of local and global community, and living with respect for the natural world."

Skepticism for Teens Magazine

Junior Skeptic (http://www.skeptic.com/junior_skeptic/): "Bound into every issue of *Skeptic* magazine, *Junior Skeptic* is an engagingly illustrated science and critical thinking publication for younger readers."

Themes Unrelated to Parenting:

Books

Russell Blackford, *Freedom of Religion and the Secular State* (Blackford, 2012b)

Sean Faircloth, *Attack Of The Theocrats! How The Religious Right Harms Us All—And What We Can Do About It* (Faircloth, 2012)

Brian Leiter, *Why Tolerate Religion?* (Leiter, 2012)

Darrel Ray, *The God Virus: How Religion Infects Our Lives and Culture* (Ray, 2009)

Al Stefanelli, *Free Thoughts—A Collection of Essays by an American Atheist* (Stefanelli, 2012a)

Katherine Stewart, *The Good News Club: The Christian Right's Stealth Assault on America's Children* (Stewart, 2012)

Online Article

Ryan Cragun, "How Secular Humanists (and Everyone Else) Subsidize Religion in the United States" (Cragun, Yeager, & Vega, 2012)

Suggested Academic-Community Partners

The James Randi Educational Foundation (JREF; http://www.randi. org/site/): "The James Randi Educational Foundation was founded in 1996 to help people defend themselves from paranormal and pseudoscientific claims. The JREF offers a still-unclaimed million-dollar reward for anyone who can produce evidence of paranormal abilities under controlled conditions. Through scholarships, workshops, and innovative resources for educators, the JREF works to inspire this investigative spirit in a new generation of critical thinkers."

The Richard Dawkins Foundation for Reason and Science (RDFRS; http://richarddawkinsfoundation.org/): "The mission of the Richard Dawkins Foundation for Reason and Science is to support scientific education, critical thinking and evidence-based understanding of the natural world in the quest to overcome religious fundamentalism, superstition, intolerance and suffering."

Secular Student Alliance (SSA; http://www.secularstudents.org/about): "The mission of the Secular Student Alliance is to organize, unite, educate, and serve students and student communities that promote the ideals of scientific and critical inquiry, democracy, secularism, and human-based ethics. We envision a future in which nontheistic students are respected voices in public discourse and vital partners in the secular movement's charge against irrationality and dogma."

The Skeptics Society and *Skeptic* Magazine (http://www.skeptic. com/): "The Skeptics Society is a nonprofit 501(c)(3) scientific and educational organization whose mission is to engage leading experts in investigating the paranormal, fringe science, pseudoscience, and extraordinary claims of all kinds, promote critical thinking, and serve as an educational tool for those seeking a sound scientific viewpoint. Our contributors—leading scientists, scholars, investigative journalists, historians, professors and teachers—are top experts in their fields. It is our hope that our efforts go a long way in promoting critical thinking and lifelong inquisitiveness in all individuals."

Secular Legal Support

Americans United for Separation of Church and State (https://www. au.org/): "Americans United for Separation of Church and State is a nonpartisan educational organization dedicated to preserving the constitutional principle of church-state separation as the only way to ensure religious freedom for all Americans."

Freedom From Religion Foundation (FFRF; http://ffrf.org/): "The history of Western civilization shows us that most social and moral progress has been brought about by persons free from religion. In modern times the first to speak out for prison reform, for humane treatment of the mentally ill, for abolition of capital punishment, for women's right to vote, for death with dignity for the terminally ill, and for the right to choose contraception, sterilization and abortion have been freethinkers, just as they were the first to call for an end to slavery. The Foundation works as an umbrella for those who are free from religion and are committed to the cherished principle of separation of state and church."

Military Religious Freedom Foundation (MRFF; http://www. militaryreligiousfreedom.org/): "The Military Religious Freedom Foundation is dedicated to ensuring that all members of the United States Armed Forces fully receive the Constitutional guarantees of religious freedom to which they and all Americans are entitled by virtue of the Establishment Clause of the First Amendment."

National Engagement Opportunities

American Atheists (http://atheists.org/about-us): "Since 1963, American Atheists has been the premier organization laboring for the civil liberties of atheists and the total, absolute separation of government and religion. It was born out of a court case begun in 1959 by the Murray family which challenged prayer recitation in the public schools. . . . Now in its 50th year, American Atheists is dedicated to working for the civil rights of atheists, promoting separation of state and church, and providing information about atheism."

Center for Inquiry (http://www.centerforinquiry.net/): "The mission of the Center for Inquiry is to foster a secular society based on science, reason, freedom of inquiry, and humanist values. To oppose and supplant the mythological narratives of the past, and the dogmas of the present, the world needs an institution devoted to promoting science, reason, freedom of inquiry, and humanist values. The Center for Inquiry is that institution."

Council for Secular Humanism (http://www.secularhumanism.org/index.php): "The mission of the Council for Secular Humanism is to advocate and defend a nonreligious lifestance rooted in science, naturalistic philosophy, and humanist ethics and to serve and support adherents of that lifestance."

Foundation Beyond Belief (http://foundationbeyondbelief.org/): "To demonstrate humanism at its best by supporting efforts to improve this world and this life, and to challenge humanists to embody the highest principles of humanism, including mutual care and responsibility."

Freedom From Religion Foundation (http://ffrf.org/)

Secular Coalition for America (http://secular.org): "The Secular Coalition for America is a 501(c)(4) advocacy organization whose purpose is to amplify the diverse and growing voice of the nontheistic community in the United States. We are located in Washington, D.C. for ready access to government, activist partners and the media. Our staff lobbies U.S. Congress on issues of special concern to our constituency."

Entertainment

It is not a coincidence that depictions of a godless world commonly occur in television and movies that take place in the future.

Babylon 5

Blake's 7

Farscape

Stargate Universe

Star Trek

NOTES

1. For why someone should care about the truth, see American philosopher Harry Frankfurt's brief but engaging book, *On Truth* (Frankfurt, 2006). Frankfurt writes, "how could a society that cared too little for truth make sufficiently well-informed judgments and decisions concerning the most suitable disposition of its public business?" (p. 15).

2. We need to clean up our language and remove the vestiges of religious ages. Here are some frequently used expressions that I'm advocating we stop using: "God bless you," "May the Lord have mercy," "The devil is in the details," "Thank God," "Soul searching," "For God's sake," "God helps those who help themselves," "God only knows," "God willing," "Thank God for small favors," "God's gift to women/men," "Godspeed," "Our thoughts and prayers are with you," "Thank you, Jesus," "God dammit," "Bless you," "Leap of faith," "Act of faith," "To act in bad/good faith," "Show good faith," "Take it on faith," "An article of faith," "An act of God," "Count your blessings," "Have faith in me," "Match made in heaven," etc. These and other expressions permeate our language in virtually every domain, for example, law ("Act in bad faith"), insurance ("Act of God"), football ("Hail Mary pass"), computing (Daemon), computer gaming

("God mode"), physics ("The God particle"), ethics ("God's eye view"), relationships ("Soul mate"), etc.

It is possible for religious language to fall into disuse. Witness the women's movement—words and titles have, in one generation, been changed—Mrs. to Ms., spokesman to spokesperson, stewardess to flight attendant, fireman to firefighter, etc.

3. In *Philosophical Investigations*, philosopher Ludwig Wittgenstein popularized the phrase *Sprachspiel*, or "language game" (Wittgenstein, 2009). "Language game" is meant to capture the idea that words have a multiplicity of uses—people use the same word across many different contexts. There's no fixed meaning of any word.

4. By 2015, my Atheism course at Portland State University will hopefully become a MOOC. The course should be free and open to the public.

5. Many people struggle with the sense of meaninglessness that the contemporary world seems to thrust upon them. The specter of relativism makes individuals think that all answers are the same—hollow and useless. God-fearing people see relativism as an enemy and meaninglessness as an inevitable result of being cut off from God.

    What figures like Nietzsche teach us is that the sense of meaninglessness is a result of millennia of dependency on mythological thinking. When myths are shown to be false, the result is a sense of despair because we've been dependent upon them for so long. The step out of meaninglessness should not be dependency on a new myth (the New Age movement, Scientology, Mormonism), but self-sufficiency and a tough-mindedness that is weary of resting the sense of meaning on what someone else has said or done or promised. We have to earn meaning for ourselves.

    The sequence of escaping myth is: dependency, despair, reawakening, and self-sufficiency that embraces the value of tough-minded living.

6. In Oregon, for example, a student Christian organization at Portland State University sponsors Louis Palau's crusade (http://www.palau.org/) along the riverfront. Teenagers by the thousands are lured to the event with

sports demonstrations and music, but they must also endure a heavy dose of evangelism. I've yet to see a single picketer at this event. Even a few dozen people with signs who picketed the entrance and warned parents that the event is not what it seems would make a difference. There's plenty of religious propaganda that could use a conspicuous, public assault by clear thinkers.

Many people are willing to picket an event, but few are willing to organize an event. Find someone who's willing to organize an event and tell them you'll attend.

7. I recently formed academic-community partnerships with the RDFRS and with the JREF. The RDFRS partnership will potentially allow students in my New Atheism course to publish their work on the RDFRS Web page: http://richarddawkinsfoundation.org/. The JREF partnership will allow students to make their work accessible on the iPad.

But beyond this, these partnerships enable me to find students who are passionate about, and committed to, spreading reason and rationality. It's an amazing opportunity for students to improve their writing, delve into a topic in great depth, and have a competitive advantage when they apply to graduate schools.

8. Conspicuously absent from the Centers for Disease Control and Prevention's information Web page are epistemologists: "From the food you eat, to the air you breathe, to staying safe wherever you are, CDC's mission touches all aspects of daily life. CDC researchers, scientists, doctors, nurses, economists, communicators, educators, technologists, epidemiologists and many other professionals all contribute their expertise to improving public health" (CDC, 2012).

We need to institutionalize the way we deal with cognitive contamination by virulent epistemologies. Future generations will likely view the eradication of epistemological contagions in the same way that previous generations viewed the importance of eradicating smallpox and polio.

9. When I told my father that K–12 educational systems should promote the value of epistemological rigor, he replied incredulously, "Are you kidding

me? High school dropout rates are hovering around 33 percent in most [U.S.] cities. We can't even teach kids how to read. What makes you think we'd be any more successful with instilling 'epistemological rigor?'"

Whether or not we can be successful in helping people see value in epistemological rigor is an empirical question. I have my own speculation that this can be accomplished through pop culture—for example, comic books and TV shows for children that personify new heroes, Epistemic Knights, and new villains, Faith Monsters.

10. Tax revenues could then be put into public health programs that attempt to contain faith and promote reason. Additional monies and incentives could aim at: reforming colleges of education that grant promotion and tenure to faculty who attempt to reconstruct reason and conduct community outreach work in the public understanding of reason and science; institutionalizing critical thinking curricula in grades K–12; sponsoring public outreach campaigns that reframe the value of faith; funding music, movies, and TV shows that portray faith (not the faithful but the process and consequences of faith) in a negative light; etc.

11. In Germany and even Ireland and Italy, there is growing support for taxing the Catholic Church, their holdings, donations, and lands. I don't, however, see this happening in the United States within the next five years. Yet I can imagine a single, enlightened U.S. government official recognizing the hypocrisy of taxing a nonprofit dedicated to feeding the impoverished or curing cancer, while Scientologists continue to build their empire, tax free—this is the kind of change we can demand as society learns to value and promote reason.

12. For every dollar spent by FFRF or Americans United, the Christian ministries (in coalition) spend more than $150 (Brown, 2012; A. Seidel, personal communication, December 5, 2012). They employ special interest law firms whose primary mission is to petition appellate and supreme courts to either sue or file friends-of-the-court briefs on issues ranging from public school release time for religious instruction, to bans on abortion, to programs designed to stop contraception.

13. The American Psychiatric Association's description of the DSM reads,

the "DSM . . . contains descriptions, symptoms, and other criteria for diagnosing mental disorders. These criteria for diagnosis provide a common language among clinicians—professionals who treat patients with mental disorders. By clearly defining the criteria for a mental disorder, DSM helps to ensure that a diagnosis is both accurate and consistent; for example, that a diagnosis of schizophrenia is consistent from one clinician to another, and means the same thing to both of these clinicians, whether they reside in the U.S. or other international settings. It is important to understand that appropriately using the diagnostic criteria found in DSM requires clinical training and a thorough evaluation and examination of an individual patient" (American Psychiatric Association, 2012).

ACKNOWLEDGMENTS

First and foremost, thanks to my wife. I could never have done this without her tireless support. She is my rock. She is my place of safety in chaos. Thanks to my daughter for her patience and to my son for allowing me to bounce ideas off of him. Thanks to my mother and father for a lifetime of kindness, generosity, and unconditional love. Mom, you were my best friend. You are missed beyond measure: your grace, humor, compassion, irreverence, and unconditional love are models I strive to emulate. My goal is to do for my children what you have done for me. Thank you for sharing your life with me. I love you and will always love you.

Thank you Jason Stevens and Matthew Hernandez for exceptional research contributions. (Jason was literally an atheist in a foxhole.) Jason and Matthew worked diligently in helping me fact-check, cite, and research sometimes obscure topics. Ryan Marquez, Renee Barnett, and Anna Wilson also helped me hammer out and research important details. Thanks to Corey Van Hoosen for creating the front cover and illustration in appendix C. (Corey [corey.vanhoosen@pdx.edu] also makes the custom images for my presentations.) Thank you to my childhood friend and amateur historian Jimmy Farrell for helping me with footnote 12 in chapter 7, and Tom O'Connor for helping me with footnote 8 in chapter 6. Thanks to Micah Barnott for doing so much to advance reason, but asking for so little in return.

Thanks to Renee Barnett for being an inspiring friend and an ever-dependable source of support. Renee has an incredible career ahead of her. Thank you Guy P. Harrison, Brom Anderson, and John W. Loftus for friendship and patience in answering my questions. Thanks to Avram Hiller for his incredibly helpful contributions to all of my presentations.

Thank you to those at Portland State University who supported me, most notably the Philosophy Department chair, Tom Seppalainen. Tom, thank you again for providing me with an opportunity when nobody else would. You are the last believer in the meritocracy. Special thanks to my colleague who told me, "Even if you published ten critically received books from Harvard you'd never get tenure here." Your words are a constant source of motivation.

Locally, thanks to Center for Inquiry (CFI)–Portland and Sylvia Benner; Humanists of Greater Portland and Del Allen; Oregonians for Science and Reason and Jeanine DeNoma; Josh Fost, Christof Teuscher, Erik Bodegom, and Amanda Thomas for your contributions to reason, rationality, critical thinking, and the public understanding of science. You're making our community better.

Nationally, thanks to Mike Cornwell, Elisabeth Cornwell, Suzy Lewis, Joel Guttormson, Todd Stiefel, Kurt Volkan, D. J. Grothe, Greg Stikeleather, and Sean Faircloth. You didn't know me, but you were very kind to me. Your efforts at making our society more rational and more thoughtful matter.

Thanks to Dan Barker, Annie Laurie Gaylor, and the Freedom From Religion Foundation for your practical, applied efforts in fighting irrationality in a way that I never could. In particular I'd like to thank Andrew Seidel for being on the frontline. Your efforts are making a difference.

Thanks to my past and present students for engaging and challenging me.

Thanks to everyone who read drafts and commented on *A Manual for Creating Atheists*: Sylvia Benner, Steven Brutus, Bruce Carter, John

Diggins, Steve Eltinge, Alan Litchfield from "The Malcontent's Gambit" (http://www.malcontentsgambit.com/), Gary W. Longsine, Justin Vacula, and Bob Williams.

Thank you to Massimo Pigliucci and Stephen Law for their original contributions to this book.

Thanks to my old, dear friend and editor, Christopher Johnson. Before I realized his e-mail signature is "Your best friend!" I was under the assumption—for years—that he thought that I thought that we were best friends.

Thanks to William Guy Hart for (unbeknownst to me) starting and maintaining my Facebook page. Thanks to Steven Humphrey from the *Portland Mercury* for taking a gamble on my articles. Samantha Russell, thank you for your lovely paintings and for your continued support.

Especially profound and heartfelt thanks to Steve Goldman and Matt Thornton for their invaluable help, council, advice, and authentic friendship. When I have questions about philosophy, Steve is my go-to. Steve and Matt were kind enough to let me record our conversations and copy our e-mail correspondence. Portions of those conversations are found throughout the book.

Thanks to Paul Pardi and philosophynews.com for hosting some of my content, driving down to Portland to review my "Easter Bunny" talk, being incredibly supportive of my work, and interviewing me for my first podcast.

Many people helped me with this project. Please accept my apologies if I failed to mention anyone, and thank you to all my supporters.

Finally, thanks in advance to those who've agreed to let me sleep on their couch when I go into hiding after the publication of this book.

APPENDIX A

CONSENSUS STATEMENT REGARDING CRITICAL THINKING AND THE IDEAL CRITICAL THINKER

We understand critical thinking [CT] to be purposeful, self-regulatory judgment which results in interpretation, analysis, evaluation, and inference, as well as explanation of the evidential, conceptual, methodological, criteriological, or contextual considerations upon which that judgment is based. CT is essential as a tool of inquiry. As such, CT is a liberating force in education and a powerful resource in one's personal and civic life. While not synonymous with good thinking, CT is a pervasive and self-rectifying human phenomenon. The ideal critical thinker is habitually inquisitive, well-informed, trustful of reason, open-minded, flexible, fair minded in evaluation, honest in facing personal biases, prudent in making judgments, willing to reconsider, clear about issues, orderly in complex matters, diligent in seeking relevant information, reasonable in the selection of criteria, focused in inquiry, and persistent in seeking results which are as precise as the subject and the circumstances of inquiry permit. Thus, educating good critical thinkers means working toward this ideal. It combines developing CT skills with nurturing those dispositions which consistently yield useful insights and which are the basis of a rational and democratic society (American Philosophical Association, 1990, p. 2).

APPENDIX B

"INTRODUCING SOCRATES" SYLLABUS

Instructor:
Peter Boghossian

Course Description:
In this 8-hour critical thinking class we will think through some difficult questions together, articulate our responses to those questions, and assess our reasoning.

Objectives:
1) Learn how to identify consequences
2) Learn how to reason through a problem (problem-solving)
3) Learn how to assess our thinking
4) Learn how to assess our current relationships
5) Learn how to articulate our ideas
6) Develop higher stages of moral reasoning
7) Develop verbal self-control
8) Understand how our identities are formed
9) Understand the roles that pleasure-seeking and gratification play in our lives

Class Structure:
The class has two separate parts: (1) Discussion Questions, and (2) Discussion Analysis.

Part I
Discussion Questions
Every 25 minutes we will start with a question that is taken, in some form, from the Platonic dialogues (on occasion we may start with a reading from the dialogues). For example, a typical question could be, "How much control do we have over who we are?" We will then think through the question, and pose possible answers. I will participate in the discussion as a guide.

The discussion could take any one of a number of unexpected turns. It is okay if it does—evaluating different responses and analyzing those responses is part of the practice of learning. Until you become accustomed to the way that issues will be discussed, this may be perceived as a lack of structure. Also, if you are used to more formal class settings where exactly what you will learn is mapped out in detail beforehand, then this way of teaching class may initially be difficult for you. This is something that you need to be aware of in our discussions.

Part II
Discussion Analysis
The next 5 minutes we will analyze the discussion. We will identify the stages and process of our reasoning, assess our thinking, and attempt to figure out how we could have been more effective both in our reasoning and in our articulation. We will use what we have learned in the next discussion.

I have the following expectations:

- That you will be respectful of others. This does not mean that you have to agree with someone else's viewpoint, but you do need to let them speak without *personally* criticizing them.
- That you will ask if you have any questions, or if something is unclear.

If something is bothering you, then you need to tell me.

- At times in our discussion I may say "STOP!" If I do, this means that we need to stop what we are doing, and I will direct you to write about what we are discussing.

What are the expectations that you have of me?

Finally

We can make this a very rewarding experience for everyone involved. It is an opportunity for us to explore issues and ideas in a way that challenges us intellectually. We will have an opportunity to think about ideas that everyone has wondered about, but few have had an opportunity to explore in depth in a classroom setting. My role is to help you articulate your thoughts and give you a process to evaluate critically your ideas. But there is only so much that I can do. Ultimately, you must take responsibility for your own learning. So perhaps our first question should be, "What does it mean to take responsibility for our learning?"

DISCUSSION QUESTIONS

The following are questions that we will be asking ourselves throughout this course. I have listed the names of where these ideas can be found in the event that you would like to read more on your own. Unless otherwise stated, all names refer to works written by Plato.

- What is it to be a man? What is it to be virtuous? (*Apology, Meno*)
- What is courage? (*Laches*)
- Do people knowingly do bad things? (*Gorgias, Protagoras, Hippias Minor*)
- What is justice? (*Republic*)
- Are people responsible for who they become? (*Republic*)
- Can a man be unjust toward himself? Can one be too modest? (Immanuel Kant's "Metaphysics of Virtue," in the first part of the *Metaphysics of Morals, Gorgias*, Aristotle's *Nicomachean Ethics*)
- Why obey the law? (*Crito, Republic*)
- What's worth dying for? (*Apology, Crito*)
- When is punishment justified? (*Gorgias, Crito*)

- How important is personal responsibility? What does "character counts" mean? (*Republic, Gorgias, Laws*)
- Are customs and conventions important? What kinds of customs and conventions are there (styles, manners, laws, social class)? (*Republic*)
- What's the best life? What are the possible lives we can lead? Is the life of the tyrant the best life? (*Republic*)
- How much control do we have over who we are? (*Republic*)
- What obligations do we have toward others? (*Republic*)
- What are the claims of loyalty and friendship? (*Republic, Lysis*)
- What are our obligations toward our families? (*Republic*)
- What makes a way of life appealing to us? What attaches people to the way of life? (*Republic*)

APPENDIX C

ANTIRELATIVISM ROADMAP

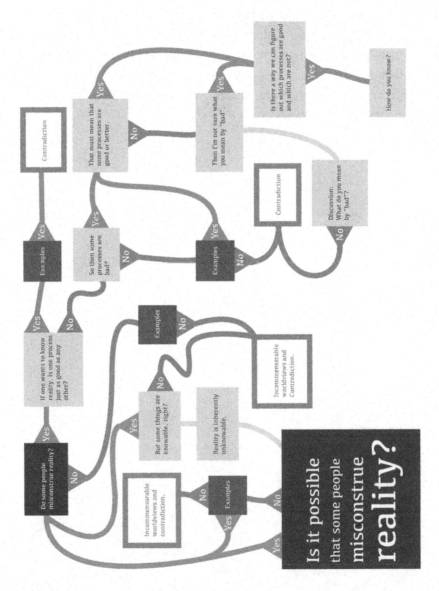

GLOSSARY

Agnostic
Someone who's unsure whether or not God(s) exist.

Apologetics
A defense of the faith. (The word "apologetics" is often misunderstood as an apology for faith or for having faith.)

Aporia
Confusion, puzzlement, perplexity. The state of pause caused by philosophical examination.

Atheist
1. A person who does not think there's sufficient evidence to warrant belief in God(s), but who would believe if shown sufficient evidence.
2. A person who doesn't pretend to know things he doesn't know with regard to the creator of the universe.

Auditing
A practice in the Church of Scientology in which a minister or a minister-in-training gives "auditing commands" to a person, referred to as a "preclear." Auditing commands are questions or directions.

Augustine (St. Augustine of Hippo) (354–430)
A medieval Christian philosopher of enormous authority and influence.

Azande
An ethnic group of approximately one million people living in and around central Africa.

Bayes' Theorem
Provides the probability of an event given measured test probabilities.

Chaerephon
Socrates's close friend. Chaerephon appears in Plato's *Apology*, *Charmides*, and *Gorgias*.

Coherence theory of truth
States that a proposition is true if it coheres or fits with other propositions.

Confirmation bias
The tendency to privilege confirming evidence and disregard disconfirming evidence.

Critical thinking
A skill set and an attitude. For a description and definition of the ideal critical thinker, see appendix A.

Cruise, Tom (human body: 1962–) (Thetan: several trillion years)
American film actor and producer. Awarded Scientology's Freedom Medal of Valor in 2004.

Delusion
1. The current DSM-IV definition of delusion can be found on page 765.
2. German psychiatrist and philosopher Karl Jaspers (1883–1969) offers three criteria for delusion: certainty (someone is absolutely positive their belief is true), incorrigibility (the belief is incapable of revision), and impossibility or falsity of content (bizarre or highly improbable content) (Maher, 2001).

Deepak Chopra
Indian-born American. New Age guru. Deepity black belt.

Deepity
A statement that is seemingly profound yet trivial on one level and meaningless on the other.

Defensive posture
Self-protection from criticism, personal shortcomings, whatever challenges one's worldview, or that which is perceived as threatening.

Doxastic
Belief and reasoning about belief. "Doxastic" comes from the ancient Greek word "doxa," which means belief.

Doxastic closure
A belief or a belief system that cannot be revised. (Systems of belief and individual beliefs have degrees of closure.)

Doxastic openness
A belief system or belief that can be revised. (Systems of belief and individual beliefs have degrees of openness.)

Empirical claim
A claim about the world.

Enlightenment (New Enlightenment)
"The growing up stage in man's development, his determination to put away childish things, to stand upon his own two feet, to be no longer under tutelage, and above all, to use his reason and to think for himself" (Thrower, 2000).

Epistemic
Of or related to knowledge or knowing.

Epistemology
The study of knowledge.

Evidence
That which justifies belief and guides one toward truth.

Falsifiable
Capable of being shown false. Usually applied to hypotheses.

Faith
1. Pretending to know things one doesn't know
2. Belief without evidence
3. An irrational leap over probabilities

Feminism
Equal rights for women.

Foundationalism (also, Foundationalist theory of truth)
Beliefs receive justification from "basic" or "foundational" beliefs.

Four Horsemen
Richard Dawkins, Daniel Dennett, Sam Harris, and Christopher Hitchens. The phrase "Four Horsemen" comes from the New Testament's Book of Revelation.

God
An undetectable metaphysical entity that caused all of existence to come into being but whose existence was not caused.

Genetic fallacy
The endorsement or condemnation of a claim based upon its past as opposed to its merit. The original source of an idea is or is not a reliable basis for evaluating truth. For example, Massachusetts Representative Michael Capuano favors higher taxation on the wealthy; Marx had the same economic way of thinking; therefore, Capuano is wrong.

Hadith
Actions or statements attributed to the Muslim prophet Muhammad not found in the Koran.

Hermeneutic circle
The impossibility of stepping back from one's experiences and objectively interpreting a text, work of art, event, or phenomena.

Humanism
A practice and a worldview focusing on human values, concerns, and issues. Humanists come to decisions, particularly moral decisions, completely independent of supernatural considerations.

Institutional Review Board (IRB)
Approves, monitors, and reviews all research involving human subjects (people).

Intervention (see "Treatment")

Justification
Sufficient reason to believe.

Knowledge
Justified True Belief (K = J T B.) Knowledge claims must satisfy these three criteria: they must be justified, true, and believed. This formula for knowledge was originally articulated in Plato's *Theaetetus*.

Knowledge claim
Mind-independent, objective statements of fact about the world.

Logical possibility
A logically possible statement can be asserted without implying a contradiction. For example, "There exists a golden mountain," is logically possible. There could be a mountain made of gold. However, "A square is a circle," is not logically possible because the definition of a square precludes it from being a circle. (If you can imagine something, then it doesn't contradict the laws of logic.)

Luther, Martin (1483–1546)
German theologian. A pivotal figure in the Protestant Reformation.

Manu
From Hindu mythology, the gods created Manu who became the progenitor of humanity.

Meme
A concept that spreads from one person to another.

Multiculturalism
A doctrine stating that a community containing multiple cultures can peacefully coexist.

Metaphysics
The branch of philosophy that studies "being," "first cause," and "what there is."

Pathogenic belief
A belief that directly or indirectly leads to emotional, psychological, or physical pathology.

Pedagogy
The method and practice of teaching.

Pluralism
The peaceful coexistence of two or more states, entities, cultures, or phenomena.

Pythia, The
Also known as the Oracle of Delphi. The Pythia was a priestess at the Temple of Apollo, located on Mount Parnassus, who was a source of wisdom and who made prophecies.

Quantum mechanics
A branch of physics that provides a mathematical description of the behavior and interaction of energy and matter at the atomic and subatomic level.

Relativism
Either there is no absolute truth or it's not possible to know the absolute truth.

Scientific method
A process by which one can make an objective investigation.

Selection bias
"Selection bias comes in two flavors: (1) self-selection of individuals to participate in an activity or survey, or as a subject in an experimental study; (2) selection of samples or studies by researchers to support a particular hypothesis." The Skeptics Dictionary: http://skepdic.com/selectionbias.html

Shermer, Michael (1954–)
The founding publisher of *Skeptic* magazine, the executive director of the Skeptics Society, a monthly columnist for *Scientific American*, the host of the Skeptics Society, and bestselling author.

Śrīmad Bhāgavatam (also, Bhāgavata Purāna)
A Hindu sacred text. (The story recounted in chapter 3 has to do with Daksha and his daughter Dakshayani, one of whose names is Sati. She is the wife of Shiva the Destroyer and is considered the goddess of marital happiness. She immolates herself on her divine husband's funeral pyre as a final act of loyalty and is later reincarnated as Paravati. The human woman who does this for her husband is patterning her action after a divine prototype described in one of India's most ancient texts. The Bhāgavata is sometimes called the fifth Veda—this goes to the idea that its source is ancient.)

Subjective claim
A statement of preference that is neither true nor false.

Supernatural
Outside of the natural world.

Therapeutic alliance
The bond between the therapist and the client that allows the client to make therapeutic progress. This term, also referred to as "therapeutic relationship," has been appropriated from Edward Bordin's 1979 article, "The Generalizability of the Psychoanalytic Concept of the Working Alliance" (Bordin, 1979).

Thetan
The Scientologist's belief that a spirit is "stuck" in a human body.

Treatment
A therapeutic process in which something that is damaged becomes whole.

Truth
Beliefs that are in lawful alignment with reality.

Truth claim
A statement of fact.

Urantia Book, The
"*The Urantia Book*, first published by Urantia Foundation in 1955, claims to have been presented by celestial beings as a revelation to our planet, Urantia. The writings in *The Urantia Book* instruct us on the genesis, history, and destiny of humanity and on our relationship with God the Father. They present a unique and compelling portrayal of the life and teachings of Jesus. They open new vistas of time and eternity to the human spirit, and offer new details of our ascending adventure in a friendly and carefully administered universe." Urantia Foundation, custodian and publisher of *The Urantia Book*: http://www.urantia.org/urantia-book

Vector
An organism that spreads an infectious pathogen but shows no symptoms.

Warrant
Sufficient justification for a claim.

Wittgenstein, Ludwig (1889–1951)
Austrian philosopher. One of the most important figures in philosophy in the twentieth century whose work continues to influence contemporary thinkers.

REFERENCES

Acock, A. C., & Bengtson, V. L. (1980). Socialization and attribution processes: Actual versus perceived similarity among parents and youth. *Journal of Marriage and Family, 42,* 501–515.

Agee, J. (2009). *A death in the family* (Centennial ed.). New York, NY: Penguin Books.

Ali, M., & Ali, H. Y. (2004). *The soul of a butterfly: Reflections on life's journey.* New York, NY: Simon & Schuster.

American Philosophical Association. (1990). *Critical thinking: A statement of expert consensus for purposes of educational assessment and instruction. "The Delphi Report."* Millbrae, CA: The California Academic Press.

American Psychiatric Association. (2000). *Diagnostic and Statistical Manual of Mental Disorders DSM-IV* (4th ed.). Washington, DC: American Psychiatric Association.

American Psychiatric Association (2012). *APA DSM-5.* Frequently Asked Questions. Retrieved from http://www.dsm5.org/ABOUT/Pages/faq.aspx

Anderson, S. D. (2010). *Living dangerously: Seven keys to intentional discipleship.* Eugene, OR: Wipf & Stock Pub.

Andrews, D. A., & Friesen, W. (1987). Assessments of Anticriminal Plans and the Prediction of Criminal Futures. *Criminal Justice and Behavior, 14*(1), 33–37.

Andrews, D. A., Zinger, I., Hoge, R. D., Bonta, J., Gendreau, P., & Cullen, F. T. (1990). Does correctional treatment work? A clinically-relevant and psychologically-informed meta-analysis. *Criminology, 28*(3), 369–404.

Andrews, S. (2013). *Deconverted: A journey from religion to reason.* Denver, Colorado: Outskirts Press.

Argyle, M. (2000). *Psychology and religion: An introduction.* London, England: Routledge.

Baltag, A., Rodenhäuser, B., & Smets, S. (2011). *Doxastic attitudes as belief-revision policies.* (Unpublished manuscript). ILLC, University of Amsterdam. Amsterdam, Netherlands.

Bandura, A. (1990). Mechanisms of moral disengagement. In W. Reich (Ed.), *Origins of terrorism: Psychologies, ideologies, theologies, states of mind* (pp. 161–191). Washington, DC: Woodrow Wilson Center Press.

Bandura, A. (1999). Moral disengagement in the perpetration of inhumanities. *Personality and Social Psychology Review, 3,* 193–209. doi:10.1207/s15327957pspr0303_3

Bandura, A. (2002). Selective moral disengagement in the exercise of moral agency. *Journal of Moral Education, 31*(2), 102–119. doi:10.1080/0305724022014322

Bartlett, T. (2012, August 13). Dusting off God: A new science of religion says God has gotten a bad rap. *The Chronicle of Higher Education.* Retrieved from http://chronicle.com/article/Does-Religion-Really-Poison/133457/

Barker, D. L. (Performer). (2012). *Making the case for atheists.* [Web Video]. Retrieved from http://www.youtube.com/watch?v=e7y5slO kwaU&feature=player_embedded

Barker, D. (2008). *Godless: How an evangelical preacher became one of America's leading atheists.* Berkeley, CA: Ulysses Press.

Bausell, R. B. (2007). *Snake oil science: The truth about complementary and alternative medicine.* Oxford: Oxford University Press.

Bering, J. (2011). *The belief instinct: The psychology of souls, destiny, and the meaning of life.* New York, NY: W.W. Norton & Company, Inc.

Berns, G. S., Bell, E., Capra, C. M., Prietula, M. J., Moore, S., Anderson, B.,... Atran, S. (2012). The price of your soul: Neural evidence for the non-utilitarian representation of sacred values. *Philosophical Transactions of The Royal Society, 367*(1589), 754–762. doi:10.1098/rstb.2011.0262

Bernstein, R., & Gaw, A. (1990). Koro: Proposed classification for DSM-IV. *The American Journal of Psychiatry, 147*(12), 1670–1674.

Bishop, B. (2008). *The big sort: Why the clustering of like-minded America is tearing us apart.* New York, NY: Houghton Mifflin Company.

Blackford, R. (2012a, August, 8). Islam, racists, and legitimate debate. Talking Philosophy: The Philosophers' Magazine Blog. Retrieved from http://blog.talkingphilosophy.com/?p=5305

Blackford, R. (2012b). *Freedom of religion and the secular state.* West Sussex, England: Wiley-Blackwell.

Blume, A. W., Schmaling, K. B., & Marlatt, G. A. (2000). Revisiting the self-medication hypothesis from a behavioral perspective. *Cognitive and Behavioral Practice, 7*(4), 379–384. doi:10.1016/S1077-7229(00)80048-6

Boghossian, P. A. (2006c). *Fear of knowledge: Against relativism and constructivism.* Oxford: Clarendon Press.

Boghossian, P. (under review). Doxastic closure: Why I ain't wrong and you is.

Boghossian, P. (2002a). Socratic pedagogy, race and power. *Education Policy Analysis Archives, 10,* 3. Retrieved from http://epaa.asu.edu/ojs/article/view/282

Boghossian, P. (2002b). The Socratic method (or, having a right to get stoned). *Teaching Philosophy, 25*(4), 345–359. doi:10.5840/teachphil200225443

Boghossian, P. (2003). How Socratic pedagogy works. *Informal Logic, 23*(2), TS17-25.

Boghossian, P. (2004). *Socratic pedagogy, critical thinking, moral reasoning and inmate education: An exploratory study.* (Unpublished doctoral dissertation). Portland State University. Portland, OR.

Boghossian, P. (2006a). Socratic pedagogy, critical thinking, and inmate education. *Journal of Correctional Education, 57*(1), 42–63.

Boghossian, P. (2006b). Behaviorism, constructivism, and Socratic pedagogy. *Educational Philosophy and Theory, 38*(6), 713–722. doi:10.1111/j.1469-5812.2006.00226.x

Boghossian, P. (2010). Socratic pedagogy, critical thinking, and offender programming. *Offender Programs Report, 13*(5), 65–80.

Boghossian, P. (2011a). Critical thinking and constructivism: Mambo dog fish to the banana. *Journal of Philosophy of Education, 46*(1), 73–84. doi:10.1111/j.1467-9752.2011.00832.x

Boghossian, P. (2011b). Socratic pedagogy: Perplexity, humiliation, shame and a broken egg. *Educational Philosophy and Theory, 44*(7), 710–720. doi:10.1111/j.1469-5812.2011.00773.x

Boghossian, P. (2011c, July). Should we challenge student beliefs? *Inside Higher Ed.* Retrieved from http://www.insidehighered.com/views/2011/07/192/boghossian

Boghossian, P. (2012). Faith no more. *The Philosophers' Magazine, 59*, 15–16.

Bogue, B., Diebel, J., & O'Connor, T. P. (2008). Combining officer supervision skills: A new model for increasing success in community corrections. *Perspectives, Spring, 2*(32), 30–45.

Bonta, J., & Andrews, D. (2010). Viewing offender assessment and rehabilitation through the lens of the risk-needs-responsivity model. In F. McNeill, P. Rayner & C. Trotter (Eds.), *Offender supervision: New directions in theory, research and practice* (pp. 19–40). New York: Willan Publishing.

Bordin, E. S. (1979). The generalizability of the psychoanalytic concept of the working alliance. *Psychotherapy: Theory, Research, and Practice, 16*(3), 252–260.

Bortolotti, L. (2010). *Delusions and other irrational beliefs*. Oxford: Oxford University Press.

Bostrom, N. (2003). Are you living in a computer simulation? *The Philosophical Quarterly, 53*(211), 243–255.

Bostrom, N. (May/June 2008). Where are they?: Why I hope the search for extraterrestrial life finds nothing. *MIT Technology Review.* Retrieved from http://www.technologyreview.com/article/409936/ where-are-they/

Boyer, P. (2001). *Religion explained: The evolutionary origins of religious thought.* New York, NY: Basic Books.

Boyer, P. (2004, March/April). Why is religion natural? *Skeptical Inquirer, 28.2,* Retrieved from http://www.csicop.org/si/show/why_ is_religion_natural/

Braithwaite, V. & Levi, M. (Eds.). (1998). *Trust and governance (Russell Sage Foundation series on trust, volume 1).* New York, NY: Russell Sage Foundation.

Brock, T. C., & Balloun, J. L. (1967). Behavioral receptivity to dissonant information. *Personality and Social Psychology, 6*(4, Pt.1), 413–428. doi:10.1037/h0021225

Brodie, R. (1996). *Virus of the mind: The new science of the meme.* Carlsbad, CA: Hay House, Inc.

Brown, S. (2012, October 2). The 10 most dangerous religious right organizations. *Network for Church Monitoring.* Retrieved from http:// churchandstate.org.uk/2012/10/the-10-most-dangerous-religious-right-organizations/

Brutus, S. (2012). *Religion, Culture, History: A Philosophical Study of Religion.* Portland, OR: Daimonion Press.

Carrier, R. (2012). Atheism IS an identity. Retrieved from http:// freethoughtblogs.com/carrier/archives/337/

CBS News. (2012, August 16). *More Americans identifying as atheists.* Retrieved from http://www.cbn.com/cbnnews/us/2012/August/ More-Americans-Identifying-as-Atheist/

CDC. (2012). *Centers for Disease Control and Prevention.* Retrieved from http://www.cdc.gov/24-7/CDCFastFacts.html

Chambers, A. (2009). *Eats with sinners: Reaching hungry people like Jesus did.* Cincinnati, OH: Standard Pub.

Christian, J. L. (Ed.). (2011). *Philosophy: An introduction to the art of wondering.* (11th ed., pp. 51). Boston, MA: Wadsworth.

Christina, G. (2012). *Why are you atheists so angry? 99 things that piss off the Godless*. Charlottesville, VA: Pitchstone.

Clarke, M. L. (1968). *The Roman mind: Studies in the history of thought from Cicero to Marcus Aurelius*. New York, NY: W.W. Norton & Company, Inc.

Clark, C. M. (1992). Deviant adolescent subcultures: Assessment strategies and clinical interventions. *Adolescence, 27*(106), 283.

Clifford, W. (2007). The ethics of belief. In D. Basinger, W. Hasker, M. Peterson & B. Reichenbach (Eds.), *Philosophy of religion: Selected readings* (3rd ed., pp. 104–109). New York, NY: Oxford University Press, Inc.

CNN. (2008). *Election exit polls*. Retrieved from http://www.cnn.com/ELECTION/2008/results/polls/

Comfort, R. (2009). *You can lead an atheist to evidence, but you can't make him think*. Los Angeles, CA: WorldNetDaily.

Coffey, C. (2009). *As I see it*. Bloomington, IN: AuthorHouse.

Covey, S. R. (2004). *The 7 habits of highly effective people*. New York, NY: Free Press.

Cragun, R., Yeager, S., & Vega, D. (2012). How secular humanists (and everyone else) subsidize religion in the United States. *Free Inquiry, 32*(4). Retrieved from http://www.secularhumanism.org/index.php?section=fi&page=cragun_32_4

Craig, W. L. (n.d.). Christian apologetics: Who needs it? *Reasonable Faith*. Retrieved from http://www.reasonablefaith.org/christian-apologetics-who-needs-it

Craig, W. L. (2003). *Hard questions, real answers*. (pp. 35). Wheaton, IL: Crossway Books.

Curtis, J. T., Silberschatz, G., Sampson, H., Weiss, J., & Rosenberg, S. E. (1988).

Developing reliable psychodynamic case formulations: An illustration of the plan diagnosis method. *Psychotherapy: Theory, Research, Practice, Training, 25*(2), 256–265.

Dacey, A. (2012). *The future of blasphemy: Speaking of the sacred in an age of human rights*. London: Continuum.

Davis, R. (2012, February 28). Apology for Afghan Quran burning was right. *The Daily Athenaeum*. Retrieved from http://www.thedaonline.com/opinion/column-apology-for-afghan-quran-burning-was-right-1.2801610

Dawkins, R. (Performer). (2005). *Richard Dawkins: Why the universe seems so strange.* [Web Video]. Retrieved from http://www.ted.com/talks/richard_dawkins_on_our_queer_universe.html

Dawkins, R. (2006a). *The god delusion.* London, England: Bantam Press.

Dawkins, R. (2006b). Why I won't debate Creationists. The Richard Dawkins Foundation for Reason and Science. Retrieved from http://old.richarddawkins.net/articles/119-why-i-won-39-t-debate-creationists

Dawkins, R. (2007, October). In W.H. Pryor (Moderator) debate between Richard Dawkins and John Lennox. The God delusion debate, Birmingham, AL. Retrieved from http://old.richarddawkins.net/audio/1707-debate-between-richard-dawkins-and-john-lennox

Dawkins, R., & McKean, D. (2011). *The magic of reality: How we know what's really true.* New York, NY: Free Press.

Dennett, D. (2007). *Breaking the spell: Religion as a natural phenomena.* New York, NY: Penguin Group.

Dennett, D., & LaScola, L. (2010). Preachers who are not believers. *Evolutionary Psychology, 8*(1), 121–50.

DeWitt, J., & Brown, E. (2013). *Hope after faith: An ex-pastor's journey from belief to atheism.* Cambridge, MA: Da Capo Press.

DiClemente, C. C., & Prochaska, J. O. (1998). Toward a comprehensive, transtheoretical model of change: Stages of change and addictive behaviors. In W. R. Miller & N. Heather (Eds.) *Treating Addictive Behaviors* (2nd ed.) (pp. 3–24). New York, NY: Plenum Press.

Doumit, P. E. (2010). *A unification of science and religion.* Pittsburg, PA: RoseDog Books.

Dozier, V. (2006). C.L. Shattuck & F.H. Thompsett (Eds.), *Confronted by God: The essential Verna Dozier* (pp. 118). New York, NY: Church Publishing Inc.

Dubrow-Eichel, S. K. (1989). *Deprogramming: An investigation of change processes and shifts in attention and verbal interactions* (pp. 43–49, 52–53, 182–216). Philadelphia, PA: University Of Pennsylvania.

Dye, J. (2007, February 7). *Socratic method and scientific method.* Retrieved from http://www.niu.edu/~jdye/method.html

Earley, D., & Wheeler, D. (2010). *Evangelism is . . .: How to share Jesus with passion and confidence.* Nashville, TN: B&H Academic Publishing Group.

Edwards, J. W. (1984). Indigenous Koro, a genital retraction syndrome of insular Southeast Asia: A Critical Review. *Culture, Medicine and Psychiatry, 8,* 1–24.

Erikson, J. A. (1992). Adolescent religious development and commitment: A structural equation model of the role of family, peer group, and educational influences. *Journal for the Scientific Study of Religion, 31*(2),131–152.

Faccini, L. (2009). The incredible case of the shrinking penis: A Koro-like syndrome in an [sic] person with intellectually disability. *Sexuality and Disability, 27*(3), 173–178. doi:10.1007/s11195-009-9120-5

Falk, R. (2012, March 9). Koran burning in Afghanistan: Mistake, crime, and metaphor. [Web log message]. Retrieved from http://richardfalk.wordpress.com/2012/03/09/koran-burning-in-afghanistan-mistake-crime-and-metaphor/

Faircloth, S. (2012). *Attack of the theocrats! How the religious right harms us all—and what we can do about it.* Charlottesville, VA: Pitchstone.

Fish, S. (2007, June 17). Atheism and evidence. [Web log message]. Retrieved from http://opinionator.blogs.nytimes.com/2007/06/17/atheism-and-evidence/

Foerst, A. (2001). Do androids dream of bread and wine? In W. Richardson & G. Slack (Eds.). *Faith in science: Scientists search for truth* (pp. 197). New York, NY: Routledge.

Frankfurt, H. G. (2006). *On truth.* New York, NY: Alfred A. Knopf.

Froján-Parga, M. X., Calero-Elvira, A., & Montaño-Fidalgo, M. (2011). Study of the Socratic method during cognitive restructuring. *Clinical Psychology & Psychotherapy, 18*(2), 110–123.

Gal, D., & Rucker, D. D. (2010). When in doubt, shout!: Paradoxical influences of doubt on proselytizing. *Psychological Science, 21*(11), 1701–1707.

Gamponia, H. L. (2010). *Great prescriptions to a better you.* Pittsburgh, PA: RoseDog Books.

Gassner, S., Sampson, H., Weiss, J., & Brumer, S. (1982). The emergence of warded-off contents. *Psychoanalysis and Contemporary Thought, 5*(1), 55–75.

Gervais, W. M., & Norenzayan, A. (2012). Analytic thinking promotes religious disbelief. *Science, 336*(6080), 493–496. doi:10.1126/science.1215647

Grimley, D., Prochaska, J. O., Velicer, W. F., Blais, L. M., & DiClemente, C. C. (1994). The Transtheoretical Model of Change. In T.M. Brinthaupt & R. P. Lipka (Eds.). *Changing the self: Philosophies, techniques, and experiences* (pp. 201–228). Albany, NY: SUNY Press.

Gross, N., & Simmons, S. (2007). "The social and political views of American professors." Unpublished manuscript, Harvard University, Cambridge, MA.

Habermas, G. R. (1996). *The historical Jesus: Ancient evidence for the life of Christ.* Joplin, MO: College Press Publishing Company, Inc.

Habermas, G. R. (1997). *In defense of miracles: A comprehensive case for God's action in history.* Downers Grove, IL: InterVarsity Press.

Habermas, G. R., & Licona, M. R. (2004). *The case for the resurrection of Jesus.* Grand Rapids, MI: Kregel Publications.

Hallowell, B. (2012, May 15). A world without faith would be a world on the path to tragedy & disaster. *The Blaze.* Retrieved from http://www.theblaze.com/stories/tony-blair-a-world-without-faith-would-be-a-world-on-the-path-to-tragedy-disaster/

Hanson, R. (1998, September 15). The great filter: Are we almost past it? Retrieved from http://www.webcitation.org/5n7VYJBUd

Harris, A. (forthcoming). *I Wonder.*

Harris, S. (2004). *The end of faith: Religion, terror and the future of reason.* New York, NY: W.W. Norton & Company, Inc.

Harris, S. (2007, April 18). The empty wager [Web log message]. Retrieved from http://newsweek.washingtonpost.com/onfaith/panelists/sam_harris/2007/04/the_cost_of_betting_on_faith.html

Harris, S. (2007b). Aspen Ideas Festival. Retrieved from http://www.youtube.com/watch?v=H9_WbWLiWKg

Harrison, G. P. (2008). *50 reasons people give for believing in a god.* Amherst, NY: Prometheus Books.

Harrison, G. P. (2013). *50 simple questions for every christian.* Amherst, New York: Prometheus Books.

Haught, J. F. (2008). *God and the new atheism: A critical response to Dawkins, Harris, and Hitchens.* Louisville, KY: John Knox Press.

Henriques, D. B. (2006a, October 11). Religion-based tax breaks: Housing to paychecks to books. *The New York Times.* Retrieved from http://www.nytimes.com/2006/10/11/business/11religious.html?_r=2&oref=slogin&pagewanted=all

Henriques, D. B. (2006b, October 9). Where faith abides, employees have few rights. *New York Times.* Retrieved from http://www.nytimes.com/2006/10/09/business/09religious.html?pagewanted=all

Hitchens, C. (1995). *The missionary position: Mother Teresa in theory and practice.* London: Verso.

Hitchens, C. (2007). *The portable atheist: Essential readings for the nonbeliever.* Philadelphia, PA: Da Capo.

Höfele, A., & Laqué, S. (Eds.). (2011). *Humankinds: The renaissance and its anthropologies.* Berlin/New York: Walter de Gruyter GmbH.

Hoge, D. R., Petrillo, G., & Smith, E. (1982). Transmission of religious and social values from parents to teenage children. *Journal of Marriage and the Family, 44,* 569–579.

Holt, J. (2012, August 2). The basic question: Why does the world exist? *The New York Times.* Retrieved from http://www.nytimes.com/2012/08/05/books/review/why-does-the-world-exist-by-jim-holt.html?_r=1&emc=eta1

Horowitz, L. M., Sampson, H., Siegelman, E. Y., Weiss, J., & Goodfriend, S. (1978). Cohesive and dispersal behaviors: Two classes of concomitant change in psychotherapy. *Journal of Consulting and Clinical Psychology, 46*(3), 556–564.

Horvath, A. O., & Luborsky, L. (1993). *Journal of Consulting and Clinical Psychology, 61*(4), 561–573. doi:10.1037/0022-006X.61.4.561

Iannaccone, L .R. (1990). Religious practice: A human capital approach. *Journal for the Scientific Study of Religion, 29*, 297–314.

Jacobsen, K. A. (2011). *Yoga powers: Extraordinary capacities attained through meditation and concentration.* Leiden, Netherlands: Brill.

James, W. (1897). *The will to believe: And other essays in popular philosophy.* New York, NY: Longmans Green and Co.

Jaschik, S. (2012, October 24). Survey finds that professors, already liberal, have moved further to the left. *Inside Higher Ed.* Retrieved from http://www.insidehighered.com/news/2012/10/24/survey-finds-professors-already-liberal-have-moved-further-left

Johnson, N. (2001). *Living with diabetes: Nicole Johnson, Miss America 1999.* Washington, DC: LifeLine Press.

Jones, J. M. (2011, July 8). In U.S., 3 in 10 say they take the Bible literally. *Gallup.* Retrieved from http://www.gallup.com/poll/148427/say-bible-literally.aspx

Kahneman, D. (2011). *Thinking, fast and slow.* New York, NY: Farrar, Straus and Giroux.

Keohane, J. (2010, July 11). How facts backfire: Researchers discover a surprising threat to democracy. *Boston Globe.* Retrieved from http://www.boston.com/bostonglobe/ideas/articles/2010/07/11/how_facts_backfire/

Kim, B. (1979). Religious deprogramming and subjective reality. *Sociological Analysis, 40*(3), 197–207.

Kinast, R. L. (1999). *Making faith-sense: Theological reflection in everyday life.* Collegeville, MN: The Liturgical Press.

Krauss, L. (2012). *A universe from nothing: Why there is something rather than nothing.* New York, NY: Free Press.

Kübler-Ross, E., & Kessler, D. (2005). *On grief and grieving: Finding the meaning of grief through the five stages of loss.* New York, NY: Scribner.

Kurtz, H. (2005, March 29). College faculties a most liberal lot, study finds. *The Washington Post*. Retrieved from http://www.washingtonpost.com/wp-dyn/articles/A8427-2005Mar28.html

Lamb, C. M. (1981, March). Legal foundations of civil rights and pluralism in America. *The ANNALS of the American Academy of Political and Social Science, 454*(1), 13–25. doi:10.1177/000271628145400103

Law, S. (2011). *Believing bullshit: How not to get sucked into an intellectual black hole.* Amherst, NY: Prometheus Books.

Law, S. (2012). *Really, really big questions.* New York, NY: Kingfisher books.

Leiter, B. (2012). *Why tolerate religion?* Princeton, NJ: Princeton University Press.

Lindsay, J. A. (2012, December 8). Defining faith via Bayesian reasoning. *God Doesn't; We Do*. Retrieved from http://goddoesnt.blogspot.com/2012/12/defining-faith-via-bayesian-reasoning.html

Livneh, H. (2009). Denial of chronic illness and disability part I. Theoretical, functional, and dynamic perspectives. *Rehabilitation Counseling Bulletin*, 225–236. doi:10.1177/0034355209333689

Loftus, J. W. (2008). *Why I Became an Atheist: Personal Reflections and Additional Arguments.* Victoria, BC: Trafford.

Loftus, J. W. (2010). *The Christian Delusion: Why Faith Fails.* Amherst, NY: Prometheus Books.

Loftus, J. W. (2012). Victor Reppert now says he doesn't have faith! Debunking Christianity. Retrieved from http://debunkingchristianity.blogspot.com/2012/10/victor-reppert-now-says-he-doesnt-have.html

Loftus, J. W. (2013). *The outsider test for faith: How to know which religion is true.* Amherst, NY: Prometheus Books.

Longsine, G., & Boghossian, P. (2012, September 27). Indignation Is Not Righteous. *Skeptical Inquirer*. Retrieved from http://www.csicop.org/specialarticles/show/indignation_is_not_righteous/

Luce, M. R., Callanan, M. A., & Smilovic, S. (2013). Links between parents' epistemological stance and children's evidence talk. *Developmental Psychology, 49*(3), 454–461. doi:10.1037/a0031249

Lukianoff, G. (2012). *Unlearning liberty: Campus censorship and the end of American debate*. New York, NY: Encounter Books.

Maher, B. A. (2001). Delusions. In H. E. Adams & P. B. Sutker (Eds.), *Comprehensive handbook of psychopathology, third edition* (3rd ed., pp. 312). New York, NY: Springer Science.

Malik, M. (2010, September 14). Benghazi murders: revisit free speech. *SFGate*. Retrieved from http://www.sfgate.com/opinion/article/Benghazi-murders-Revisit-free-speech-3866748.php

McCormick, M. S. (2011). The defeasibility test. http://www.provingthenegative.com/2011/02/defeasibility-test.html

McCormick, M. S. (2012). *Atheism and the case against Christ*. Amherst, NY: Prometheus Books.

McCreight, J. (2012, August 19). Atheism+. *Freethought Blogs*. Retrieved from http://freethoughtblogs.com/blaghag/2012/08/atheism/

McElveen, F. C. (2009). *Faith of an atheist: Do you have enough faith to be an atheist?* (pp. 11). Riverside, CA: Big Mac Publishers.

McGowan, D. (2007). *Parenting beyond belief: On raising ethical, caring kids without religion*. New York: American Management Association.

McGowan, D. (2009). *Raising freethinkers: A practical guide for parenting beyond belief*. New York: AMACOM, American Management Association.

McLaren, B. D. (1999). *Finding faith: A search for what is real*. (pp. 3). Grand Rapids, MI: Zondervan.

McNamara, P. (2009). *The neuroscience of religious experience*. Cambridge, MA, MA: Cambridge University Press.

McNeill, F., Raynor, P., & Trotter, C. (Eds.). (2010). *Offender Supervision: New Directions in Theory, Research and Practice*. New York: Willan Publishing.

Mehta, H. (2012). *The young atheist's survival guide: Helping secular students thrive*. Engelwood, Colorado: Patheos Press.

Mele, A. R. (2009). Have I unmasked self-deception or am I self-deceived? In C. Martin (Ed.). *The philosophy of deception*. New York, NY: Oxford University Press, Inc.

Meiland, J. W., & Krausz, M. (1982). *Relativism, cognitive and moral.* Notre Dame, IN: University of Notre Dame Press.

Migliore, D. L. (1991). *Faith seeking understanding: An introduction to Christian theology.* (2nd ed.). Grand Rapids, MI: Wm. B. Eerdmans Publishing Co.

Miller, W. R., Rollnick, S. (2002). *Motivational interviewing: Preparing people for change, vol. 2.* New York: Guilford.

Miller, R. (2006). *Why Christian's don't vote for Democrats.* Maitland, FL: Xulon Press.

Moberg, D. O. (1962). *The church as a social institution; the sociology of American religion.* Englewood Cliffs, NJ: Prentice-Hall.

Muran, J. C., & Barber, J. (Eds.). (2010). *The therapeutic alliance: An evidence based guide to practice.* New York, NY: The Guilford Press.

Myers, S. M. (1996). An interactive model of religiosity inheritance: The importance of family context. *American Sociological Review, 61,* 858–866.

Newberg, A. (2006). The neurobiology of spiritual transformation. In J. Chioino, P. J. Hefner (Eds.). *Spiritual transformation and healing: Anthropological, theological, neuroscientific, and clinical perspectives* (pp. 189–205). Lanham, MD: AltaMira Press.

Norville, R., Sampson, H., & Weiss, J. (1996). Accurate interpretations and brief psychotherapy outcome. *Psychotherapy Research, 6*(1), 16–29.

Nussbaum, M. (1994). *The therapy of desire: Theory and practice in Hellenistic ethics.* Princeton, NJ: Princeton University Press.

Orenstein, A. (2002). Religion and paranormal belief. *Journal for the Scientific Study of Religion, 41,* 301–311.

Partlow, J., & Londono, E. (2011, April 1). Mob protesting Koran burning kills 7 at U.N. compound in Kabul. *The Washington Post.* Retrieved from http://www.washingtonpost.com/world/12-killed-in-attack-on-un-compound-in-northern-afghanistan/2011/04/01/AFrb5iHC_story.html

Paulos, J. A. (2008). *Irreligion: A mathematician explains why the arguments for God just don't add up.* New York, NY: Hill and Wang.

Pigliucci, M. (2012, August 29). On A+, with a comment about Richard Carrier's intemperance. Rationally Speaking. Retrieved from http://rationallyspeaking.blogspot.com/2012/08/on-with-comment-about-richard-carriers.html

Plantinga, A. (2000). *Warranted Christian belief.* New York, NY: Oxford University Press.

Pariser, E. (2012). *The filter bubble: What the Internet is hiding from you.* New York, NY: The Penguin Group.

Previc, F. H. (2006). The role of the extrapersonal brain systems in religious activity. *Consciousness and Cognition, 15,* 500–539.

Prochaska, J. O., Norcross, J. C., & DiClemente, C. C. (1994). *Changing for good: The revolutionary program that explains the six stages of change and teaches you how to free yourself from bad habits.* New York: W. Morrow.

Rawls, J. (2005). *A theory of justice.* Boston, MA: Belknap Press of Harvard University Press.

Ray, D. W. (2009). *The God virus: How religion infects our lives and culture.* Bonner Springs, KS: IPC Press.

Robbins, T., & Anthony, D. (1982). Deprogramming, brainwashing, and the medicalization of deviant religious groups. *Social Problems, 29*(3), 283–297.

Rothman, S. Lichter, S. R., & Nevitte, N. (2005). Politics and professional advancement among college faculty. *The Forum, 3*(1), 1–16.

Ryan, A. (2012). *The making of modern liberalism.* Princeton, NJ: Princeton University Press.

Sampson, H. (1994). Repeating pathological relationships to disconfirm pathogenic beliefs: Commentary on Steven Stern's "needed relationships." *Psychoanalytic Dialogues, 4*(3), 357–361.

Sausa, D. (2007). *The Jesus tomb: Is it fact or fiction? Scholars chime in.* Fort Meyers, FL: The Vision Press.

Schick, T., & Vaughn, L. (2008). *How to think about weird things: Critical thinking for a new age.* (5th ed.). New York, NY: McGraw-Hill Education.

Secular News Daily. (September 6, 2012). "I Wonder" by Annaka Harris teaches children it's OK to question and not know. Retrieved from http://www.secularnewsdaily.com/2012/09/i-wonder-by-annaka-harris-teaches-children-its-ok-to-question-and-not-know/

Shermer, M. (1997). *Why people believe weird things: Pseudoscience, superstition, and other confusions of our time.* New York, NY: Henry Holt and Company, LLC.

Shermer, M. (2012). *The believing brain: From ghosts and gods to politics and conspiracies: How we construct beliefs and reinforce them as truths.* New York, NY: Henry Holt and Company, LLC.

Sieff, K. (2012, February 21). Afghans protest burning of Korans at U.S. base. *The Washington Post.* Retrieved from http://www.washingtonpost.com/world/asia_pacific/afghans-protest-improper-disposal-of-koran-at-us-base/2012/02/21/gIQAjhBqQR_story.html

Silberschatz, G., Curtis, J. T., Sampson, H., & Weiss, J. (1991). Mount Zion Hospital and Medical Center: Research on the process of change in psychotherapy. In L.E. Beutler & M. Crago (Eds.), *Psychotherapy research: An international review of programmatic studies* (pp. 56–64). Washington, DC: American Psychological Association.

Skonovd, L. N. (1981). *Apostasy: The Process of Defection from Religious Totalism.* Ph.D. thesis. University of California, Davis.

Smith, G. H. (1979). *Atheism: The case against God.* Amherst, NY: Prometheus Books.

Solomon, L. D. (2006). *From Athens to America: Virtues and the formulation of public policy.* Lanham, MD: Lexington Books.

Souter, A. (1917). *A pocket lexicon to the Greek New Testament.* Oxford: Clarendon Press.

Stefanelli, A. (2011). *A Voice Of Reason In An Unreasonable World: The Rise Of Atheism On Planet Earth.* Fairbanks, AK: UAF Publications.

Stefanelli, A. (2012a). *Free thoughts—A collection of essays by an American atheist.* Fairbanks, AK: UAF Publications.

Stefanelli, A, (2012b, October 31). When religious people attribute the acts of Hitler, Stalin and Pol Pot to atheism. *God Discussion.* Retrieved from http://www.Goddiscussion.com/103457/when-religious-people-attribute-the-acts-of-hitler-stalin-and-pol-pot-to-atheism/

Stenger, V. J. (2007). *God: The failed hypothesis: How science shows that God does not exist.* Amherst, N.Y.: Prometheus Books.

Stenger, V. J. (2011). *The fallacy of fine-tuning: Why the universe is not designed for us.* Amherst, NY: Prometheus Books.

Stenger, V. J. (2013). *God and the atom.* Amherst, NY: Prometheus.

Stenger, V. J., & Barker, D. (2012). *God and the folly of faith: The incompatibility of science and religion.* Amherst, NY: Prometheus Books.

Stewart, K. (2012). *The Good News Club: The Christian Right's stealth assault on America's children.* New York, NY: PublicAffairs.

Strobel, L. (2004). *The case for a creator: A journalist investigates scientific evidence that points towards God.* Grand Rapids, MI: Zondervan.

Sunstein, C. R. (2009). *Going to extremes: How like minds unite and divide.* Oxford: Oxford University Press.

Szimhart, J. (2009). Razor's Edge Indeed: A Deprogrammer's View of Harmful Cult Activity. *Cultic Studies Review, 8*(3), 231–265. Retrieved from the TESC Online Journal database.

Tassi, A. (1982). Modernity as the transformation of truth into meaning. *International Philosophical Quarterly, 22*(3), 185–193.

The Global Religious Landscape. (2012, December 18). *Pew Forum on Religion & Public Life.* Retrieved from http://www.pewforum.org/global-religious-landscape.aspx

Thrower, J. (2000). *Western atheism: A short history.* Amherst, NY: Prometheus Books.

Tillich, P. (1957). *Dynamics of faith.* New York, NY: Harper Collins Publishers, Inc.

Tobin, G. A., & Weinberg, A. K. (2006). Political beliefs & behavior of college faculty. Institute for Jewish & Community Research.

Torres, P. (2012). *A crisis of faith: Atheism, emerging technologies, and the future of humanity.* England: Dangerouslittlebooks.

Turner, S., & Ehlers, T. B. (2003). *Sugar's life in the hood: The story of a former welfare mother.* Austin, TX: University of Texas Press.

United States Department of State, Bureau of Democracy, Human Rights and Labor. (2011a). *July–December, 2010 international religious freedom report* (Excerpt). Retrieved from http://translations.state.gov/st/english/texttrans/2011/09/20110913111820su0.204366.html

United States Department of State, Bureau of Democracy, Human Rights and Labor. (2011b). *International religious freedom report for 2011* (192947.pdf). Retrieved from http://www.state.gov/documents/organization/192947.pdf

Vos, M. S., & de Haes, J. C. (2007). Denial in cancer patients, an explorative review. *Psychooncology,16*(1), 12–25.

Wade, N. (2009). *The faith instinct: How religion evolved and why it endures.* New York, NY: The Penguin Press.

Warraq, I. (2003). *Leaving Islam: Apostates speak out.* Amherst, NY: Prometheus Books.

Warren, R. (2002). *What on Earth am I here for?* Grand Rapids, MI: Zondervan.

Weiss, J., & Sampson, H. (1986). *The psychoanalytic process: Theory, clinical observation, and empirical research.* New York: Guilford Press.

Williams, T. (2012, March 9). Koran-burning & sacrilege: Religion matters in diplomacy. *Capital Commentary.* Retrieved from http://www.capitalcommentary.org/afghanistan/koran-burning-sacrilege-religion-matters-diplomacy

Winell, M. (1993). *Leaving the fold.* Oakland, CA: New Harbinger Publications.

Wittgenstein, L. (2009). *Philosophical investigations.* (G.E.M. Anscombe, P.M.S. Hacker, J. Schulte, Trans.). (4th ed.). Malden, MA: Blackwell Publishing Ltd.

Wright, L. (2013). *Going Clear: Scientology, Hollywood, and the prison of belief.* New York: Alfred A. Knopf.

Zuckerman, P. (2009). Why are Danes and Swedes so irreligious? *Nordic Journal of Religion and Society, 22*(1).

INDEX

OTHER TITLES FROM PITCHSTONE

Attack of the Theocrats!:
How the Religious Right Harms Us All—and What We Can Do About It
by Sean Faircloth

Candidate Without a Prayer:
An Autobiography of a Jewish Atheist in the Bible Belt
by Herb Silverman

The Citizen Lobbyist:
A How-to Manual for Making Your Voice Heard in Government
by Amanda Knief

The Ebony Exodus Project:
Why Some Black Women Are Walking Out on Religion—and Others Should Too
by Candace R. M. Gorham, LPC

God Bless America:
Strange and Unusual Religious Beliefs and Practices in the United States
by Karen Stollznow

PsychoBible:
Behavior, Religion & the Holy Book
by Armando Favazza, MD

What You Don't Know about Religion (but Should)
by Ryan T. Cragun

Why Are You Atheists So Angry?:
99 Things That Piss Off the Godless
by Greta Christina

Why We Believe in God(s):
A Concise Guide to the Science of Faith
by J. Anderson Thomson, Jr., MD, with Clare Aukofer

ABOUT THE AUTHOR

Dr. Peter Boghossian is a full-time faculty member in Portland State University's philosophy department. He was thrown out of the doctoral program in the University of New Mexico's philosophy department.